Data Protection Handbook

SECOND EDITION

Other titles available from Law Society Publishing:

Company Law Handbook
Stephen Griffin

Drafting Confidentiality Agreements, 2nd edn
Mark Anderson and Simon Keevey-Kothari

Execution of Documents, 2nd edn
Mark Anderson and Victor Warner

Freedom of Information Handbook, 2nd edn
General Editors: Peter Carey and Marcus Turle

Insolvency Law Handbook, 2nd edn
Vernon Dennis

Intellectual Property Law Handbook
Bird & Bird, Edited by Lorna Brazell

All books from Law Society Publishing can be ordered from good bookshops or direct (by telephone 0870 850 1422, email law.society@prolog.uk.com, or by visiting our online bookshop at **www.lawsociety.org.uk/bookshop**).

DATA PROTECTION HANDBOOK

SECOND EDITION

General Editor: Peter Carey

The Law Society

© The Law Society 2008

ISBN 978–1–85328–773–2

First edition published in 2004

This second edition published in 2008 by the Law Society
113 Chancery Lane, London WC2A 1PL

Typeset by J&L Composition Ltd, Filey, North Yorkshire
Printed by TJ International Ltd, Padstow, Cornwall

FSC
Mixed Sources
Product group from well-managed
forests and other controlled sources

Cert no. SGS-COC-2482
www.fsc.org
© 1996 Forest Stewardship Council

The paper used for the text pages of this book is
FSC certified. FSC (The Forest Stewardship Council)
is an international network to promote responsible
management of the world's forests.

Contents

About the editor and contributors

ABOUT THE EDITOR

Peter Carey is a consultant solicitor with Charles Russell in London, where he is head of the Information Law team. After gaining a Masters Degree in International Business Law in the United States in 1993, Peter spent six years as a senior lecturer at the College of Law. Peter has established a reputation as one of the UK's leading data protection and privacy experts. He is author of *Data Protection: A Practical Guide to UK and EU Law* (Oxford University Press, 2004) and is the editor of the journal, *Privacy & Data Protection*. Peter advises commercial organisations of varying sizes on all aspects of information law compliance. His clients include a major water utility, several charities, a global telecommunications services provider, one of the world's largest medical data suppliers, local authorities and several e-commerce companies.

ABOUT THE CONTRIBUTORS

Sally Annereau is a data protection analyst in the London office of Taylor Wessing LLP. She has over 16 years' experience of providing advice on data protection issues including six years working at the Information Commissioner's office), in addition to data protection compliance roles with marketing, broadcast and new media companies. Sally co-presents the Direct Marketing Association's Data Protection Compliance Award and is co-author of the data protection chapter for Sweet & Maxwell's *Practical Commercial Precedents*.

Kate Brimsted is of Counsel at Herbert Smith LLP and a founder member of the firm's Data Privacy Group. Kate's practice focuses on commercial data protection and privacy law and she regularly advises clients based in the UK and internationally on a wide variety of domestic and international data protection matters, such as tactical advice on handling subject access requests in a litigious context and compliance and exploitation strategies. Kate contributes to a range of professional journals on topical data protection and privacy, intellectual property and IT issues. She speaks regularly on data protection at conferences and professional seminars, and is a member of the editorial board of the legal journal, *Privacy & Data Protection*.

Gary Brooks is a freelance data protection and information rights lawyer with his own consultancy business. As well as advising his own clients, Gary works as a consultant for Privacy Laws & Business and for the law firm Berwin Leighton Paisner, where he was formerly head of the Data Protection Unit. He has provided data protection compliance advice to some of the UK's leading businesses, including a client secondment to Tesco where he worked as the data protection manager. He also advises on freedom of information compliance issues. Gary is a regular contributor to legal and industry journals on a range of topics in the field of data protection and privacy, and has spoken at conferences on data protection and e-privacy issues.

Sue Cullen is a solicitor specialising in information law and director of Amberhawk Training Ltd, which she founded with Dr Chris Pounder in August 2008. She was for over seven years a member of the Information Law Team at Pinsent Masons LLP, providing training and advice principally on data protection and freedom of information, but also on human rights and the Regulation of Investigatory Powers Act, and the re-use of public sector information. She regularly contributed case reports to the *Encyclopaedia of Data Protection* and was Data Protection Officer for Pinsent Masons. She is an accredited trainer for the ISEB qualifications in data protection, FOI and IT Law, and as well as delivering training and advice to clients, she speaks and writes on current information law topics.

Daniel Pavin is a partner in the London office of Taylor Wessing LLP. He advises in relation to a broad range of information technology and intellectual property matters, both non-contentious and contentious, with a particular focus on data protection. Daniel helped to set up the UK Direct Marketing Association's Data Protection Compliance Award and is a contributor to the British Bankers' Association's *Data Protection – Practical Guidance for Banks*. He has a degree from Cambridge University in Computer Science and Physics and worked as a computer programmer before qualifying as a solicitor. He has a Diploma in Intellectual Property Law and Practice from Bristol University.

Louise Townsend is a senior associate in the Outsourcing, Technology and Commercial Group at Pinsent Masons LLP, specialising in information law. She advises on data protection issues, including carrying out data protection compliance audits, advising on overseas transfers, information security, website compliance and marketing. She provides training on data protection and freedom of information, holds the ISEB qualifications in data protection and freedom of information, and is an accredited ISEB trainer. Lousie has contributed to a number of publications on information law, is on the editorial board of *Privacy & Data Protection* and speaks widely on these topics.

Gayle Trigg is an associate and professional support lawyer at Wragge & Co LLP with experience in IT contracts, procurement and outsourcing, and specialising in e-commerce and information law. She has advised a wide range of organisations in the public and private sector on compliance strategies and audits, processing arrangements, privacy policies and other consents, marketing issues and obtaining, providing or restricting access to information under the legislation, both domestically and internationally. As a professional support lawyer, Gayle regularly provides training both to members of the firm and clients on data protection and freedom of information issues.

Eduardo Ustaran is the head of the Privacy and Information Law Group at Field Fisher Waterhouse and an internationally recognised expert in privacy and data protection law. He is a dually qualified English solicitor and Spanish abogado. Eduardo advises on the impact of EU data protection and e-commerce law on the operational activities of all types of organisations, including FTSE 100 companies and public sector bodies. He advises a number of international clients on the adoption of global privacy strategies. Eduardo regularly manages teams of lawyers across many jurisdictions and has assisted data protection regulators from different countries to align their positions and interpretation of the law. Eduardo has experience of drafting and negotiating data protection Binding Corporate Rules. He is co-chairman of KnowledgeNet London, editor of *Data Protection Law & Policy* and co-author of *E-Privacy and Online Data Protection* (Tottel Publishing, 2007).

Preface

This book consists of a series of extended essays on selected important and practical topics within the field of data protection law. Each chapter is written by a leading expert in the data protection field.

There have been several significant developments since the last edition of this book, including the Information Commissioner's clarification of the meaning of 'personal data', the introduction of a new method to justify intra-company overseas transfers, and the upgrading of the Commissioner's powers to include the ability to fine errant organisations. In addition, the Information Commissioner's Office (ICO) has been prolific in its production of new guidance on various aspects of data protection practice, including on the use of CCTV cameras and handling requests for information. This guidance, whilst not 'law' *per se*, is nevertheless useful to data controllers, and those who advise them, in understanding the Information Commissioner's thinking.

Data protection has caught the attention of the media in recent months. Scarcely a week goes by without a data protection story making front page news. This seems to have focused the attention of many organisations on their data protection responsibilities in a way that the Information Commissioner could never have hoped to achieve on his own.

As before, this book is an essential general guide for the legal practitioner or the data protection officer, consisting of 10 chapters written by the UK's foremost data protection experts in clear and easy-to-follow language. The chapters are designed to be self-contained, although references are made to topics discussed in other chapters where appropriate. The views of the author of each chapter are not necessarily held by the remaining authors.

Most of the authors of the chapters in this book are regular contributors of articles to the legal journal, *Privacy & Data Protection*. Readers wishing to stay in touch with developments in this rapidly changing area of legal practice are referred to the journal's website, which can be accessed at **www.pdpjournals.com**.

The main statutory provision discussed in this book is the Data Protection Act 1998. The 1998 Act is referred to throughout this book as 'the DPA'. Where other statutes are mentioned, their full title is included. The DPA was passed to give effect to Directive 95/46/EC on the protection of individuals with regard to the processing of personal data and on the free movement of such data ('the Directive' or 'the Data Protection Directive').

The other significant statutory provision discussed in this book is the Privacy and Electronic Communication (EC Directive) Regulations 2003, SI 2003/2426 (PEC Regulations) which were passed to give effect to Directive 2002/58/EC on the protection of privacy in the electronic communications sector.

One unique feature of this book is that it contains specific data protection compliance guidance for law firms (see especially Chapter 10). In my experience of conducting data protection compliance reviews (or 'audits') for law firms, I have discovered that there are a number of areas where law firms commonly fall foul of their legislative requirements. The processing undertaken by a law firm can be more extensive than that notified by the firm to the ICO (a criminal offence) and law firm security arrangements frequently breach the basic requirements of the Seventh Data Protection Principle (law firm compliance officers or managing partners are referred to Chapters 4 and 7, dealing with notification and security respectively). Firms with clients or associated offices located outside the European Economic Area often make tranfers of client or staff data without giving appropriate thought to restrictions on international transfers in the Eighth Data Protection Principle (see Chapter 8). Law firms should ensure that they adhere to the opt-in requirement (or the terms of the exemption from that requirement) in regulation 22 of the PEC Regulations when sending marketing e-mails to clients or potential clients (see Chapter 9). While excessively poor data protection compliance by law firms is rarely due to firms' other legal and quasi-legal obligations, firms should ensure that they pay attention to data protection compliance issues for the reasons referred to in this book. Further, commercial clients are increasingly requiring law firms to certify that they are 'data protection compliant'.

I am indebted to the authors of the chapter for their time, patience and dedication in producing this work. I trust that you, the reader, will find it of great practical value in your professional life.

Peter Carey, Solicitor
Data Protection Consultant
peter.carey@dataprotectionlaw.com
July 2008

Table of cases

Table of statutes

Table of statutory instruments

Table of European legislation

Decisions

Regulations

CHAPTER 1

Determining needs

Gayle Trigg[1]

1.1 INTRODUCTION

Ten years ago, the Data Protection Act 1998 (DPA) and several associated statutory instruments were entered onto the statute books in the UK. They came into force on 1 March 2000, repealing the Data Protection Act 1984.

Since then, data protection has grown significantly in importance, with organisations that breach its principles appearing regularly in the national news.

However, data protection is not a black and white area of law. It is instead a principles-based piece of legislation, leaving many aspects of compliance to the discretion and subjective opinion of the data controller. The words of the legislative document may be the law, but the spirit of the Act will help data controllers (and those advising them) interpret those words into actions where their meanings are not entirely clear from the text itself.

This chapter, on determining needs under the DPA, will therefore introduce you to the legislative framework, but would not be complete without an understanding and appreciation of the spirit of the DPA. Advising on data protection issues is not just about reading the DPA and relaying the law applicable to the particular set of circumstances described by a client. Frequently, a large element of any such advice will take the form of a risk analysis so that the client is equipped to make a business decision, based not just on the law but also on the consequences of compliance and non-compliance, in the context of its business operations.

Needless to say, the positive consequences of compliance must be carefully weighed up against the negative consequences of non-compliance, including not just the direct legal consequences, but also loss of opportunity and adverse publicity. A good adviser will help a client through this evaluation process, whether simply by arming the client with the requisite knowledge or by helping in the evaluation itself. To do this effectively and efficiently, it is imperative to have a clear grasp of the legislative and regulatory framework for data protection compliance in the UK.

---

[1] Based on an original contribution by Cinzia Biondi.

1

This chapter will go on to examine the kind of issues which data protection advisers should explore in order to ensure that an organisation's data protection needs are fully understood and addressed. This process will also help with the risk analysis exercise.

Data protection is, and should be strongly promoted as, an efficient management tool for business operations. This message is not always easy to sell, but is one that will give data controllers the commercial, as well as legal, drive to commit to a programme of data protection audit and compliance. This chapter will provide some useful arguments to help sell this message as well as practical guidance on how to engage effectively the attention of the important parties in a data controller's organisation on such issues.

Finally, it is essential to keep fully up to date with changes to data protection compliance practice. New guidance is issued by the Information Commissioner's Office on almost a weekly basis and significant decisions are now emerging from the courts. Whilst this book is a valuable introduction to the law and practice of data protection, readers are referred to the practical compliance journal, *Privacy & Data Protection* (see **www.pdpjournals.com** and the Information Commissioner's website **www.ico.gov.uk**), in order to remain fully appraised of relevant changes and updates.

1.2 LEGISLATIVE FRAMEWORK

Data protection legislation in the UK is no longer a new phenomenon. The Data Protection Act 1984 (now repealed) was introduced to provide certain protections to individuals in respect of the way in which information relating to them was handled, primarily (but not exclusively) by larger business organisations and especially in the context of emerging information technology.

In tandem, in Europe the requirement of the protection of personal privacy was seen as a natural progression from the provisions of the European Convention on Human Rights. The Committee of Members was asked by the Council of Europe to propose recommendations in respect of data protection in the public and private sectors. Following these recommendations, the Council of Europe Convention on Data Protection was established in January 1981. Due to the lack of take up by Member States of the Convention, the European Commission proposed a directive on the subject of data protection and information security. Following lengthy discussion sessions in the European Parliament, the Commission adopted a proposal for a directive on the processing of personal data and on the free movement of such data. This proposal, as amended, became Directive 95/46/EC (the Directive). Member States were required to adopt the Directive into national law within three years, subject to transitional provisions.

2

Thus came into life in the UK the Data Protection Act 1998.

The DPA was enacted with several aims in mind, the most important being:

- to implement the Directive and thereby harmonise the law in this area throughout the European Union;
- to provide consumer protection in the area of personal privacy;
- to provide individuals with certain rights and powers, and therefore control, over the way in which their personal information is dealt with by third parties.

Although those already complying with the 1984 Act had a good head start, complying with the DPA required even these organisations to take a fresh look at their handling of personal information.

The first key difference related to who assumes responsibility for data processing operations.

The 1984 Act allowed for both data controllers and computer bureaux to have direct responsibilities under the Act. The DPA, however, makes no reference to computer bureaux, but retains the category of data controller and introduces the concept of 'data processor' in place of computer bureau. The definitions of these terms can be found in the glossary provided at the end of this book. The DPA imposes direct responsibilities only on the data controller, and ensures that a data controller will be liable under the DPA for the processing activities which are carried out by data processors (third parties acting on its behalf).

From a commercial perspective alone this necessitates a review of contractual arrangements between data controllers and data processors to ensure that data controllers have placed appropriate contractual obligations on data processors, which are linked to the data controller's own obligations under the DPA. In essence, a back-to-back arrangement is called for. But in case this commercial drive was not enough, the DPA, in Schedule 2, sets out statutory requirements for a contractual link between controller and processor. These require that:

- such arrangements are governed by a contract in writing; and
- the contract states that the data processor will only process personal data in accordance with the data controller's instructions; and
- the data processor agrees to comply with obligations equivalent to those set out in the Seventh Principle of the DPA (that is, using appropriate technical and organisational measures to prevent the unauthorised or unlawful or accidental loss, damage or misuse of personal data).

The DPA (together with its associated statutory instruments) is not the only piece of legislation which forms the legislative framework for data protection.

In 1997, a directive was adopted which dealt with personal data in the telecommunications sector. Directive 97/66/EC of the European Parliament and of the Council of 15 December 1997 concerning the processing of personal data and the protection of privacy in the telecommunications sector became known as the Telecoms Directive. This Directive was implemented in the UK as the Telecommunications (Data Protection and Privacy) Regulations 1999, SI 1999/2093 followed by the Telecommunications (Data Protection and Privacy) (Amendment) Regulations 2000, SI 2000/157. Given the pace of developments within the technology sector, it was felt that a more technology-neutral directive was required. Certain practices, such as 'spamming', had emerged swiftly and to a scale not entirely expected (and have become a great nuisance) as a result of greater capabilities of technology since the time when the 1997 Directive was conceived. It was felt that a further directive was required to address such issues and concerns.

As a result, Directive 2002/58/EC of the European Parliament and of the Council of 12 July 2002 concerning the processing of personal data and the protection of privacy in the electronic communications sector (Directive on Privacy and Electronic Communications) was adopted. Following much debate in the UK amongst industry sectors and regulatory bodies, the UK adopted the Directive in the shape of the Privacy and Electronic Communications (EC Directive) Regulations 2003, SI 2003/2426, replacing the Telecommunications (Data Protection and Privacy) Regulations 1999, which were repealed. These Regulations came into force on 11 December 2003. It is important to note that the Regulations do not relieve any person of his obligations under the DPA in relation to the processing of personal data (see reg.4 of the Regulations); instead, the Regulations supplement the DPA's requirements in areas such as marketing activities by telephone, fax and, more importantly, e-mails/SMS/MMS and the use of cookies on websites.

1.3   FUTURE DEVELOPMENTS

The European Council, as required under Directive 95/46/EC, produced its first report on the operation of the Directive within Member States in May 2003. The report follows a detailed consultation exercise carried out within Member States. It is clear that some Member States believe that there are certain parts of the Directive which require clarification, if not complete amendment. Although advisers should not be advising clients to change business methods and practices solely to align them with any potential new legislation before it has been drafted, they can be aware of the perceived inadequacies of the Directive (and, in certain respects therefore, the DPA) and put their advice in this context.

The Commission's first report on the implementation of the Directive states that it 'considers that results of the review on balance militate against proposing modifications to the Directive at this stage'. Apparently very few contributors explicitly favoured such modifications, the exceptions being Austria, Sweden, Finland and the UK who submitted a joint paper with proposals for amendments (later retrospectively adopted by the Netherlands). The Commission does, however, agree that further analysis of some of the proposals and issues raised during the consultation exercise should be undertaken and that such new proposals would be reviewed in light of greater experience of the Directive's implementation as time goes by. If at a later stage it is deemed appropriate for the Directive to be modified given such greater experience of its implementation, then the Commission will consider taking such a step at the relevant time. The Commission recognises that some issues need to be reviewed sooner rather than later.

As a priority, the Commission is concerned with the harmonious application of the rules relating to the transfer of data to third countries. In addition, because of the different ways in which the Directive has been implemented in various Member States, there are some diverse interpretations and/or practices which are causing difficulties in the internal market. This will not be new to advisers who regularly advise their clients on data protection issues. The Commission hopes these divergences will be remedied by way of closer co-operation amongst supervising authorities of the Member States rather than by amendments to the Directive.

The Commission was also particularly concerned with evidence which suggests that there is an under-resourced enforcement effort among supervising authorities. It appears likely that the Commission will investigate this aspect further as it is concerned to prevent a lack of resources being a reason for limited regulation and enforcement activities.

The UK's implementation of the Directive is also potentially subject to possible action by the European Commission for non-compliance with the Directive. This is primarily as a result of the decision of the Court of Appeal in *Durant* v. *FSA* [2003] EWCA Civ 1746 (discussed in Chapter 2) and subsequent initial guidance from the Information Commissioner's Office. This decision and guidance potentially narrows the definition of personal data, and therefore limits the protection available to individuals in respect of that data. The Information Commissioner has recently updated the guidance, seeking to reconcile it with guidance on the definition of personal data issued by the Article 29 Working Party, but the Court of Appeal's decision will retain precedence unless overruled by a higher court or change in legislation. Vague details of correspondence between the UK and the Commission have been published in the press, but specific details of any potential enforcement action have not been made public.

Such action notwithstanding, the UK regulator, the Information Commissioner, is actively encouraging a review of data protection legislation across Europe. Whilst he cannot amend the Directive directly, he has in 2008 appointed independent think-tank RAND Europe to carry out a review of European Data Protection Law.

The Information Commissioner can, however, recommend changes to the DPA as long as these proposed changes fall within, and accord with, the requirements of the Directive. In 2007, the Prime Minister asked Richard Thomas (the current Information Commissioner) and Dr Mark Walport of the Wellcome Trust to carry out a review into data sharing. This development handed the review team a wide remit to consider whether there should be any changes to the way the DPA operates and the options for implementing any such changes. As well as considering the extent to which the sharing of personal information should and can be regulated or even facilitated, it will look in particular at the powers and sanctions available to the regulator and courts in the legislation governing data sharing and data protection.

Keeping abreast of legal and regulatory changes involves monitoring the following on a regular basis:

1. Court decisions. For example, the Naomi Campbell case (*Naomi Campbell* v. *MGN Limited* [2003] 1 All ER 224, CA, [2004] UKHL 22) usefully confirmed that photographic images amount to personal data, although ultimately her claims under the DPA could add nothing to her claim for breach of confidence; the ruling in *R* v. *Wakefield Metropolitan Council* [2002] QB 1052 clarified issues on the proper use of personal data for specific purposes and led to changes in electoral register use; *Durant* v. *FSA* [2003] EWCA Civ 1746 focused on the meaning of 'relevant filing system' and 'personal data' and the court's discretion under the DPA in respect of enforcing data subject access requests (see Chapter 10 for further details); *Johnson* v. *Medical Defence Union* [2007] EWCA Civ 262, which related to the fairness of processing data, and whether decisions taken as a result of processing data could be challenged on these grounds.
2. Information Tribunal cases.
3. New statutory instruments.
4. The Information Commissioner's Office (ICO) website (**www.ico.gov.uk**) and Annual Reports which detail assessments, enforcement action and case studies.
5. Other legislation amending the DPA, such as the Freedom of Information Act 2000.
6. Quality periodicals containing regular updates and practical guidance on developments in data protection, such as the *Privacy & Data Protection* journal.

The way in which data protection is managed in practice in the UK (and other Member States) is also influenced by the outcomes of the ongoing debates and development within the European Union. In particular, the work carried out by the Article 29 Working Party (a body set up under Directive 95/46/EC to examine and make recommendations to the Council on data protection issues) is particularly persuasive. The work of the Article 29 Working Party not only sheds light on the spirit of data protection legislation, but also proves to be a good indication of future potential legal developments in this area.

Helping clients to develop and maintain systems and processes which are flexible enough to accommodate such future potential developments will lessen the expense and inconvenience for clients at a later date.

1.4   REGULATORY FRAMEWORK

The ICO has previously been known as the Office of the Data Protection Registrar and the Office of the Data Protection Commissioner. Its latest title is a result of the Freedom of Information Act 2000, and reflects its remit in the fields of both data protection and freedom of information. The current Information Commissioner is Richard Thomas. The ICO is tasked with regulating and enforcing the data protection regime within the UK. The Information Commissioner, amongst other functions, is there to provide guidance, promote good practice and issue codes of practice in relation to various matters which fall under the data protection regime. The ICO also provides day-to-day assistance through the operation of a helpline (see Appendix 4). A more detailed assistance service is offered whereby a written request for clarification on certain issues can be submitted for consideration and response by the Information Commissioner.

It must be borne in mind, however, that any advice, assistance or guidance provided by the Information Commissioner, although very persuasive, is only his interpretation of the DPA. It is ultimately for the courts, which may consider the Information Commissioner's view, to decide on such interpretation. The Information Commissioner's view will undoubtedly prove influential and persuasive, but not necessarily conclusive.

The Information Commissioner has developed and issued many good practice and technical guidance notes and other leaflets, documents and papers to help with the interpretation, and implementation, of a data controller's obligations and a data subject's rights under the DPA. It is a legal adviser's task to be as familiar with these as with the DPA itself. Arguably, of most importance amongst those papers are the codes of practice which set out, in practical terms, the steps which the Information Commissioner considers must be taken by data controllers to comply with their obligations under the DPA in the context of specific processing activities.

Codes of practice include:

- CCTV Code of Practice;
- Employment Practices Code (covering Recruitment and Selection; Records Management; Monitoring at Work and Medical Information);
- Code of Practice on Telecommunications Directory Information and Fair Processing; and
- Framework code of practice for sharing personal information.

Technical Guidance Notes cover a wide variety of topics including:

- access to personal information held by schools;
- dealing with subject access requests involving other people's information;
- determining what is personal data;
- FAQs and answers about relevant filing systems;
- filing defaults with credit reference agencies;
- privacy enhancing technologies; and
- subject access requests and legal proceedings.

The codes of practice are not law. Whether a data controller has complied with the codes of practice will, however, be taken into account by a court and the Information Commissioner in deciding whether a breach of the DPA has occurred. In the absence of any clearly unjustifiable and/or adverse processing, compliance with the codes should be treated as compliance with the DPA itself.

It is fair to say that the Information Commissioner, as with most data protection regulatory authorities within the Member States, is limited in his regulatory and enforcement activities by lack of resources. Recognising this to be the case, although campaigning strongly for resources to be increased, the Information Commissioner has been forced to prioritise the areas of data protection compliance in which he is most interested and, more often than not, these are selected by means of an analysis of the extent and level of adverse impact such areas could have on individuals. Accordingly, as the Information Commissioner's 2007 consultation on Data Protection Enforcement Strategy highlights, the Information Commissioner has set priorities by focusing most attention on situations where there is a real likelihood of serious harm, and where intervention is most likely to make a long-term as well as a short-term difference. In his reports 'What Price Privacy?' and 'What Price Privacy Now?' he called for stronger enforcement and penalties for the offences of unlawfully obtaining and/or disclosing and/or processing and/or selling personal data (that is, recklessly or knowingly doing so without the data controller's consent). This approach is no doubt due to the greater potential for adverse impact on the data subject involved.

A legitimate part of providing advice is to help a client to undertake a risk analysis of the likelihood of enforcement action or criminal prosecutions being taken against it.

1.5 SANCTIONS AND PENALTIES

In addition to the threat of criminal prosecution, the Information Commissioner has other powers at his disposal. Briefly, these are:

1. Assessment following a request by a person directly affected by any processing of personal data. The Information Commissioner must look at such a request and issue an assessment to the requesting party as to whether it is likely or unlikely that the processing has been or is being carried out in compliance with the provisions of the DPA (see DPA, s.42).
2. An Information Notice (or Special Information Notice in respect of the 'special purposes': journalism, artistic and literary purposes; DPA, s.3). Whether as a result of a request for assessment received or for the purposes of generally checking compliance with the DPA, the Information Commissioner may serve an Information Notice on a data controller requiring such to provide certain information (DPA, ss.43, 44). Failure to comply amounts to a criminal offence (DPA, s.47).
3. An Enforcement Notice, which is the most serious notice that can be issued by the Information Commissioner. It can be of any nature and extent; it is open to the Information Commissioner to order a data controller to do something in relation to processing of personal data or to refrain from processing personal data in specified ways. Failure to comply with an Enforcement Notice is a criminal offence (DPA, s.47).
4. The Information Commissioner has powers of entry and inspection in order to carry out its investigations and satisfy itself of the state of compliance of the Act by a data controller. A warrant is required before such power can be exercised.
5. Prosecution in respect of offences of failing to notify when required to be notified, and unlawfully obtaining and/or disclosing and/or processing and/or selling personal data (that is, recklessly or knowingly doing so without the data controller's consent).
6. The Criminal Justice and Immigration Act 2008 introduced a new power for breach of the data protection principle of imposing civil monetary penalties. This power has not yet come into force.

More details on these sanctions and penalties can be found in Chapter 3.

1.6 OTHER CONSEQUENCES

Individuals have a civil right of action under the DPA. They are entitled to claim damages for loss caused by any contravention of the DPA as well as compensation for distress caused by such contravention. Normal quantification rules will apply.

One of the biggest fears regarding compliance (and therefore one of the strongest drivers to get it right) is its effect on a data controller's reputation, and the adverse impact that damage to such reputation would have on consumer trust and confidence.

An organisation's success relies on market positioning and reputation. The brand of an organisation is an invaluable asset and represents trustworthiness, quality, fair dealing and stability of an organisation. Damage to this brand can cause unquantifiable loss; lack of trust and confidence of the public in a brand can seriously undermine the future viability of an organisation. It would be a shameful waste to allow adverse publicity for non-compliance with the DPA to render worthless the time, energy and resources invested by an organisation in building its brand. The effect should not be underestimated and, therefore, certain decisions in respect of compliance with data protection legislation (or indeed any other type of legislation) should be escalated to the appropriate level of seniority within an organisation if the brand and reputation of the organisation are at stake.

Those operating within other regulated sectors should be aware that breach of the DPA can frequently lead to breach of their own regulation. For example, the Financial Services Authority has shown itself to be a strong protector of personal information within the financial services sector, imposing fines of over £1million on organisations which fail to protect their customers' personal data.

1.7 BEST PRACTICE

In addition to the legislative and regulatory requirements, which themselves will be modified from time to time, it is vital for advisers to have an understanding of accepted best practice in respect of the application of the DPA within particular industry sectors. This gives the adviser a fuller picture of the issues/demands faced by the client and the adviser is then better placed to assist with the risk analysis exercise, which is discussed later in this chapter.

The following are places to look for information about best industry practice:

1. Industry sector guidance such as that issued by the DMA, OFTEL, ASA, FSA and BBA puts data protection compliance in the context of, and bearing in mind the issues faced by, particular industry sectors.
2. Lessons learned from the experiences of implementing data protection in practice can be invaluable. Advisers should encourage clients to carry out internal reviews to monitor whether their processes/procedures remain efficient and valid for a client's organisation. Other people's mistakes – whether learned of through the media or in networking circles – can be valuable lessons on what not to do!

Having considered some of the background that will influence the way in which lawyers will advise clients on data protection compliance, the next section will consider in more detail the ways in which lawyers might help clients in determining and protecting their data protection needs, and offers some tools to help with this process in practice.

1.8 ADVISER'S ROLE

Data protection is, rightly or wrongly, seen as a compliance and regulatory issue and therefore tends to have negative connotations. As such, it is not unusual for it to be a 'mental block' issue for some organisations. When these organisations seek advice and assistance from a legal adviser on data protection compliance issues, it is important for the legal adviser to understand carefully the client's wants and needs and to be able to turn what is expected to be a negative experience into a positive one.

How can clients be convinced that data protection can be a positive thing which reaps rewards beyond just compliance with the law?

Data protection is an efficient management tool for business operations. If properly approached, the process of devising and implementing a data protection compliance programme will be advantageous. There are three key areas which an adviser should bear in mind not only when providing advice on data protection compliance but also when trying to persuade a client of the importance and benefits of such programmes.

1.8.1 Improving business efficiency

Every organisation can benefit from a review of the way it carries out its business operations. This review can be carried out for several reasons and under different guises. For the purpose of this book, it is enough to understand that in the process of conducting such an audit, an adviser and/or a client who has been advised on the process by an adviser, should always remain aware of the bigger business picture. Do not only look at what processing is being carried out but ask at the same time whether what is being done is the best way of achieving the aim of the processing. Consider whether there is a better way to carry out the same processing/function. Look out for duplication of work: experience of audits has proved that duplication of effort in respect of data processing activities (for example, duplication of data inputs) costs an organisation money in terms of salary for the people to do such work (where they could be redeployed elsewhere) as well as a waste of resources such as IT capacity. Data protection audits are an effective means of reporting any inefficiencies within an organisation and may spark ideas as to how to streamline processes which in turn will benefit overall business activity.

1.8.2 Improving flexibility

Data processing activities are just one set of activities within the context of business operations. It is therefore important to bear in mind that data processing activities must be flexible enough to accommodate all of the business needs, whether they be operational needs or strategy needs. The processes being reviewed and revised at any given time should have built-in flexibility to be able to deal with future and more long-term business strategies. The last thing a client should have to do is to revise and carry out a further data protection (or any other kind of) audit a short period of time after the previous one simply because of the introduction of a new business practice. Organisations have short-term, medium-term and long-term business plans. These should be reviewed in the context of providing advice on data protection issues (for example, an audit or the decision to outsource certain processing activities) and organisations should ensure that any new processes which are put in place are not only compliant with the law but are flexible enough to accommodate future business needs. An audit can after all be a costly, time-consuming and potentially painful process for an organisation. The investment in an audit should not be undermined in the short term.

1.8.3 Maximising commercial use/value of data

Data are valuable. We live in an information age where the collection of data in respect of customers and potential customers is of immense commercial significance. A good adviser will encourage and help a client to maximise the potential commercial use of its data. If a client's collection and general management of its data is compliant and flexible enough to accommodate different potential business processes, such as a variety of marketing schemes, then this data will become even more valuable. This is particularly so in the event that customer lists are to be bought, sold or shared either on their own or as part of a sale or purchase of a business.

In addition to ensuring that data are managed in such a way as to ensure freedom of use of the data in most business activities, an adviser should promote a data protection compliance programme which offers the greatest revenue generation potential for the client (assuming that this is a consideration for the client). Consider, for example, whether a client could collect and manage data in such a way as to be able to share data with new business partners as part of, for example, introductory and commission-based arrangements.

These benefits flow very easily and naturally from proper data handling processes and their importance cannot be over-emphasised.

1.8.4 Engaging the right people

It is likely that there will always be someone who does not see the need for time or money to be spent on data protection compliance programmes. There are different ways to engage people's attention and to motivate them into believing otherwise. Set out below are a selection of the types of obstacles which may be faced and some practical tips on how to overcome them.

Senior management

If an organisation does not have the 'buy-in' to a data protection compliance programme at the highest levels, then it is going to be very difficult for the task to succeed. The right message must be seen to emanate from senior management and trickle its way down through the organisation. If senior management/directors do not take it seriously, neither will those who handle data on a day-to-day basis. Obtaining senior management buy-in can be achieved in several ways:

1. It is not surprising that the threat of personal liability can be a very effective persuasion technique. Directors, or other responsible office holders, may be held personally liable for criminal offences under the DPA. This could lead to a fine (currently £5,000 in the magistrates' court, unlimited in the Crown Court) but, most importantly, may lead to such directors losing office and being unable to hold office in other organisations. It is not clear whether it was intended from the outset for the DPA to create such a powerful provision. It does, however, have the desired effect.
2. Directors and other senior management will have a stake in the business. If the business does well, then so too will the directors. They are likely to benefit not only financially through bonuses and other incentivisation schemes but also in terms of their own reputation within a successful and thriving organisation. They should be under no illusion of the damage which bad data handling processes can cause. This is particularly the case with a consumer-centric business. Such organisations are, and remain, in business because of the confidence held in them by consumers.

13

Consumers very easily lose this confidence if they feel that their personal data are being misused for the commercial gain of the organisation.

The Information Commissioner recently (prior to high profile data loss within the public sector) carried out research into the public's attitude towards data protection. Confidence is already low, with 60 per cent of the population strongly believing that individuals have lost control over the way that their information is used. Loss of confidence in an organisation also leads to a bad reputation. This in turn affects the organisation's brand and it becomes worthless.

Marketers

Marketers quite rightly see themselves as promoting the organisation in order to help it improve its image as well as to increase its business activity and profits. They are out to sell the product or services of an organisation and they may believe that legal requirements get in the way of this process. Marketers may be persuaded by the adage 'no pain, no gain'. It may be seen as a painful exercise to review the marketing department's policies and procedures and to overhaul them, but the benefits will outweigh such pain. Once the marketers are clear in the way in which data are intended to be used throughout the organisation, they can collect them in a more effective manner (e.g. accommodating third-party sharing arrangements in data protection notices) and therefore help the organisation to meet its business objectives. In addition, the use of standardised documentation (standard data protection notices and privacy policies) enables day-to-day operations to become quicker, easier and smoother and should help minimise the internal approval processes. This could result in greater autonomy – every marketer's dream!

IT

IT managers will see the advantages of data protection compliance through better records management. Centralised databases and systems will help with their management of the organisation's systems and will help streamline their processes, thereby making support and maintenance easier. Centralised records management and databases also allow for easier and better security to be put in place such as, for example, more sophisticated restricted access rights.

The role of legal advisers

Where legal advisers fully understand and appreciate the obstacles faced by a client (whether political or business sensitivities, or practical constraints such as system limitations) they are best placed to manage client expectations from a data protection compliance programme and in the wider business operational sense. Advice can be tailored to ensure that it is practical for clients to follow in particular circumstances.

An adviser's role can, however, be much more than just giving legal advice. At times it calls upon the adviser to be a challenging voice and to test the client's decisions.

1.9   RISK ANALYSIS AND PRIVACY IMPACT ASSESSMENTS

There may be instances where a client is not persuaded by the arguments of improving business efficiency, flexibility or maximising data potential, or is persuaded but nonetheless is not driven by them in relation to its data protection compliance programme. It may even be the case that, in limited circumstances, such arguments are not relevant to the client's organisation. In such circumstances, additional, if not total, focus is required on the risk analysis.

A risk analysis should be undertaken in all circumstances of providing data protection advice. The trick is to ask the right questions in order to determine the consequences for the client in:

- not acting in accordance with data protection advice; and
- acting in accordance with data protection advice.

These consequences will be weighed up by the appropriate person within the client organisation as part of taking the commercial decision on the matter. The identity of the appropriate person will depend on the issue at hand and, indeed, the perceived outcome of the risk analysis. If the matter is particularly sensitive or political, a senior person within the client organisation should take the decision. The risk analysis matrix (see Table 1.1) is a useful tool for exploring issues with a client.

In some cases, the risk analysis will be a quick exercise, but sometimes the opposite will be true. The case study in Table 1.2 illustrates a risk analysis matrix for a fictional company which is considering whether to change its data protection notice.

The ICO has recently launched its *Privacy Impact Assessment Handbook* which can be found on the ICO website (**www.ico.gov.uk**). Data controllers are encouraged to include 'privacy by design'.

The scale of effort that is appropriate to invest in a privacy impact assessment (PIA) depends on the circumstances. Large-scale projects, with significant inherent risks to privacy warrant much more investment than those with a limited privacy impact.

Table 1.1 Risk analysis maxtrix

To Act or Not to Act? Issue	Effect	Probability H/M/L Impact H/M/L	Negative Consequences	Probability H/M/L Impact H/M/L	Benefits	Probability H/M/L Impact H/M/L
Note the DP issue, e.g. • Change DP notices – see case study *Or* • Insist on indemnity in data processing agreement? *Or* • Outsource data processing activities outside EEA	Consider the effect of the actions from a legal viewpoint, e.g. • Amounts to breach of the Act or Regulations? • Amounts to a criminal offence? • Adverse impact on the data subject? • Breach of applicable Code of Practice/Best Practice/ Guidance?	How likely are these to be the case? • High • Medium • Low What is the likely impact? • High Risk • Medium Risk • Low Risk	Consider the consequences of a course of action, e.g. • Costs* • Resources • Business impact • Impact on reputation • Lost opportunity • Organisational (re-structuring required?) • Market holding affected? • Criminal prosecution? • Action by OIC? Civil action?	How likely are these to be the case? • High • Medium • Low What is the likely impact? • High risk • Medium risk • Low risk	What are the benefits to be achieved from a course of action? • Improved efficiency • Flexible processes/ systems • Maximise commercial use of data • Increase customer confidence/ trust ** • Compliant with law	How likely are these to be the case? • High • Medium • Low What is the likely impact? • High benefit • Medium benefit • Low benefit

* i.e. the medium- to long-term cost of not achieving the benefits

** The OIC conducted research in 2003 which showed that over 80% of the population say they will stop business with an organisation if they find that personal information is being processed in an unfair way.

© Wragge & Co LLP

Table 1.2 Case study: change Data Protection Notice risk analysis

Client 'Virtual Party Limited'* operates an online party organising business. Potential clients are asked to submit contact details (name, address, email address, payment information) as well as details of the birthday party to be arranged, special messages for the cake, etc. The client has been advised that its Data Protection Notice is inadequate for several reasons including:

- it is not prominent to user on the data collection page (or any other page) so it may not be read;
- it does not give all of the information required;
- it does not allow for sharing of data with third parties.

The risk analysis matrix may look like this:

Issue	Effect	Probability/Impact	Negative consequences	Probability/Impact	Benefit(s)	Probability/Impact
CHANGE DP NOTICE						
1. Act	• Compliant with law and guidance	P-High I-Low risk	• Cost of changes to website • Resources to draft new DP notice	P-High I-Medium risk P-High I-Low risk	• Increased consumer confidence • Increased business reputation • Maximise commercial potential of data, e.g. allowing business arrangements such as introductory arrangements	P-High I-High benefit P-High I-High benefit P-High I-High benefit
2. Do not act	• Breach of Act/Regulations • Breach of guidance	P-High I-High risk P-High I-High risk	• Action by Information Commissioner • Bad publicity • Lose customers	P-Low I-High risk P-Medium I-High risk P-Medium to high I-High risk		

*names and circumstances are fictitious
© Wragge & Co LLP

The Handbook anticipates a range of different PIAs from those which simply check compliance with privacy laws, and in particular with the provisions of the DPA, to those which consider every aspect of the design of a project and identify how the impact on privacy can be minimised.

The intention is that such assessments should take place at a very early stage, before decisions have been taken about the project, to allow privacy to drive the process, rather than technology application or business processes.

1.10 ISSUES TO EXPLORE WITH THE CLIENT

An adviser cannot fully determine a client's data protection needs without probing the state of current compliance of the organisation. This is not restricted to cases where a full data protection audit is being undertaken.

All data protection work involves an element of review (experienced advisers will know that the word 'audit' has negative connotations and it is therefore recommended that it be avoided if possible). An examination of data processing practices is often necessary for relevant and adequate advice to be given in relation to all data protection matters, no matter how small they may appear to be.

Box 1.1 shows a checklist of issues which should be explored with the client.

BOX 1.1   Determining needs checklist

THE BASICS: Does DPA apply? What data are involved? Notification

Questions to ask:

   (a) Is client established in the UK? (see DPA, s.5). Examine whether the client organisation is based in the UK in some way (e.g. company registered in UK; branch exists in UK) and data is processed in the context of such. Alternatively, is processing done using equipment in the UK?
   (b) Are personal data or sensitive personal data being processed? If not, DPA does not apply. If so, establish the basic information.
   (c) Is the client notified with the Information Commissioner? If so, for what purposes and are these accurate/comprehensive? Is there any issue of group companies' notifications?
   (d) What personal data are being processed and for what purpose? These may need to be split down by category of data, e.g. contact details, and health information.
   (e) With what justification (Schedule 2/Schedule 3) are personal data (and/or sensitive personal data) being processed? Is this valid?
   (f) Does the client use privacy/DP notice(s)? Review and challenge where appropriate, e.g. are the purposes valid?

INTERNAL PROCESSES: How does the client organisation address DP issues internally?

Questions to ask:

    (a) Is there a DP manager/officer? Who is responsible for day-to-day DP management? Make contact with this person quickly – they will be an invaluable source of information.
    (b) What is the escalation process? Find out who should be consulted and in what circumstances.
    (c) If dealing with a group of companies or multi-office company, find out about intra-company/office DP management.
    (d) Are there policies/procedures in place? Ask to see a copy for review.
    (e) How does client deal with subject access requests? Ask to see any applicable documentation such as subject access response forms.
    (f) Does client have a complaints-handling procedure? Find out what it is. (Good complaints handling reduces SARs.)
    (g) Test level of awareness of DP responsibilities and policies/procedures within the organisation. Are members of staff trained?

EXTERNAL RELATIONS: Knowing about third-party involvement helps with the provision of advice but also completion of the risk analysis matrix

Questions to ask:

    (a) Who are the data subjects? How are they affected by proposed action/non-action?
    (b) Does client use any data processors or intend to do so (or might do) in future? Examine data processing contractual documentation.
    (c) Do clients have third-party sources of data?
    (d) Are there third parties with whom client shares/transfers information?
    (e) Is the client a multinational organisation which shares data?

Attitude to risk

Explore with the client where it may be prepared to take some risk and where not. Smaller organisations may consider cost to be the most influential factor while multinationals may be prepared to absorb cost but not take any risk with their reputation/brand. A clear steer on this is likely to come from someone relatively senior. Examine past projects and determine important factors for clients.

Future business strategy also comes into play here; maybe the current data protection work is in the context of a bigger project. Explore the risks that this other project might represent.

Resources

Examine the resources available to the client. This will help determine not only what the client should do but the timescale and ability in which to do so. It will also help with scoping issues and gives an adviser an insight into the client's limitations. What can the client cope with?

Determine whether:

    (a) the right people are available at the right time
    (b) the requisite expertise exists within the organisation to conduct revisions/implement changes

(c)   there is an availability of funds for the audit and compliance project
(d)   the client has got support/buy-in from the right people
(e)   there are/are not any related dependencies

Politics/sensitivities

Be aware of the potential obstacles. Try to predict what these may be and devise strategies to overcome/manage them. Determine the messages which people want to hear and deliver them in the most appropriate ways.

© Wragge and Co. LLP

1.11   SCOPING ISSUES

Determining a client's data protection needs is not just about understanding the state of data protection compliance within the organisation and determining the programme to address any compliance issues. It is also about assessing the nature and level of input required from an adviser. Some compliance activities are, where resources permit, best undertaken by the client itself. This may be for cost reasons or because the client's staff have more appropriate knowledge/skills to conduct the review. Working with the client in allocating tasks from the outset benefits the adviser by establishing clear instructions and lines of responsibility.

1.12   CONCLUSION

Proper data protection compliance requires an effective determination of needs from the outset and throughout the advising process. Needs change over time and must be reviewed on a regular basis to ensure they remain relevant and are always taken into consideration in the appropriate way.

This chapter does not introduce new, earth-shattering concepts; rather its aim has been to provide information and tools, gained through experience in this field, to help advisers do what they should always do: keep a client's best business interests at heart.

CHAPTER 2

Defining 'personal data'

Kate Brimsted

The concept of 'personal data' lies at the heart of the DPA: only information which qualifies as 'personal data' is affected by the obligations, limitations and rights created by the DPA.

'Personal data' means 'data' (information in a defined format) which relate to a living individual who can be identified:

(a) from those data alone; or
(b) from those data and other information in the possession of, or likely to come into the possession of, the data controller.

Personal data do not have to be factual or relate to something that has happened; they can be an expression of opinion about an individual (e.g. 'I think Mr Smith lacks motivation') or an indication of the intentions of the data controller or any other person in respect of the individual (e.g. 'Mrs Jones is being considered by the company for redundancy').

In some cases it will be clear whether particular information is 'personal data' but, in many other situations, uncertainty remains. Examples of information capable of being (but not always necessarily amounting to) personal data are: an individual's name, address, telephone number, CCTV image, graffiti 'tag', fingerprint, X-ray image, national insurance number, car number plate and the Internet protocol (IP) address of a computer he is using to connect to the Internet. Information about legal entities per se, e.g. the registered office of a limited company, is not personal data and so cannot be protected by the DPA.

Before looking at the component parts of personal data, it is important to mention some current problems surrounding the interpretation of this concept.

There is considerable uncertainty regarding the scope of the 'personal data' definition. This confusion does not derive simply from the general language of the definition and the dearth of case law. It has a more usual explanation. Data protection law in the UK has reached a surprising juncture where the courts on one hand, and the Information Commissioner on the other, appear to have adopted significantly different approaches to determining what is 'personal data'. This is explained in more detail later in the chapter but, in brief, the courts' interpretation of 'personal data' appears significantly narrower than that adopted by the Information Commissioner.

The chapter explores the meaning of 'personal data' and 'data' and summarises the most relevant case law and guidance from the Information Commissioner.

2.1 'PERSONAL DATA' AS DEFINED IN THE DPA

The definition in s.1 of the DPA states:

> 'personal data' means data which relate to a living individual who can be identified –
> (a) from those data, or
> (b) from those data and other information which is in the possession of, or is likely to come into the possession of, the data controller,
> and includes any expression of opinion about the individual and any indication of the intentions of the data controller or any other person in respect of the individual.

'Personal data' can therefore be seen as comprising three main components:

- data;
- which relate to a living individual; and
- that individual is identifiable from just those data or when they are supplemented by other information.

2.1.1 Data

This term is defined in the DPA as:

(a) information processed by means of equipment operating automatically in response to instructions given for that purpose (e.g. information held on a computer) or information recorded with the intention that it should be processed by such equipment (e.g. manuscript notes that are to be typed up later);
(b) information recorded as part of a 'relevant filing system', as defined in s.1 of the DPA, (i.e. paper records held in a highly structured kind of filing system – see below for further explanation);

(c) information which falls into neither of the above categories but which is an 'accessible record', as defined in s.68 of the DPA (e.g. specific kinds of education or health records); or

(d) recorded information held by public authorities that does not fall within one of the above categories (e.g. paper records held by a public authority that are not in an organised, highly-structured filing system).

Only if information meets one of these four criteria can it be 'data' and therefore potentially relevant to the DPA. The concept of a 'relevant filing system' is described in more detail later in this chapter.

2.1.2   'Personal data', 'relating to' and 'identifiable'

No further definitions are provided in the DPA on the meaning of 'relating to' or 'identifiable' contained in the 'personal data' definition. It is on the meaning of 'relating to' where the greatest disparity between the courts (more precisely the Court of Appeal's judgment in *Durant* v. *The Financial Services Authority* [2003] EWCA Civ 1746) and the Information Commissioner's guidance can be seen.

The Court of Appeal proposed a three-stage test in *Durant*, based on a requirement that the information must affect an individual's privacy. The Information Commissioner's view is that, to be personal data, data need only 'relate' to an identifiable individual in a broad sense. Current guidance from the Information Commissioner[1] explains his view that data will relate to an individual sufficiently to constitute personal data if:

- the data are obviously about him, or, if not,
- they are being processed for the purposes of learning, recording or deciding something about him; or
- as an incidental consequence of the processing, something may be learned or recorded about the individual, or it may have an impact on, or affect, him.

2.2   *DURANT* ON 'PERSONAL DATA'

The Court of Appeal found there are three concepts (the *Durant* concepts) which should be considered when determining whether information amounts to personal data:

1. It must affect an individual's privacy.

In determining this, the court suggested it may be helpful to apply the following additional criteria:

2. It should be biographical in a significant sense.
3. It should have the individual as its focus.

The main aspects of the case are summarised at the end of this chapter in Box 2.1.

In 2003, this judgment was initially welcomed by data privacy specialists and commentators, as it appeared to shed light on a difficult area. A finding, that the scope of personal data was narrower than had generally been thought, also appeared to reduce the compliance burden on data controllers; this was, naturally, viewed positively by businesses and other organisations. However, it became clear fairly quickly that any practical assistance provided by the *Durant* concepts was limited because the question of whether or not the criteria are met can often be highly dependent on the particular context. One example given in *Durant* of information that would not be personal data was meeting minutes recording the mere attendance of a person at a business meeting. However, in certain situations it may have a considerable impact on an individual's privacy to demonstrate that he was at a particular meeting at a particular time. It is respectfully suggested that a pronouncement that information of this kind cannot be 'personal data' is unhelpfully rigid. It has been suggested by some commentators that, contrary to the commonly held view, the Court of Appeal was not suggesting the *Durant* concepts as a universal test for personal data, but rather that they were merely offered as a tool in borderline cases (as per Buxton LJ). This view does not have widespread endorsement.

In summary, the *Durant* concepts can be difficult to apply and it is understood that the correctness of the approach has been called into question by the European Commission in confidential discussions with the UK government over the UK's implementation of the Data Protection Directive (95/46/EC) (see **2.3** for further details).

2.3 THE INFORMATION COMMISSIONER ON 'PERSONAL DATA'

The Information Commissioner is, of course, bound by legal precedent (including *Durant*) and this makes the apparent departure in his published guidance from *Durant* appear surprising at first. However, the Information Commissioner's approach to the 'personal data' concept was not formulated in isolation; it is, in fact, consistent with the view of the other EU Member States' data protection regulators and the European Commission, which is understood to be considering a legal challenge to the UK government's implementation of Directive 95/46/EC based on a number of issues. The details of the talks between the UK government and the European Commission are not publicly known, but some of the European Commission's concerns reportedly arise from the narrow interpretation given to 'personal data' (and 'relevant filing system') under the law in the UK.

2.3.1 The guidance on personal data

If the European Commission ultimately brings infringement proceedings against the UK government this could have an impact on the meaning of personal data in English law, but this is not likely to occur soon. In the meantime, the Information Commissioner has published guidance on determining what information is 'personal data' (the Personal Data Guidance).[2] The Personal Data Guidance is consistent with views expressed by the Article 29 Working Party (an advisory committee to the European Commission composed of representatives of the EU Member States' national data protection authorities).[3] The views of the Information Commissioner (like those of the Working Party) are influential but not legally binding. Significantly, the Personal Data Guidance does not cite the *Durant* concepts.

The Personal Data Guidance examines the meaning of 'relates to' and 'identified/identifiable', as briefly summarised below.

2.3.2 'Relates to an individual'

The Personal Data Guidance suggests that it will often be clear where data 'relates to' a particular individual. Where data are 'obviously about' a particular individual, for example, medical history or criminal record, then this will relate to him because the content of the information determines its relationship with the individual.

Where data are not obviously about an identifiable individual, the Information Commissioner takes the view that:

(1) where data are being processed, or could easily be processed, to *learn, record or decide* something about an identifiable individual; or
(2) as an incidental consequence of the processing, either (a) you could *learn or record something* about an identifiable individual or (b) the processing could have an *impact on*, or *affect*, an identifiable individual,

then the data relate to that individual.

To help answer these questions, the Personal Data Guidance contains a list of supplemental questions, questions 4–8 of which are summarised in Table 2.1.

Table 2.1 Supplemental questions to establish whether data is personal data

Supplemental question	Examples of personal data
1 Are the data linked to an individual so as to provide particular information about him? If yes, they are personal data. If no, go to next question.	Salary details advertised for a job vacancy which are later linked to the individual who is appointed to it.
2 Are the data used, or are they to be used, to inform or influence actions or decisions affecting an identifiable individual? If yes, they are personal data. If no, go to next question.	Data about an individual's mobile phone account (this determines what he will be billed).
3 Do the data have any biographical significance for the individual? If yes, they are personal data. If no, go to next question.	An individual listed as an attendee in meeting minutes (records where he was for that period of time).
4 Does the information concentrate on the individual? If yes, it is personal data. If no, go to next question.	Meeting minutes which record the investigation of a grievance brought by an employee will relate to him.
5 Do the data impact, or have the potential to impact on an individual, whether in a personal, family, business or professional capacity? If yes, they are personal data. If no, the information is not personal data.	Information about the output of a biscuit machine where this is used to access the productivity of the operator.

The Personal Data Guidance recognises that there may still be situations where it is not clear whether information is personal data in the sense of 'relating to' a particular person. The advice from the Information Commissioner is: when in doubt, information should still be treated as personal data and held and disposed of securely.

2.3.3   Identified or identifiable

Although a name is the most common way of identifying someone, it is, of course, not the only way. Examples are given in the Personal Data Guidance of situations where a person's name is not known but he is still identifiable, such as 'the tall, elderly man with a dachshund who lives at number 15 and drives a Porsche Cayenne' or a combination of data about gender, age and grade or salary which enables an employee to be identified without knowing his name.

Where an individual's name is not known, then when determining whether he is nevertheless identifiable, regard has to be had to 'all the means likely reasonably to be used either by the controller *or by any other person* to iden-tify the said person' [emphasis added]. The Personal Data Guidance explains that 'it should be assumed that you are not looking just at the means reason-ably likely to be used by the ordinary man in the street, but also at the means that are likely to be used by a determined person with a particular reason to want to identify individuals'; examples given in the Personal Data Guidance of determined persons include investigative journalists, estranged partners, stalkers or industrial spies. However, in order for a person to be 'identifiable' from the information, there must be more than a very slight hypothetical chance of identifying the individual.

Technological advances are likely to have an impact on the ease with which individuals can be identified; the Information Commissioner's view is that organisations cannot assume that, because information they hold does not allow the identification of individuals at a particular point in time, this will always remain the case. Data controllers are expected to keep under review their decision as to the 'identifiability' question.

The Appendix to the Personal Data Guidance provides some further commentary on the question of anonymisation and how to treat information which is personal data about more than one individual.

2.4 'RELEVANT FILING SYSTEM'

A relevant filing system is one of the four types of 'data' described above in **2.1**. This section looks at the statutory definition, the Court of Appeal's view in *Durant* and the Information Commissioner's guidance.

2.4.1 Definitions in the DPA

A 'relevant filing system' is defined at s.1 of the DPA as:

> any set of information relating to individuals to the extent that, although the infor-mation is not processed by means of equipment operating automatically in response to instructions given for that purpose, *the set is structured*, either by refer-ence to individuals or by reference to criteria relating to individuals, *in such a way that specific information relating to a particular individual is readily accessible.* [emphasis added]

Relevant filing systems contain 'manual' information about people; they do not comprise any computerised or digital-form information. A common example of a relevant filing system is an employee's paper personnel file, containing sub-divided sections for 'leave', 'employment contract and benefits' and 'annual appraisals'.

2.4.2 'Relevant filing system' according to *Durant*

The meaning of 'relevant filing system' was considered by the Court of Appeal in *Durant*. This case is summarised at the end of this chapter in Box 2.1. Auld LJ, giving the lead judgment, stated

> 'a relevant filing system' . . . is limited to a system (1) in which the files forming part of it are structured or referenced in such a way as clearly to indicate at the outset of the search whether specific information capable of amounting to personal data of an individual requesting it under section 7 is held within the system and, if so, in which file or files it is held and (2) which has . . . a sufficiently sophisticated and detailed means of readily indicating whether and where in an individual file or files specific criteria or information about the applicant can be readily located.

2.4.3 The Information Commissioner's guidance on 'relevant filing system'

The Information Commissioner's guidance[4] appears broadly to follow the Court of Appeal's approach. The 'frequently asked questions' on relevant filing systems contains a 'temp test' intended to give a quick, general indication as to whether the Information Commissioner is likely to consider a particular collection of files to be a relevant filing system:

> If you employed a [reasonably competent temp, who had had an induction/explanation about the system], would they be able to extract specific information about an individual without any particular knowledge of your type of work or the documents you hold?

If the temp could locate specific information, then the system is likely to qualify as a relevant filing system.

The 'frequently asked questions' document also contains a series of questions for determining whether there is a relevant filing system which are set out as a flow diagram in Figure 2.1.

In practical terms, to be a 'relevant filing system' a collection of papers needs to be organised in a highly structured way, so that particular information about specific individuals is 'readily accessible', i.e. without the need to look through the file.

If an employee's personnel file is simply ordered by date (and not further subdivided), then it may not be considered (by either the courts or the Information Commissioner) to be a relevant filing system, and therefore its contents would not be personal data (unless held by a public authority). As with so many aspects of data protection law, it should not be regarded as an absolute rule that a file merely organised in chronological order cannot be a relevant filing system.

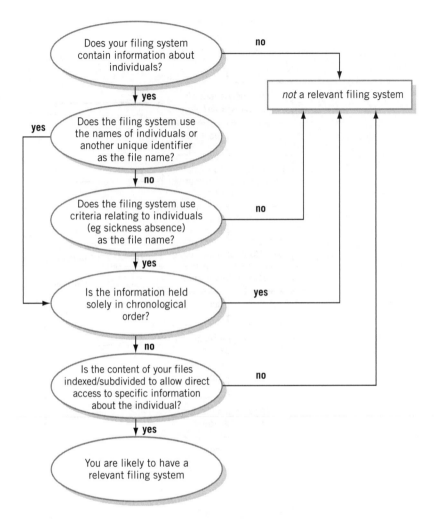

Figure 2.1 Quick guide to understanding the DPA definition of 'relevant filing systems'

'Relevant filing system' is another area where the European Commission is understood to have concerns about the correctness of the UK's implementation of the Directive. At the date of publication, new guidance from the Information Commissioner on 'relevant filing system' was awaited; it will be interesting to see whether the future guidance reveals a preference by the Information Commissioner for a broader 'European' view of the concept.

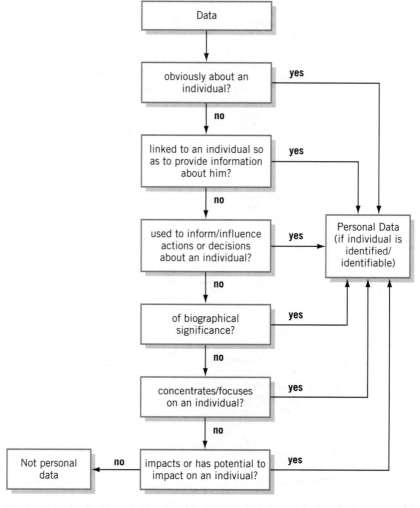

Figure 2.2 Information Commissioner's test for personal data

2.5 CONCLUSION

The Information Commissioner is bound by the Court of Appeal's judgment in *Durant* and, therefore, unless and until the decision is overturned, or the DPA is amended, the narrower view of personal data represents the law. However, in practice aggrieved individuals are more likely to complain to the Information Commissioner, than to sue for breach of the DPA.

Bearing in mind that:

(a) the Information Commissioner is the first independent 'port of call' for most people with a data protection-related grievance; and
(b) very few data protection disputes ever become the subject of court proceedings;

the Information Commissioner's view of personal data can be expected to prevail in day-to-day data protection matters subject to appeals to the Information Tribunal (derived from the Personal Data Guidance). This is likely to be of significant practical importance.

The Information Commissioner's test for personal data is set out in the flow diagram in Figure 2.2.

Until greater clarity is achieved, it may be prudent for organisations to adopt the Information Commissioner's view of the personal data concept, in particular when addressing their compliance obligations.

BOX 2.1   *Durant* v. *FSA* [2003] EWCA Civ 1746

In what arguably remains the most influential English data protection decision, the Court of Appeal declined to order the FSA to provide access by the applicant, Mr Durant, to information he sought from them pursuant to subject access requests. In forming its judgment, the Court narrowed the type of information falling within the definition of 'personal data'.

Facts

Mr Durant was initially in dispute with Barclays Bank in connection with a loan made to Mr Durant's company. He then made a complaint to the Financial Services Authority (FSA) concerning Barclays' conduct. Dissatisfied with their investigation of Barclays, he subsequently made two subject access requests (DPA, s.7) to the FSA, requesting his personal data held by them in both electronic and manual forms.

The FSA supplied Mr Durant with copies of his data which they held in electronic form but refused to give him access to his manual data, arguing that the data were not recorded as part of a relevant filing system.

The Court of Appeal examined the following issues in detail:

• What makes data 'personal data'?
• What is meant by a 'relevant filing system'?
• On what basis should a data controller consider it 'reasonable' to comply with a request where the data include information about a third party who has not consented to such disclosure? (This point is not discussed further in this summary.)

Personal data

The court held that, to be an individual's 'personal data', information must affect an individual's privacy; it must be biographical in a significant sense. The data must also have the individual as their focus and must go beyond merely recording an individual's involvement in a matter that has no privacy connotations.

The court started from first principles, namely that the DPA gives rights to individuals to protect their privacy. The lead judgment of Auld LJ, proposed a test for personal data, described below.

> Mere mention of the data subject in a document held by a data controller does not necessarily amount to his personal data. Whether it does so in any particular instance depends on where it falls in a continuum of relevance or proximity to the data subject as distinct, say, from trans-actions or matters in which he may have been involved to a greater or lesser degree. **It seems to me that there are two notions that may be of assistance. The first is whether the information is biographical in a significant sense,** that is, going beyond the recording of the putative data subject's involvement in a matter or an event that has no personal connotations, a life event in respect of which his privacy could not be said to be compromised. **The second is one of focus.** The information should have the putative data subject as its focus rather than some other person with whom he may have been involved or some transaction or event in which he may have figured or have had an interest, for example, as in this case, an investigation into some other person's or body's conduct that he may have instigated. **In short, it is information that affects his privacy, whether in his personal or family life, business or professional capacity.**
> [emphasis added]

The other two judges agreed, although Buxton LJ qualified his agreement by commenting that he thought the test was useful in borderline cases (and therefore, implicitly, not a universal test); he commented that this was very far from being a borderline case.

Applying the law to the facts, Auld LJ stated 'I do not consider that the information of which Mr Durant seeks further disclosure – whether about his complaint to the FSA about the conduct of Barclays Bank or about the FSA's own conduct in investigating that complaint – is "personal data" within the meaning of the Act. Just because the FSA's investigation of the matter emanated from a complaint by him does not . . . render infor-mation obtained or generated by that investigation, without more, his personal data.' Buxton LJ agreed. He said that the material held by the FSA did not relate to Mr Durant but rather to his complaint. He added that only if the FSA expressed an opinion about Mr Durant would that information 'relate to him'. Access to the material sought, he said, 'could not possibly be necessary for or even relevant to any protection by Mr Durant of his privacy'.

Relevant filing system

The court held that manual systems will only fall within the subject access request regime if they allow access to specific information with an ease comparable to that of comput-erised systems. Auld LJ stated

> 'a relevant filing system' . . . is limited to a system (1) in which the files forming part of it are structured or referenced in such a way as clearly to indicate at the outset of the search whether specific information capable of amounting to personal data of an individual requesting it under section 7 is held within the system and, if so, in which file or files it is held and (2) which has . . . a sufficiently sophisticated and detailed means of readily indicating whether and where in an individual file or files specific criteria or information about the applicant can be readily located.

It must be possible to judge from the outset whether a system is a relevant filing system or not. An ability readily to identify and locate whole files, even those organised chrono-logically or by reference to an individual's and others' names, was not enough according to the Court of Appeal.

The court considered four categories of files:

(a) a file in two volumes relating to systems and controls that Barclays was required to maintain. It was arranged in date order and contained a few documents relating to part of Mr Durant's complaint against the bank;

(b) a file with sub-dividers ordered alphabetically by reference to the name of complainants, including, behind a divider marked 'Mr Durant', some documents relating to his complaint, in date order;

(c) an FSA file relating to cases concerning Barclays, including a sub-file marked 'Mr Durant' containing documents relating to his complaint, not indexed in any way; and
(d) a sheaf of papers in an unmarked folder held by the FSA's Company Secretariat relating to Mr Durant's complaint, not organised by date or any other criterion.

The court held that none of these files was a relevant filing system.

The Court of Appeal concluded that none of the information sought by Mr Durant was his personal data and therefore his right to access under s.7 of the DPA was not engaged. The question of the court's discretion to order provision of the information was also, therefore, not engaged.

Endnotes

1. Data Protection Technical Guidance – Determining What is Personal Data (Information Commissioner's Office, 21 August 2007). (Available on ICO website.)
2. Ibid.
3. Opinion WP 136 (available at **http://ec.europa.eu/justice_home/fsj/privacy/workinggroup/index_en.htm**).
4. Data Protection Technical Guidance Note – Frequently Asked Questions and Answers about Relevant Filing Systems (Information Commissioner's Office, 21 August 2007). (Available on ICO website.)

CHAPTER 3

Risks of non-compliance

Kate Brimsted

3.1 INTRODUCTION

3.1.1 Outline

This chapter describes the consequences which can result from failures to comply with the DPA. To put these in context, the full mechanics of the enforcement process are set out, whether this is enforcement by the ICO or by individual data subjects taking steps to exercise their rights directly. An overview of the enforcement routes available is given in Figure 3.1. As well as describing the framework, this chapter also discusses the broader, non-statutory impact of poor data protection practices on organisations.

Data protection is just one component of an increasingly intricate mosaic of statutes and laws encompassing human rights, freedom of information and anti-terrorism legislation. The complex interrelationship of those laws is outside the scope of this chapter.

3.1.2 Key elements of the DPA

At its most basic, the DPA's effect can be reduced to the following key elements:

1. Defining the standard which data controllers must achieve when they process personal data. This can be summarised as the obligation to comply with the eight Data Protection Principles (s.4(4)).
2. Defining the rights of individuals (data subjects) regarding their personal data and how they may exercise and enforce those rights.
3. Defining the enforcement powers of the Information Commissioner.
4. Creating a range of criminal offences capable of being committed by data controllers, individuals or even the staff of the Information Commissioner.

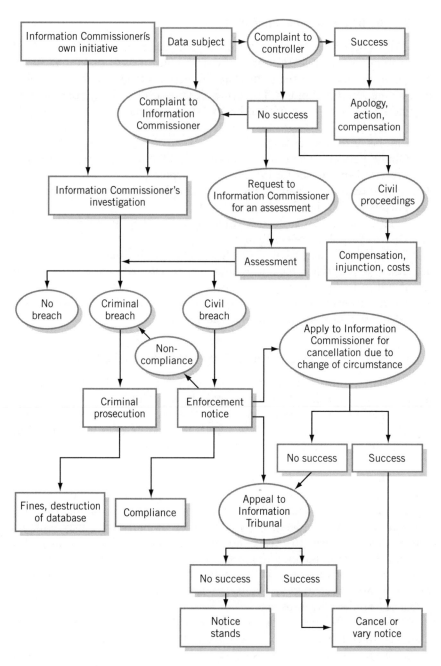

Figure 3.1 The compliance framework within the DPA

3.1.3   The Data Protection Principles

The Data Protection Principles form the foundations of the DPA, s.4(4) of which imposes an obligation on every data controller to process personal data in accordance with the eight Data Protection Principles (the Principles) unless an exemption applies. The Principles are dealt with in more detail in Chapters 5–9 but are summarised below for convenience.

1. Process fairly and lawfully.
2. Obtain personal data only for specified and limited purposes and do not process them further for incompatible purposes.
3. Ensure data are adequate, relevant and not excessive in relation to the purposes for which they are processed.
4. Ensure data are accurate and, where necessary, kept up to date.
5. Do not keep data longer than necessary.
6. Process data in accordance with the rights of individuals (data subjects).
7. Take appropriate technical and organisational measures against unauthorised processing of, loss of, or damage to, personal data.
8. Do not transfer personal data to countries outside the EEA which lack adequate protection for data subjects' rights.

3.1.4   What are the sanctions for failing to comply with the Principles?

It is a common misconception that any breach of the DPA, including the mere breach of a Principle, is a criminal offence. This is not necessarily the case. While the commission of a criminal offence will inevitably involve a breach of one or more of the Principles, the opposite does not follow. The criminal offences created by the DPA are set out in detail later in this chapter.

Breach of one or more of the Principles will, however, give rise to civil liability. The sanctions take a number of forms, including a data subject's right to apply for a court order compelling compliance and/or awarding compensation. Alternatively, the Information Commissioner may issue an Enforcement Notice to bring about compliance. More recently, the Information Commissioner has been accepting contractual undertakings from organisations found to be breaching the DPA. The undertakings are a non-statutory alternative to issuing an Enforcement Notice, and they are published on the ICO website.

In May 2008 the DPA was amended to give the Information Commissioner the power to issue fines (referred to as Monetary Penalty Notices) against data controllers for serious breaches of the Principles, likely to cause substantial damage or distress, which are committed deliberately or recklessly. This power is not in force at the time of publication and import-ant details, such as the maximum level of fine, are still to be determined.

Civil breaches and their consequences are described in more detail later in this chapter.

3.1.5 The role of the Information Commissioner

The Information Commissioner is appointed by the Queen and is an independent officer reporting directly to Parliament. The current incumbent is Richard Thomas, who took up the post in December 2002, and is expected to step down in 2009.

The duties of the Information Commissioner and his office include bringing prosecutions for offences under the DPA, maintaining the register of data controllers required to notify (i.e. register) their processing, promoting good practice and compliance with the DPA, raising awareness of the DPA and encouraging the development of codes of practice. The Information Commissioner also has significant responsibilities in relation to the Freedom of Information Act 2000 and the Environmental Information Regulations 2004, SI 2004/3391. The ICO website includes a number of codes of practice and legal guidance on particular aspects of data protection. The online Register of Data Controllers can also be accessed via the website.

3.2 INFORMATION COMMISSIONER'S REGULATORY POWERS

The DPA creates a number of means by which the Information Commissioner may investigate apparent breaches of the DPA, whether (as is more usually the case) these are breaches which have been alleged by an individual or are apparent breaches which have come to the Information Commissioner's notice in some other way, without a complaint having been received.

In the year ending 31 March 2008, the ICO handled almost 25,000 cases. Most of these cases (40 per cent) were resolved by advice and guidance being provided. The business area which generated the most complaints in the year 2007/08 was lenders, which gave rise to nearly five times more complaints than the next area ('general business'). Overall, the processing activities responsible for the most complaints were: subject access (47 per cent of cases), inaccurate data (11 per cent) and disclosure of data (9 per cent).

3.2.1 Request for assessment

Under s.42 of the DPA any person may make a 'request for assessment' to the Information Commissioner if he knows or believes himself to be directly affected by a data controller's processing of his personal data. The assessment carried out is of whether a data controller's processing is likely to be compliant with the DPA. (This is not to be confused with the less frequently-used power of the Information Commissioner to make an assessment of a data controller's processing, with the data controller's consent, under s.51(7) of the DPA.) Figure 3.2 shows an overview of the typical stages in the assessment process, although the precise procedure followed may vary from case to case.

The person requesting the assessment should preferably complete the standard complaint form, which can be downloaded from the ICO website. The form requires the individual to provide detailed information about the processing in question, including when he became aware of the matter he wishes to be assessed, who the complaint is about and evidence to support the complaint. The Information Commissioner has discretion to treat complaints and information provided other than via the complaint form as requests for assessment (however a complaint is made, there is no requirement for the word 'assessment' to be mentioned). Generally, the Information Commissioner will not consider requests for assessment where the alleged breach occurred more than 12 months previously.

Requests must meet the assessment criteria or they may be refused. Grounds for refusal include the request being made by someone other than the person directly affected, unclear requests and difficulty in being confident of the identity of the person who made the request (according to the ICO's Annual Report for 2007/08, more than 17 per cent of complaints failed to meet the assessment criteria). Once a request or complaint is made which meets the assessment criteria, the Information Commissioner must make an assessment 'in such manner as appears to him to be appropriate', i.e. he has some discretion as to how he carries it out. In exercising that discretion, the Information Commissioner may have regard to:

- the extent to which the request appears to raise a matter of substance;
- any undue delay in making the request; and
- whether or not the person making the request is entitled to make an application under s.7 in respect of the personal data in question.

Following receipt of a completed form, the Information Commissioner will decide whether or not to conduct an assessment. The Information Commissioner has produced guidance called Policy on Handling Assessments (third edn, 8 January 2003) which is available on the website. Requests for assessment fall into two main categories:

- assessments relating to, or including, a potential criminal offence; and
- those relating solely to a breach of one or more of the Principles.

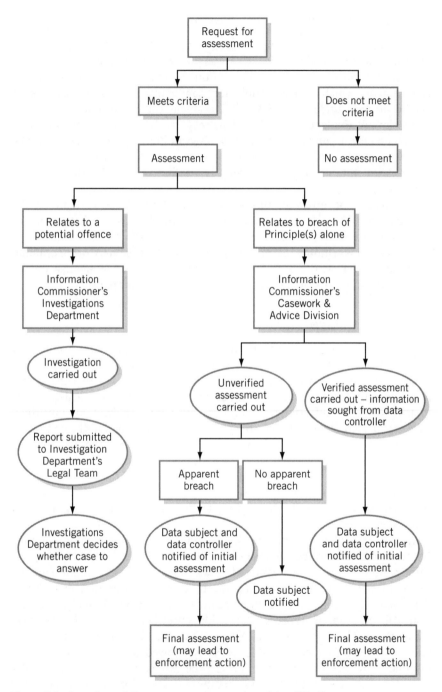

Figure 3.2 Overview of the assessment procedure (simplified)

Investigation of potential criminal breaches

Where a request for assessment reveals an apparent criminal offence and the Information Commissioner decides to pursue the matter, the data controller will be informed and the Information Commissioner's Investigations Department, which is responsible for conducting field investigations of alleged offences under the DPA, will investigate the matter under the Police and Criminal Evidence Act 1984. This may involve interviewing witnesses, taking statements under caution, obtaining and executing search warrants, reviewing evidence and preparing prosecution files. The Information Commissioner refers to this process as an 'investigation' rather than an assessment.

The results of investigations are considered by the legal team in the Investigations Department, and a decision is reached as to whether or not there is a case to answer. In the event that the Information Commissioner considers that a criminal offence has been committed, he may bring criminal proceedings against the data controller and, if appropriate, against one or more of the directors of the data controller, if it is a company.

Assessment of alleged civil breaches

Where the request for assessment involves only an alleged contravention of one or more of the Principles, the Information Commissioner's Casework and Advice Division will make an initial assessment as to whether the allegation is such that an Enforcement Notice might be issued if the allegation were to be proven. If enforcement action is considered unlikely, an unverified assessment is conducted, based solely on the facts presented in the complaint submitted. If, as a result of the unverified assessment, the Information Commissioner considers that a contravention is unlikely to have occurred, he will inform only the person making the request. Conversely, if the Information Commissioner considers a contravention is likely to have occurred, he will inform both the person who made the request and the data controller.

If it appears from the information provided that enforcement action may be required, a verified assessment will take place. This involves the Information Commissioner asking the data controller for information and an explanation of events surrounding the processing in question in order to determine whether a contravention has in fact taken place. Usually, information will be sought through correspondence between the Information Commissioner's Casework and Advice Division and the data controller. Generally, an initial period of 28 days is allowed for data controllers to respond to requests for information. To the extent that the data controller fails to provide any requested information necessary for the conduct of the assessment, the Information Commissioner may, in due course, issue an

Information Notice, which legally obliges the data controller to provide the information requested.

At the end of the period for assessment, the Casework and Advice Division will issue an initial assessment of processing and inform the person making the request and (if a verified assessment) the data controller of its preliminary conclusions. The parties are then usually allowed a further period of 28 days in which to make representations to the Information Commissioner if they disagree with any part of the initial assessment. The Information Commissioner will consider any representations made and issue a final assessment.

3.2.2 Adverse assessments

Where an adverse assessment has been made – whether following the verified or unverified route – the Information Commissioner has discretion as to whether or not to take any further action (such as seeking a written undertaking from the data controller or issuing an Enforcement Notice). An adverse verified assessment was made against 11 banks and financial institutions in early 2007 as a result of their disposal of customer information being in breach of the DPA (they were found to have discarded personal information in bins outside their premises). The result of this was that each organisation gave a written undertaking to the Information Commissioner, confirming that it had amended its practices to prevent such breaches in the future. The undertakings can be read on the ICO website.

A data controller which receives notice of an adverse assessment of processing may not necessarily be obliged to take any action. For example, the unlawful processing could relate to an historic incident and the organisation could have independently updated its procedures to prevent it happening again. An assessment represents the opinion of the Information Commissioner and there are no consequent legal penalties (although it may be given some weight, for example, in court proceedings brought by an individual for compensation under s.13 of the DPA).

During the year ending 31 March 2007, the Information Commissioner received nearly 24,000 written complaints, enquiries and requests for assessment.

3.2.3 Notices: general

To assist him in his enforcement role, there are three kinds of notice which the Information Commissioner can issue. These are:

- Enforcement Notices;
- Information Notices; and
- Special Information Notices.

Service on a data controller of any of the three types of notice does not constitute a criminal sanction. However, if the data controller does not comply with the terms of a notice within the time period specified in the notice, this can be a criminal offence under DPA, s.47 (see 'Failure to comply with a notice' later in this chapter). In most situations, the time limit for compliance with the notice will start to run from the date it is served on the data controller. It is a defence for the data controller to prove that it exercised all due diligence in order to comply with the notice. There is also a right of appeal to the Information Tribunal against the service of a notice.

Before serving a notice, the Information Commissioner will usually issue a preliminary notice to the data controller as a 'shot across the bows' and to allow the Information Commissioner to demonstrate that he has used all due diligence before exercising his enforcement powers. A preliminary notice demonstrates to a data controller that the Information Commissioner is minded to serve a formal notice if the data controller does not comply with the requests that have been made by the Information Commissioner and if the Information Commissioner does not receive a response from the data controller within a short, stipulated period of time. The preliminary notice will also usually state that, if the data controller intends to comply with its terms or if there is some reason why the data controller believes that a formal notice should not be served, the controller should contact the Information Commissioner. In either case, the onus is on the data controller to contact the Information Commissioner.

Therefore, another function of a preliminary notice is to allow the data controller an opportunity to object prior to the issuing of a formal notice; for example, in the case of an Information Notice, where the data controller is genuinely unclear what information is being requested by the Information Commissioner, or it no longer has the information requested. Any such objections by the data controller should be made to the Information Commissioner in writing.

There is a right of appeal to the Information Tribunal (DPA, s.48) against the service of a notice, and its decision may be appealed, on a point of law only, to the High Court. Schedule 6 to the DPA sets out the procedure for appeals. Each notice must contain details of the right of appeal. Appealing a notice suspends its effect.

In January 2008, Enforcement Notices were issued against two sister telecom companies, both of which were found to be breaching the subject access right and the requirement to process data securely, and were also failing to keep customer data up to date. The Enforcement Notices required the companies to take specified corrective steps within 35 days of the date of the notice. During the year ending 31 March 2008, nine Enforcement Notices were issued against six police authorities, two telecom companies and a well-known high street retailer. During the same period, nine sets of formal undertakings were obtained, including from three government departments.

3.2.4   Enforcement Notices

Where the Information Commissioner considers that a data controller is contravening, or has contravened, any of the Principles, he can serve an Enforcement Notice on that data controller. Compliance with the terms of an Enforcement Notice should bring about compliance with the Principles. The Enforcement Notice may require the data controller to do one of the following:

- stop processing any personal data;
- stop processing personal data of a particular description;
- stop processing in a certain manner; or
- take certain steps to remedy the situation (e.g. rectify or delete data) and may set out a timeframe within which this must be done.

In deciding whether or not to serve an Enforcement Notice, the DPA requires the Information Commissioner to consider whether a contravention has caused, or is likely to cause, any person damage or distress (DPA, s.40(2)).

3.2.5   Information Notices

The Information Commissioner may serve an Information Notice on a data controller in the following circumstances (DPA, s.43):

- in the course of carrying out an assessment, in which case the notice must explain that the notice is for that purpose and specify the processing which is the subject of the assessment; or
- where, of his own volition, the Information Commissioner reasonably requires information in order to decide whether or not a data controller has complied with the Principles. The notice must state why the Information Commissioner regards the information requested as being relevant for the purpose of determining whether there has been a breach of the Principles.

Where a preliminary Information Notice has been issued and has not been complied with or responded to, an Information Notice will usually follow. The Information Notice will require the data controller to provide the Information Commissioner with certain information in the form specified in the notice and within a set period of time.

Information Notices (and Special Information Notices) cannot require the recipient to provide the Information Commissioner with information which would reveal:

43

- the content of any communication between a lawyer and a client where the client's obligations, liabilities or rights under the DPA are the subject of the communication; or
- the content of any communication between a lawyer and a client, or between a lawyer or a client and any other person, made in connection with, or in contemplation of, proceedings under the DPA (including proceedings before the Information Tribunal) and for the purposes of such proceedings.

In addition, information which would incriminate the recipient of the notice (other than in relation to an offence under the DPA) does not have to be provided.

3.2.6 Special Information Notices

A Special Information Notice (DPA, s.44) is essentially a kind of Information Notice applicable where information is sought about processing carried out for the special purposes (see **3.2.7**). A Special Information Notice may be served on a data controller by the Information Commissioner in the following circumstances:

- if the Information Commissioner has received a request for assessment, in which case the notice must explain that it is for that purpose and must specify the processing which is the subject of the request; or
- where, in a case where proceedings have been stayed under s.32, the Information Commissioner has reasonable grounds for suspecting that personal data are not (contrary to the controller's assertion or the court's view) being processed only for the special purposes. Alternatively, a Special Information Notice may be served where there are stayed proceedings under s.32 and the Information Commissioner has reasonable grounds for suspecting that personal data are not (contrary to the controller's assertion or the court's view) being processed with a view to the publication by any person of any journalistic, literary or artistic material not previously published by the data controller. In either case, the notice must give the reasons for the Information Commissioner's suspicions.

As with Information Notices, Special Information Notices cannot compel a data controller to supply the Information Commissioner with particular kinds of legally privileged or incriminating information (see above).

3.2.7 Special purposes processing

The special purposes are the following: the purposes of journalism, artistic purposes and literary purposes. The extra safeguards in the DPA in respect of processing for the special purposes are to ensure that operation of the Information Commissioner's powers under the Act does not contravene the right to freedom of expression enshrined in the Human Rights Act 1998, which brought into force most of the articles of the European Convention on Human Rights.

Independent of the right to issue a Special Information Notice, the Information Commissioner may formally determine that particular personal data are either not being processed only for the special purposes or are not being processed with a view to publication of any journalistic, literary or artistic material which has not previously been published by the data controller (DPA, s.45). The effect of such a determination is that it lifts any s.32(4) stay of court proceedings involving special purposes processing and may also enable the Information Commissioner to issue an Enforcement Notice in relation to special purposes processing (DPA, ss.32(5), 46(1)).

3.2.8 Powers of entry and inspection

Schedule 9 to the DPA sets out the circumstances in which the Information Commissioner may seek the authority to enter a data controller's premises and inspect the records it holds there. In order to do so in England and Wales, the Information Commissioner must obtain a warrant from a judge to enter and search the premises. The first step by the Information Commissioner (other than in urgent cases) will be to ask the data controller for access. It is only if this is refused, or the data controller refuses to co-operate with the Information Commissioner's requests once on the premises, that the Information Commissioner will seek a warrant.

Before issuing a warrant, the judge must be satisfied by information on oath supplied by the Information Commissioner that there are reasonable grounds for suspecting that all the following apply:

1. A data controller has contravened, or is contravening, any of the Principles, or an offence under the DPA has been, or is being, committed and in either case that evidence of the breach is to be found on any premises specified in the information.
2. The Information Commissioner has given seven days' notice in writing to the occupier of the premises in question demanding access to the premises.
3. Either:

- access was demanded at a reasonable hour and was unreasonably refused, or
- although entry to the premises was granted, the occupier unreasonably refused to comply with a request by the Information Commissioner or any of the Information Commissioner's officers, for example, to search, inspect or examine equipment.

4. The occupier has been notified by the Information Commissioner of the application for the warrant and has had an opportunity of being heard by the judge on the question of whether or not a warrant should be issued.

Provisions 2–4 do not apply if the judge is satisfied that the case is one of urgency or that compliance with the provisions would defeat the object of the entry.

A warrant will permit the Information Commissioner and his staff within seven days of the date of the warrant to search the specified premises and to inspect, examine, operate and test any equipment found there which is used, or intended to be used, for the processing of personal data. It also permits them to inspect and seize any documents or other material which provide evidence of the offence or breach of the Principles.

Certain matters are exempt from the powers of inspection and seizure conferred by a warrant under Schedule 9, e.g. legally privileged material and personal data processed for national security purposes. During the year ending 31 March 2007, seven search warrants were sought.

Depending on the urgency of the situation, the Information Commissioner may not be required to give notice to the data controller. For example, in the year ending 31 March 2002, three no-notice search warrants were granted to search data controllers' premises.

The Information Commissioner has the power under s.54A to inspect personal data recorded in certain, specified overseas databases (e.g. the Schengen information system) for the purpose of determining whether or not the processing is in compliance with the DPA.

3.2.9 Assessments or 'audits' with the data controller's consent

Under s.51(7) the Information Commissioner has the power to assess any processing of personal data for the following of good practice; however, the relevant data controller's consent is required in order to exercise this power. This could be regarded as a kind of consensual audit power. The Information Commissioner considers that his office requires a general right to inspect the processing of personal data in order properly to discharge its functions (see *Data Protection Powers and Penalties, The Case for Amending the Data*

Protection Act 1998 (December 2007)). An extension of the Information Commissioner's power to audit appears likely in future.

3.2.10 Monetary Penalty Notices

In May 2008, the Information Commissioner was given the power to levy fines for serious breaches of the DPA, by issuing a Monetary Penalty Notice (MPN). This is a civil penalty and does not create a new criminal offence under the DPA. At the time of publication the power was not yet in force and a considerable amount of the detail was still to be worked out, including the maximum level of fine which can be levied. These pending details are likely to be highly significant to the effectiveness of MPNs. The new power will be contained in ss.55A–E of the DPA.

The Information Commissioner may serve a data controller with an MPN if he is satisfied that:

- there has been a serious contravention of s.4(4) by the data controller;
- such contravention was of a kind likely to cause substantial damage or substantial distress; and
- either:
  - it was committed deliberately; or
  - the data controller knew, or ought to have known, that there was a risk that the contravention would occur and that such a contravention would be of a kind likely to cause substantial damage or substantial distress, but failed to take reasonable steps to prevent the contravention.

Before an MPN can be served, the Information Commissioner must issue a Notice of Intent (s.55B of the DPA), informing the data controller that it may make written representations within a specified time in relation to the Information Commissioner's proposal to serve an MPN. The Notice of Intent must also contain other information which will be prescribed in regulations to be made by the Secretary of State.

Another preparatory step which must be taken before the MPN procedure can be used is that the Information Commissioner must produce and issue guidance about how he proposes to exercise his functions, in particular when an MPN will be considered appropriate and how the amount of the penalty will be determined (s.55C). The guidance must be laid before Parliament.

3.3   CRIMINAL OFFENCES UNDER THE DPA

A number of criminal offences are created by the DPA. One-off, minor criminal breaches will not necessarily result in a prosecution; instead, the Information Commissioner may seek written undertakings from the data controller, confirming that it will amend its processing operations to avoid future breaches of a similar nature, or he may issue a caution.

Between April 2006 and March 2007, the Information Commissioner administered five cautions in relation to offences under the DPA. This reflects the Information Commissioner's policy of administering cautions as an alternative to prosecuting, where appropriate.

Where a criminal offence is suspected, the Information Commissioner's Investigations Department will look into the data controller's processing and investigate the surrounding circumstances. This will often involve a visit to the data controller's premises – for example, 905 site visits were made by the Information Commissioner's staff during the year ending 31 March 2003.

Criminal proceedings can only be instigated by the Information Commissioner or by, or with the consent of, the Director of Public Prosecutions. Apart from the offence of obstructing the execution of a warrant (which can only be tried summarily), all offences under the DPA may be tried either in a magistrates' court or in the Crown Court. Offences under the DPA are punishable by way of a fine, with the current maximum fine on summary conviction being £5,000; in the Crown Court there is no maximum limit for a fine.

For certain offences the court has the power to order the forfeiture, destruction or erasure of material containing personal data and used in connection with the processing of personal data (documents, computer disks, etc.). This could mean that, in serious cases, entire databases have to be deleted. Similar sanctions are possible in civil proceedings.

In the year ending 31 March 2008, 11 successful prosecution cases were brought by the Information Commissioner under the DPA. The types of offence are shown in Table 3.1. The highest fine imposed during the year ending 31 March 2008 was £34,200 (together with £5,000 costs) and was

Table 3.1 Types of offence and convictions

Offence	No. of convictions
Unlawful obtaining, obtaining and selling, selling, disclosing (s. 55)	89
Failure to notify (s.17)	7
Failure to comply with Enforcement Notice (s.47)	6

Source: Information Commissioner's Annual Report and Accounts 2007/08

ordered against a private investigation company and its director for 44 counts of unlawfully obtaining personal data in breach of s.55.

3.3.1 Who can be guilty of an offence?

Offences under the DPA can be committed by:

- the data controller (which can be a body corporate or an individual);
- corporate officers of the data controller (DPA, s.61). Where an offence has been committed with 'the consent or connivance of or is attributable to any neglect' on the part of a director, manager, secretary or other similar officer, or any person who was purporting to act in any such capacity, then that person may be liable to prosecution for the same offence as that which the company has committed (three company directors and managers were found guilty of criminal offences during the period between April 2006 and March 2007);
- employees of the controller (e.g. under the unlawful obtaining offence under DPA, s.55); and
- individuals who aid, abet, counsel or procure the commission of an offence under the DPA (as a general principle of English law).

3.3.2 Types of offence

The criminal offences created by the DPA are described below. Table 3.2 summarises the offences, sanctions and relevant sections of the DPA.

Processing without notifying

Unless exempt, it is a criminal offence for data controllers to process personal data without notifying (i.e. registering with) the Information Commissioner (DPA, s.21(11)). Although a strict liability offence, failure to notify is unlikely to result in the immediate commencement of criminal proceedings.

Where the Information Commissioner determines that a data controller has not notified (and is not exempt), he will usually inform the data controller that it is required to notify and will allow it a short period of time within which to do so, failing which a criminal investigation may be initiated. In January 2008, a solicitor was convicted of failing to notify and given a six-month conditional discharge and ordered to pay £804 in costs. The requirements for notification (and the exemptions) are explained in Chapter 4.

Table 3.2 Criminal offences created under the DPA

Offence	Defence	Possible sanction	Reference in the DPA
Failure to notify the Information Commissioner of processing under s.17	None	Summary: a fine up to the statutory maximum[1] Indictment: an unlimited fine Forfeiture, destruction, erasure of data	s.21(1)
Failure to notify the Information Commissioner under s.20 of changes to information required under s.17	Exercise of all due diligence to comply with the duty	Summary: a fine up to the statutory maximum Indictment: an unlimited fine Forfeiture, destruction, erasure of data (in the case of assessable processing only)	s.21(2)
Unauthorised assessable processing	None	Summary: a fine up to the statutory maximum Indictment: an unlimited fine Forfeiture, destruction, erasure of data	s.22(6)
Failure to make certain information available upon request (relating to notification)	Exercise of all due diligence to comply with the duty	Summary: a fine up to the statutory maximum Indictment: an unlimited fine	s.24(4)

Offence	Defence	Possible sanction	Reference in the DPA
Failure to comply with an Enforcement Notice, an Information Notice or a Special Information Notice	Exercise of all due diligence to comply with the notice	Summary: a fine up to the statutory maximum Indictment: an unlimited fine Forfeiture, destruction, erasure of data (in the case of Enforcement Notices only)	s.47(1)
Making a false or reckless statement in purported compliance with a notice	None	Summary: a fine up to the statutory maximum Indictment: an unlimited fine	s.47(2)
Intentionally obstructing access to overseas information systems or failure to give assistance	Reasonable excuse		s.54A
Unlawful obtaining or disclosing of personal data	(a) Necessary for the prevention/ detection of crime or authorised by rule of law or court order (b) Acted with reasonable belief that entitled to in law (c) Reasonable belief that data controller would have consented had it know [(ca) Acted for the special purposes with reasonable belief justified in the public interest] or (d) Justified as being in the public interest	Summary: a fine up to the statutory maximum Indictment: an unlimited fine Forfeiture, destruction, erasure of data	s.55(3) [NB: (ca) NOT IN FORCE]

Offence	Defence	Possible sanction	Reference in the DPA
Selling or offering to sell personal data obtained in contravention of s.55(1)	None	Summary: a fine up to the statutory maximum Indictment: an unlimited fine	s.55(5)
Requiring production of relevant records in connection with: – recruitment – continued employment – services contract	(a) Imposition of the requirement was required/authorised by enactment, rule of law or court order or (b) Justified as being in the public interest	Summary: a fine up to the statutory maximum Indictment: an unlimited fine Forfeiture, destruction, erasure of data	s.56 [Only partially in force]
Disclosing, without lawful authority, information provided to Information Commissioner[2]	Reasonable excuse	Summary: a fine up to the statutory maximum Indictment: an unlimited fine	s.59
Intentionally obstructing the execution of a warrant or failure to give assistance	None	Summary only: a fine up to level 5	Schedule 9, paragraph 12, by virtue of s.50

1 Currently £5,000.
2 Lawful authority is defined in the DPA, s.59(2).

Change in notification particulars

Although notifications under the DPA last for a year, changes during that period should be notified as they occur, rather than at the renewal stage (DPA, s.21(2)). Data controllers must inform the Information Commissioner of any change in registrable particulars or changes to the technical and security measures taken to comply with the Seventh Principle. Failure to keep notification particulars up to date constitutes a criminal offence, although it is a defence if the controller can show it exercised all due diligence to comply.

Unauthorised assessable processing (DPA, s.22(6))

Assessable processing (not to be confused with a request for assessment under DPA, s.42) is defined in s.22(1) as meaning particular types of processing that are to be set out in an Order made by the Secretary of State and which appear particularly likely to do either of the following:

- cause substantial damage or distress to data subjects; or
- otherwise significantly prejudice the rights and freedoms of data subjects.

The Information Commissioner will not be able to make any determination regarding assessable processing under s.22 until secondary legislation has been passed by the Secretary of State. No such Order has been made to date.

After receiving a notification from a data controller, the Information Commissioner must determine whether the processing relates to assessable processing. This includes notification to the Information Commissioner of any changes to processing operations under s.20, as well as initial notifications under s.18 of the DPA. Within 28 days of receipt of the notification, the Information Commissioner has to inform the data controller whether or not it is carrying out assessable processing and, if it is, whether the assessable processing is likely to comply with the provisions of the DPA.

It is a criminal offence to carry out assessable processing after notifying unless one of the following applies:

- 28 days have elapsed from the date of receipt of the notification by the Information Commissioner (this period can be longer if the Commissioner extends it due to special circumstances – see DPA, s.22(4)); or
- before 28 days have elapsed, the data controller has received a notice from the Information Commissioner stating the Information Commissioner's opinion on whether the processing is likely to comply with the provisions of the DPA.

Failure to make certain particulars available

Where a data controller which has lawfully chosen not to notify with the Information Commissioner (i.e. its processing is exempt from the requirement to notify) receives a written request from any person for that data controller's relevant particulars, it must comply with the request within 21 days of its receipt (DPA, s.24(4)). Failure to do so is a criminal offence, although it is a defence for the controller to show it exercised all due diligence in complying.

The relevant particulars are the items set out in s.16(1) of the DPA, i.e. the information which notifying data controllers must include in their notification. The fact that a data controller's processing is exempt from the requirement to notify does not exempt the data controller from having to provide certain information to data subjects and other parties on request.

Failure to comply with a notice

As stated above, it is a criminal offence to fail to comply with an Information Notice, Special Information Notice or Enforcement Notice unless the controller charged is able to show that it exercised all due diligence to comply with the notice (DPA, s. 47(1)). Keeping detailed records of the steps taken to comply with any notice is therefore a prudent measure.

It is a criminal offence to make a materially false statement, whether knowingly or recklessly, when supplying information in response to an Information Notice or a Special Information Notice (DPA, s.47(2)).

Unlawful obtaining, disclosing or selling of personal data

It is a criminal offence for a person knowingly or recklessly, without the consent of the data controller, to obtain or disclose personal data (or the information contained in personal data), or to procure the disclosure to another person of the information contained in personal data (DPA, s.55(3)–(5)). There are defences which arise where the obtaining or disclosure is necessary for national security or in the public interest. It is also a criminal offence to sell, or offer to sell, personal data obtained in this way.

In September 2002, a tracing agency based in Portsmouth was convicted and fined for unlawfully obtaining and selling information in breach of the DPA (the fine was £1,400 with costs of £1,000). The prosecution was brought as a result of a joint investigation initiative between the Information Commissioner, the Inland Revenue and the Department for Work and Pensions, directed at clamping down on tracing agencies which often use deceptive practices in order to obtain information to which they are not entitled.

In April 2007, a private investigation company and its director were convicted of 44 counts of unlawfully obtaining personal data. The conviction related to a number of calls made to various Department of Work and Pensions offices where the caller pretended to be an employee in order to confirm the current addresses for hundreds of people being traced on behalf of finance houses.

In May 2008, s.55 was amended to confer a power on the Secretary of State to provide, by order, that a person guilty of an offence under s.55 be liable for imprisonment (up to twelve months on summary conviction and up to two years on conviction on indictment). Before making an order to amend, the Secretary of State must consult the Information Commissioner and such media organisations as he considers appropriate. In addition, s.55(2) was amended to add a new defence for the purposes of journalism and other special purposes. The defence is available where a person acted with a view to publication by any person of journalistic, literary or artistic material and in the reasonable belief that the obtaining, disclosing or procuring was justified in the public interest. At the time of publication, this amendment is not yet in force.

Prohibition of requirement of certain records

A further criminal offence is created by s.56(5) of the DPA. This provision is only partially in force (namely, in relation to information held by the Secretary of State or a body established under the Safeguarding Vulnerable Groups Act 2006) and the rest will not become operative until relevant parts of Part V of the Police Act 1997 are brought into force. This prohibits a person from requiring that another person or a third party supply a 'relevant record' (see below) or produce a 'relevant record' in connection with:

- the recruitment of another person as an employee;
- the continued employment of another person; or
- any contract for the provision of services to him by another person.

Further, a person concerned with the provision (for payment or not) of goods or services to the public must not, as a condition of providing the goods or services to another person, require that person or a third party to supply a relevant record or to produce it.

A relevant record is defined as one of a number of specified types of record which have been obtained under an individual's s.7 right of access. The records include those relating to cautions, criminal convictions and prison records. This offence is sometimes referred to as 'enforced subject access'.

It is a defence for a person charged to show that imposing the requirement to produce the record was required or authorised by or under any enactment, by any rule of law or by order of a court, or that in the particular circumstances it was justified as being in the public interest.

Disclosing the Information Commissioner's information

Unless the disclosure is made with lawful authority, it is a criminal offence knowingly or recklessly to disclose the following information which has been provided to the Information Commissioner (DPA, s.59); information which:

- has been provided to or obtained by the Information Commissioner under the DPA;
- relates to an identifiable individual or business; and
- is not, at the time of the disclosure (and has not been in the past), available to the public from other sources.

Obstructing or failing to assist in the execution of a warrant

Intentionally obstructing a person in the execution of a warrant for entry and inspection, or failing, without reasonable cause, to give any person executing such a warrant such assistance as is reasonably required, is a criminal offence (DPA, Sched.9, para.12).

3.4 CIVIL BREACH AND THE INFORMATION COMMISSIONER

Historically, the Information Commissioner's role in relation to breaches of the DPA has been more reactive than proactive, e.g. responding to and investigating complaints made by individuals. However, as explained above, the Information Commissioner has fairly extensive investigative powers, which he is entitled to – and increasingly does – exercise at his own initiative, rather than merely following up complaints. Figure 3.1 shows the routes by which either the Information Commissioner or an individual can seek to enforce the DPA's requirements.

Generally speaking, anyone can complain to the Information Commissioner about non-compliant processing; no particular locus standi is required (although only those who are, or believe themselves to be, directly affected by the processing can validly request an assessment (DPA, s.42)).

3.5 CIVIL BREACH AND THE INDIVIDUAL

Depending on the type of breach, an individual may be entitled to seek redress in the following ways (see also Figure 3.1):

- complain to the offending data controller;
- complain to the Information Commissioner;
- apply to court. In certain situations (e.g. the right to prevent processing for direct marketing purposes under s.11), before being able to apply to court for an order, an individual will have to demonstrate having given written notice to the data controller and that this has not been complied with.

3.5.1 When might an individual choose to apply to court?

An individual can take a complaint to the Information Commissioner, so why choose to commence court proceedings? In reality, court proceedings are likely to remain the less popular option but there are certain circumstances in which it could be worthwhile for individuals to apply to court. For example:

1. Where there is a sense of urgency which an individual considers is not shared by the Information Commissioner. The Information Commissioner's resources are limited and if only one individual is affected by a particular breach, the Information Commissioner may not be prepared to act with the speed which the individual believes is warranted.
2. Where significant financial damage has been, or is being, caused by a breach. The Information Commissioner has no power to order controllers in default to pay compensation to a data subject. Compensation or damages can only be obtained via a court order or through negotiation with the data controller at fault.
3. Where the Information Commissioner has already investigated the matter but the individual is not satisfied with the outcome, or considers that the outcome did not go far enough; for example, an adverse assessment which the Information Commissioner does not propose to pursue further.
4. Where there are associated breaches of other laws (e.g. contract or confidence) which the individual wants to be resolved together with the data protection breach. The Information Commissioner has no jurisdiction outside the remit of the DPA (apart from under the Freedom of Information Act 2000 and the Environmental Information Regulations 2004).

Table 3.3 sets out the sanctions available for breaches of rights of individuals under the DPA.

3.5.2 Compensation awards for individuals

So far damages awards under s.13 have been both rare and nominal in amount. One of the few instances in which damages were awarded by the court – and certainly one of the most prominent cases – was supermodel Naomi Campbell's dispute with Mirror Group Newspapers ([2002] EWHC 499). At first instance Naomi Campbell was awarded £2,500 for both breach of confidence and breach of the DPA, which decision was later overturned by the Court of Appeal ([2002] EWCA Civ 1373). Ms Campbell successfully appealed the Court of Appeal's judgment to the House of Lords ([2004] UKHL 22).

In *Adeniji* v. *London Borough of Newham* (*The Independent*, 17 October 2001) the Borough settled a s.13 claim brought against it relating to its unauthorised use of a child's photograph in an AIDS awareness campaign. The Borough is understood to have paid £5,000 in damages and costs of £50,000.

The damages award under the DPA in *Douglas* v. *Hello!* [2003] EWHC 2629 (Ch) made by Mr Justice Lindsay was a mere £50 each for Mr and Mrs Douglas.

Table 3.3 Sanctions for breaches of rights of individuals under the DPA

Key: S = data subject; C = data controller

Breach	Defence	Possible sanction	Section No.
Failure to comply with a subject access request	(a) a reasonable time has not elapsed since an earlier identical or similar request was complied with; (b) disproportionate effort (partial defence[1]); or (c) 'exempt' material; etc.[2]	S applies to court: Court may order compliance If S succeeds, court may order C to pay S's legal costs	s.7
Failure to comply with a s.10 notice (notice to stop processing likely to cause unwarranted, substantial damage or distress)	None but does not apply if any of the conditions in Sched.2, paras.1–4 are met (s.10(2))	S applies to court: Court may order compliance (including that C takes such steps for complying with the notice as the court thinks fit) If S succeeds, court may order C to pay S's legal costs	s. 10
Failure to comply with a s.11 notice (notice to stop processing for direct marketing purposes[3])	None	S applies to court: Court may order compliance (including that C takes such steps for complying with the notice as the court thinks fit) If S succeeds, court may order C to pay S's legal costs	s. 11

Breach	Defence	Possible sanction	Section No.
Failure to comply with a s.12 notice (notice to stop processing in relation to automated decision-taking)	None	S applies to court: If court satisfied that person taking decision failed to comply, court may order person to reconsider or take a new decision If S succeeds, court may order C to pay S's legal costs	s.12
Failure to comply with a s.12A notice (notice to rectify, etc. inaccurate exempt manual data or to cease holding it)	None	S applies to court: Court may order compliance (including that C takes such steps for complying with the notice as the court thinks fit) If S succeeds, court may order C to pay S's legal costs	s.12A
Compensation for damage caused by failure to comply with DPA (See **3.5.2** and summary of *Campbell* v. *Mirror Group Newspapers Limited* at the end of this chapter.)	C took such care as in the circumstances was reasonably required to comply with the particular requirement	S applies to court: Court may award compensation for damage caused (and also distress, if any[4]) Court may make associated order to address the underlying breach(es) causing the damage or distress If S succeeds, court may order C to pay S's legal costs	s.13

Breach	Defence	Possible sanction	Section No.
Processing inaccurate personal data of S (See summary of *P* v. *Wozencroft* at the end of this chapter.)	None	S applies to court: Court may order compliance (including that C takes such steps for complying as the court thinks fit, e.g. rectifying, blocking or erasing the data and any expression of opinion based on them) Court may also order C to notify third parties to whom data were disclosed of the rectification, etc. of data If S succeeds, court may order C to pay S's legal costs	s.14
Serious breach of the Principles, likely to cause substantial damage or distress, committed recklessly or deliberately	Reasonable preventative steps taken	Penalty (maximum currently unknown)	ss. 55A–55E [Not in force]

1 The data are partial in the sense that, on the strict wording of s.8(2), disproportionate effort exempts a data controller only from providing a copy in permanent form of an applicant's personal data, not from providing access to it.
2 N.B. the list of defences is not exhaustive.
3 Defined in s.11(3) as the communication (by whatever means) of any advertising or marketing material which is directed to particular individuals.
4 If processing is for the special purposes (defined in s.3), i.e. journalism, literary purposes or artistic purposes, then there is a right to compensation for distress caused by a breach, even where there is no associated loss or damage.

The right to compensation under s.13 is likely to be attractive only for those who have substantial funds and are not discouraged by the modest levels of the awards made so far and the fact that, even if successful, they are unlikely to receive all their costs. If an application for compensation is successful, then the court is likely to order the loser to bear the majority of the victor's costs (an approximate guide is that the court would order 60 per cent of the costs incurred by the victor to be paid by the loser, although the actual proportion is difficult to predict with any degree of certainty).

3.5.3 The defendant data controller's lose/lose scenario

Table 3.4 illustrates the likely alternative outcomes for a data controller defending an application for compensation under s.13 of the DPA. As can be seen in Table 3.4, the differences are fairly minimal.

Based on the information in Table 3.4, it can be seen that it will generally be in a data controller's best interests to try to avoid a data subject bringing proceedings against it in the first place or to settle such proceedings at an early stage.

Table 3.4 Outcomes for a defendant data controller

Controller loses	Controller wins
Controller bears its legal fees and probably most of the data subject's fees	Controller likely to bear at least some of its legal fees
Controller pays damages/ compensation assessed by the court (or agreed on settlement with the data subject)	N/A
Management/internal time and disruption	Management/internal time and disruption
Adverse publicity	Some (possibly adverse) publicity, e.g. prior to the outcome
Public scrutiny of the controller's data protection practices	Public scrutiny of the controller's data protection practices

3.6 NON-DPA CONSIDERATIONS

3.6.1 Commercial damage

Few organisations set out to engage in unlawful, not to mention potentially criminal, conduct. Nevertheless, even where the Information Commissioner does not consider it appropriate to take formal enforcement measures, he may require contractual undertakings from errant organisations. In such cases, the undertakings are published on the ICO website and the press frequently pick up the story, particularly in cases of prominent data protection transgressors. In 2007, 11 banks and other institutions were required to give undertakings to the Information Commissioner for poor data disposal practices; although this came to the Information Commissioner's attention as a result of investigative journalism, the publications by the ICO led to the incidents being reported widely in the mainstream press.

Particularly in the case of B2C (Business to Consumer) commerce, publicity suggesting that protection of customer data is below par or that consumers' privacy choices are not respected can be highly damaging to the reputation of a business. Even non-consumer-facing organisations need to satisfy employees and their representatives that they can be trusted with employee data, particularly if they wish to centralise the holding of these data outside the EEA, e.g. where the parent company is in the United States.

In addition to damage to reputation, substantial financial losses can flow from non-compliance. For example, making errors during the collection of personal data in circumstances where a business intends to use those data (or sell them to others) for direct marketing purposes can undermine entirely the commercial advantages to be gained. Another example is non-compliance resulting in an Enforcement Notice which blocks current and/or prospective data-processing activities by the controller, for instance, by prohibiting the export of customer personal data to a company's outsourced data processor outside the EEA or by requiring the cancellation of an imminent direct marketing campaign. The potential damage caused can be measured in a variety of ways. Taking the example of outsourced data processing, it could be in the form of:

- lost cost savings where the operations have to be carried out at the higher labour costs applicable in the EEA;
- losses associated with disruption to customer service (e.g. damage to goodwill, breach of contract with customers, disenchanted customers going elsewhere);
- the costs of putting alternative data processing arrangements in place; and
- possible liability to third parties, e.g. business partners/sponsors.

3.6.2 The impact of unlawfulness

The First Principle of the DPA requires processing to be fair and lawful; therefore, if particular processing contravenes any area of law, even one unconnected with data protection, the processing necessarily breaches the First Principle and hence the DPA. The checklist below is a non-exhaustive list of other laws which may be relevant to the processing of personal data in particular cases:

- confidentiality (which was recognised by the House of Lords in *Campbell* as including a right to prevent the misuse of private information);
- contract;
- Computer Misuse Act 1990;
- Data Retention (EC Directive) Regulations 2007, SI 2007/2199;
- defamation: common law and the Defamation Acts 1952 and 1996 and the Electronic Commerce (EC Directive) Regulations 2002, SI 2002/2013;
- Freedom of Information Act 2000;
- Human Rights Act 1998;
- Privacy and Electronic Communications (EC Directive) Regulations 2003, SI 2003/2426;
- Regulation of Investigatory Powers Act 2000;
- Telecommunications (Lawful Business Practice) (Interception of Communications) Regulations 2000, SI 2000/2699; and
- trespass.

3.6.3 The Privacy and Electronic Communications (EC Directive) Regulations 2003

The Privacy and Electronic Communications (EC Directive) Regulations 2003, SI 2003/2426 (PEC Regulations) implement Directive 2002/58/EC (concerning the processing of personal data and the protection of privacy in the electronic communications sector), the overriding aim of which is to update and clarify the impact of the existing privacy regime on newer technologies, such as e-mail and cookies. The PEC Regulations came into force on 11 December 2003. (Note that the European Commission has announced its intention to amend Directive 2002/58/EC.)

The enforcement mechanism under the PEC Regulations is closely modelled on that under the DPA, with the Information Commissioner having the prime authority for enforcement.

In terms of civil breach and individuals' rights, individuals who suffer damage as a result of any breach by another person of the PEC Regulations are entitled to sue that person for compensation (reg.30(1)). It is a defence for the other person to prove that all such care had been taken as in the circumstances was reasonably required to comply. Individuals have successfully recovered damages in both the English and Scottish courts from UK-based spammers. A Scottish court awarded an individual £750 in compensation for a single e-mail. The English court went a step further by confirming that it is not just individuals who are entitled to compensation. In *Microsoft Corporation* v. *Paul McDonald t/a Bizads UK* [2006] EWHC 3410 (Ch), [2007] Bus LR 548, the High Court awarded an Internet service provider damages, as well as an injunction.

So far as the Information Commissioner's powers in relation to a breach of the PEC Regulations are concerned, a modified version of the enforcement regime under the DPA applies. In addition, where a breach of the PEC Regulations is alleged, either OFCOM (the Office of Communications, as established by s.1 of the Office of Communications Act 2002) or an aggrieved person may request the Information Commissioner to exercise his enforcement functions in respect of that breach. However, the Information Commissioner may exercise those functions regardless of whether or not he has been requested to do so.

In addition, the Information Commissioner has powers under Part 8 of the Enterprise Act 2002 to apply to court for an enforcement order in cases where breaches of the PEC Regulations are considered harmful to individual consumers.

In the year ending 31 March 2008, five PEC Regulations Enforcement Notices were issued. Five undertakings were obtained, and undertakings under the Enterprise Act 2002 were also obtained from three companies. Since January 2007, the Information Commissioner has been taking a more robust approach to breaches of the PEC Regulations and in 2007/08 there was the first successful prosecution of the breach of an Enforcement Notice.

A summary of the powers of the Information Commissioner in relation to a breach (or suspected breach) of the PEC Regulations is set out in Table 3.5. (For more details, refer to Schedule 1 to the PEC Regulations.)

3.6.4 Codes of practice and other guidance

There are a number of potentially relevant codes of practice and guidelines which have been produced by a range of bodies, including the Information Commissioner. The general rule is that these codes do not have any direct legal effect, not even those issued by the Information Commissioner. However, breaches of particular codes are likely to be cited in any enforcement action by the Information Commissioner. Some codes have been designated as being of particular relevance for special purposes processing (see Table 3.6).

Codes of practice from the Information Commissioner

One of the general duties of the Information Commissioner is to promote compliance by data controllers with the requirements of the DPA and with

Table 3.5 Enforcement powers under the PEC Regulations

Enforcement power contained in the DPA	Available under the PEC Regulations?
Request for assessment	No
Enforcement Notice	Yes
Information Notice	Yes
Special Information Notice	No
Special Purposes Processing	N/A
Powers of entry and inspection	Yes
Right of appeal against Enforcement Notices and Information Notices	Yes

good practice standards. The Information Commissioner produces codes of practice as part of this duty (DPA, s.51). Copies of the codes of practice are available online at the ICO website, as well as in hard copy from the Information Commissioner.

Other codes and guidance

It is not only the Information Commissioner who produces codes of practice relevant to data processing that controllers need to be aware of and may need to comply with. Table 3.6 gives some illustrative examples of such other codes.

A prominent example is the British Code of Advertising, Sales Promotion and Direct Marketing (CAP Code) produced and enforced by the Committee of Advertising Practice (CAP). The CAP Code is not law, but rather industry self-regulation, and describes itself as the rule book for non-broadcast advertisements. The CAP Code does, however, reflect EU and UK regulation of distance selling and data privacy.

Where a complaint is made to CAP, it will investigate the complaint. If it concludes that the marketer has contravened the CAP Code, CAP will ask the company promptly to make any changes which are necessary for its advertisements to comply. If a company refuses to do so, there are a number of sanctions available, including negative publicity, refusal of further advertising space, removal of trade incentives and legal proceedings (under the Control of Misleading Advertisements Regulations 1988, as amended, SI 1988/915).

Table 3.6 Relevant codes of practice

Code	Date	Further Information
British Broadcasting Corporation Producers'Guidelines*	November 1996	www.bbc.co.uk
Committee for Advertising Practice (CAP) Code (11th edition) (applies to non-broadcast UK marketing communications)	March 2003	www.cap.org.uk www.asa.org.uk
Direct Marketing Association (UK) Main Code of Practice (3rd edition) Also the e-mail marketing code, SMS marketing code, automated dialling equipment code	September 2003	www.dma.org.uk
European Federation of Direct Marketing (FEDMA) Direct Marketing Code[1]	July 2003	http://europa.eu.int/comm// internal_market/privacy/docs/ wpdocs/2003/wpdocs/2003/ wp77_en.pdf
Information Commissioner's CCTV Code	January 2008	www.ico.gov.uk
Information Commissioner's Employment Practices Code Employment Practices Code – Supplementary Guidance	June 2005 June 2005	www.ico.gov.uk
Information Commissioner's Framework code of practice for sharing personal information	October 2007	www.ico.gov.uk

Code	Date	Further Information
Office of Communications (OFCOM) The Ofcom Broadcasting Code	July 2005	www.ofcom.org.uk
Press Complaints Commission Code*	August 2007	www.pcc.org.uk
Regulation of Investigatory Powers Act 2000 – codes made under this Act, e.g. the Code on Covert Human Intelligence Sources[2] and the Code on Covert Surveillance[3]	July 2002 onwards	http://security.homeoffice.gov.uk/ripa/
Treasury Guidance on money laundering and data protection	April 2002	www.hm-treasury.gov.uk/media/D/F/money_laundering.pdf

* Codes which have been designated under the Data Protection (Designated Codes of Practice) (No.2) Order 2000, SI 2000/1864. These regulations were made under the DPA, s.32(3). The significance of the designation is that, in relation to special purposes processing, in determining whether any publication would be in the public interest, regard may be had to compliance with the particular codes.

1 The European Commission has approved this Europe-wide code of practice as complying with the Data Protection Directive (95/46/EC).

2 SI 2002/1932.

3 SI 2002/1933.

3.6.5   The Information Commissioner's approach to enforcement

The Information Commissioner is 'committed to making it easier for those organisations who seek to handle personal information well – and tougher for those who do not'.

His attitude to enforcement is to adopt a risk-based approach (Data Protection – Protecting People, A Data Protection Strategy for the Information Commissioner's Office (March 2008)). The Information Commissioner has explained that his priorities for enforcement will be influenced by both (a) the seriousness of the risk of harm to individuals and society and (b) the likelihood of that risk materialising. When assessing the seriousness of harm the Information Commissioner will take account of:

• the number of individuals actually or potentially affected;
• whether these individuals are particularly vulnerable;

67

- the long-term as well as the short-term impact on those affected;
- whether the harm is a one-off or part of a trend; and
- harm that arises indirectly because public confidence in data protection is damaged.

Even if a serious risk of harm is deemed likely to arise, before intervening the Information Commissioner will consider whether, realistically, action by his office can make a difference in reducing the risk of harm and whether the outcome of an intervention is likely to represent a worthwhile return on the effort required.

3.6.6　New powers for the Information Commissioner?

For a number of years, the Information Commissioner has been seeking additional powers of enforcement and greater resources. The introduction of the power to fine is a significant development and it is interesting to put it in the context of the powers and changes which the Information Commissioner has been publicly seeking (e.g. see the First Report of the House of Commons Select Committee on Justice (December 2007)).

The main changes sought have been:

- the introduction of a new criminal offence for significant breaches of the Principles (this resulted in the power to issue a civil penalty (MPN));
- an obligation on data controllers to notify security breaches to the ICO;
- a right of audit and inspection by the Information Commissioner without the consent of the data controller affected; and
- an obligation on data controllers to include a statement in annual reports, to be signed by the chief executive or head of government department and confirming that internal security policies have been followed.

The Information Commissioner is understood to be in discussions with the Government, which, in December 2007, announced its commitment to strengthening the ICO's powers. In his 2008 Annual Report, the Information Commissioner stated:

> We hope soon to have long-awaited inspection and audit powers. Modest increases in the notification fee for the largest data controllers will give us significant resources to improve our infrastructure and make the best possible use of existing and new powers.

It appears to be a question of 'when' and not 'if' the powers of the Information Commissioner will be further increased, although this will not necessarily result in all of the powers requested becoming available to the ICO.

3.7   CONCLUSION

The likelihood of non-compliance and the associated risks are higher than they have ever been. They can also confidently be predicted to increase. Some of the reasons for this are:

- continued construction of centralised databases containing personal data and data sharing initiatives, especially in the public sector;
- greater deployment of IT generally, leading to increased opportunities to exploit electronic information;
- increasing technical sophistication of organised crime;
- greater awareness and concern by individuals regarding their rights and the dangers of identity theft, due in no small part to breaches on the scale of that by HMRC in late 2007;
- the Information Commissioner's power to issue Monetary Penalty Notices (currently pending);
- a political will to increase further the powers of the Information Commissioner and the powers and profile of the Minister responsible for data protection.

The possible negative consequences of a breach of the DPA are as follows:

- Controllers can incur criminal as well as civil liability.
- Officers of the offending controller can be personally criminally liable.
- Breaches can lead to identity theft and can even endanger individuals (e.g. in 1999 in New Hampshire, USA, an obsessed stalker obtained Amy Boyer's details from information brokers and private investigators (whose methods included pretext calls) and used the information to follow and murder her).
- Fines/compensation/orders/Enforcement Notices can be made against failing controllers (including, in future, fines by the Information Commissioner).
- Restrictions may be imposed on the way in which a controller can conduct its business and exploit the information it holds.
- Breaches can result in bad publicity and lasting damage to an organisa- tion's reputation and brand.
- Failing controllers are more likely to have their processing assessed by the Information Commissioner.
- Breaches can annoy, and even alienate, customers and business partners.
- Breaches can undermine new (particularly online) products, e.g. trials of interactive advertising services.
- Breaches can accompany breaches of other, more established areas of law where levels of damages are more substantial, e.g. breach of confi- dence, defamation, breach of contract.

This chapter has largely focused on the enforcement mechanisms and sanctions under the DPA. However, despite the increase in the Information Commissioner's enforcement powers, for most organisations the greatest risk posed by non-compliance is still likely to be in the form of reputational harm and, as a consequence, possible commercial damage. Data protection compliance is now widely seen as a component of good corporate governance. Astute organisations recognise it as an opportunity, i.e. a means by which a commercial entity can differentiate itself from its competitors. In the light of this, to use the words of the Information Commissioner, data protection compliance should essentially be a matter of enlightened self-interest.

BOX 3.1 *Campbell* v. *Mirror Group Newspapers* [2002] EWHC 499, [2002] EWCA Civ 1373

Naomi Campbell sued the *Mirror* (now the *Daily Mirror*) newspaper for damages for breach of confidence and compensation under s.13 of the DPA in respect of articles and photographs which the newspaper had published about her. The articles stated that, contrary to her previous assertions, Campbell was in fact a drug addict and attended Narcotics Anonymous meetings. The *Mirror* printed details of the meetings, as well as photographs showing Campbell leaving the meetings. At trial Campbell agreed that the *Mirror* was entitled to reveal that she was a drug addict and receiving therapy, but argued the information that she was attending Narcotics Anonymous, the photographs and details of the meetings were private and confidential and that it was not in the public interest that they be published.

At first instance Campbell succeeded on both counts on the basis that the details of the meetings were confidential and publication was detrimental to her. Although the newspaper was held to have been justified in publishing that Campbell had made false denials about her drug taking, the details of her attendance at Narcotics Anonymous meetings with accompanying photographs and captions were sensitive personal data under s.3 of the DPA because they were information relating to her physical or mental health or condition. The court held that the special purposes exemption under s.32 (which exempts processing undertaken with a view to the publication of journalistic material from complying with most of the Principles – including the First Principle – provided the controller reasonably believes publication of the material is in the public interest) only applied to pre-publication processing and not to the publication itself. The *Mirror*, therefore, had no defence under the DPA as it had published the material. Damages of £2,500 were awarded for the distress and injury to feelings caused, in addition to aggravated damages of £1,000.

The *Mirror* appealed and won. The Court of Appeal held that the publications were wholly justified in the public interest and that they did not breach the DPA. The disclosure of Campbell's attendance at Narcotics Anonymous was a legitimate part of the journalistic package, which a fair-minded person would not have considered offensive to publish. Further, the court ruled that the processing in this case was exempt from complying with the First Principle as the public interest defence in s.32 was not limited to processing prior to publication but also applied to publication as part of the processing operation.

The court held:

> [b]ecause the exemption provided by s.32(1) depends upon the processing being undertaken with a view to publication the door was open to the argument . . . that the processing could not include the publication itself. The result of this argument is an absurdity. Exemption is provided in respect of all steps in the operation of processing up to publication on the ground that publication is reasonably believed to be in the public interest – yet no public interest defence is available to a claim for compensation founded on the publication itself. . . . We do not consider that the wording of s.32 compels such a result.

Campbell appealed to the House of Lords and in May 2004 their Lordships upheld her appeal by a majority of 3 to 2, confirming that the law of confidence includes a right to prevent misuse of private information and reinstating her damages award of £3,500. However, the widely-reported judgment focuses exclusively on Campbell's claim for breach of confidence, with the House of Lords taking the view that her 'claim under the [Act] . . . adds nothing here'. The Court of Appeal's ruling as to the scope of the s.32 exemption must therefore be presumed to stand.

BOX 3.2 *P* v. *Wozencroft* [2002] EWHC 1724 (Fam)*

P separated from his wife, who subsequently refused him access to his daughter, who was living with her. P, as litigant in person, embarked on a long battle to try to secure rights of access to his child. Dr Wozencroft was a consultant child psychiatrist instructed to write a report concerning P's application for, among other things, a contact order regarding his daughter. The defendant's report was critical of P. P made a data subject access request under s.7 of the DPA to Wozencroft to try to obtain documents underlying the report. Wozencroft told P that he had already been provided with copies of all relevant material but P disputed this and applied to court for an order that documents be provided to him. P also made an application for rectification under s.14 in respect of sections of the report with which he strongly disagreed. The judge dismissed both these applications and ordered P to pay the defendant's costs.

The court noted that both ss.7 and 14 confer a discretion, not a duty, on the court to make an order. It also held that under the s.14 application, even though it did not have sufficient facts before it in order to judge whether the personal data processed were inaccurate, it could nevertheless conclude that, even if they were, the court would not exercise its discretion to order rectification of the report. This was because P had had two previous hearings at which to raise the rectification issue and had not done so.

The judge concluded:

> with confidence that it is an abuse of process to use later proceedings in order to ventilate challenges which were clearly apt to be ventilated in earlier proceedings in which the claimant was a party. I consider that the claim for rectification is an abuse of this court's process and I hereby strike out the statement of case therein.

* High Court of Justice (Family Division) before Mr Justice Wilson on 15 July 2002.

71

CHAPTER 4

Notification

Sally Annereau

4.1 INTRODUCTION

This chapter examines the notification requirements of the DPA. It sets out how to assess whether notification is needed and, where this is the case, examines the principal methods of making an application for a notification entry. Finally the chapter reviews the consequences of failing to notify.

By reading this chapter, the reader will be able to:

- understand the purpose of notification;
- decide if notification is required;
- check whether an exemption from notification applies;
- make an application for notification;
- keep the notification entry under review;
- update and make changes to the notification entry; and
- understand the criminal consequences of failing to comply.

4.2 WHAT IS NOTIFICATION?

4.2.1 Introduction

If someone intends to process personal data, an important first consideration is whether they must inform the ICO that they are doing so. Notification is a statutory process whereby a data controller provides the Information Commissioner with details of the processing of personal data carried out. The details of this processing are then published in the form of an entry in a public register. Failure to notify the Information Commissioner where this is required and failure to keep registered details up to date are criminal offences under the DPA.

4.2.2 The legal obligation

The notification process set out in the DPA replaces an earlier system of registration under the Data Protection Act 1984 and changes the law in this area to a substantial extent. Part III of the DPA deals with the notification obligation of data controllers, and s.17 of this Part sets out the specific prohibition on the processing of personal data without first having an entry on the public register of data controllers maintained by the Information Commissioner.

Although the DPA provides the framework for the notification process, other more specific details are provided in secondary legislation. The Data Protection (Notification and Notification Fees) Regulations 2000, SI 2000/188 sets out regulations covering a range of provisions relating to the notification process including:

- arrangements for exempting data controllers from the need to notify where they carry out certain personal data processing activities;
- the prescribing of the notification fee payable by data controllers; and
- providing for the Information Commissioner to determine the actual form that notifications should take.

The Data Protection (Fees under Section 19(7)) Regulations 2000, SI 2000/187 prescribe the fee to be paid to the Information Commissioner for a certified copy of any data controller's entry on the register (currently £2). Uncertified copies of entries are, however, available free of charge at any time from the ICO website.

4.2.3 The purpose of notification

The key objective behind the notification process is to provide openness concerning the processing of personal data so that members of the public can easily find out information about who is processing personal data, and why. They can then use this knowledge to exercise their rights under the DPA in respect of that processing.

Transparency is also important in helping the Information Commissioner to target advice and enforce compliance with the data protection Principles of the DPA. It is worth noting, however, that there is no link between notification and compliance with the Principles. The Information Commissioner can enforce the Principles against any data controller, irrespective of whether the data controller needs to notify under the DPA. The Information Commissioner can choose whether to separately investigate and prosecute a data controller who is obliged to notify but does not do so, and can also investigate and enforce any breaches of the Principles.

The notification process additionally has some value as a means of revenue generation.[1] Following an agreement with the former Department for Constitutional Affairs (now the Ministry of Justice) and with the consent of the Treasury, the Information Commissioner can retain revenue derived from notification fees collected since 1 April 2005 for expenditure on data protection purposes.

4.3 WHO NEEDS TO NOTIFY?

4.3.1 Data controllers

A legal person such as an individual, a company or other corporate body who makes the decisions about how personal data are processed must, as a data controller, notify this processing with the Information Commissioner unless an exemption applies. The requirement to notify the details of personal data processing to the Information Commissioner only applies to data controllers. An organisation that merely processes personal data on behalf of a data controller (described by the DPA as a processor) is not required to notify that processing. Only one notification entry is allowed per data controller.

Identifying the legal person responsible for determining how personal data are processed is not always straightforward. Complex organisational structures and data-sharing arrangements can often mean that that there is more than one legal entity processing personal data as a data controller, in which case, where no relevant exemption applies, each must separately notify the processing it undertakes.

4.3.2 Identifying the data controller – examples

Groups of companies

Where individual companies within a group each process personal data as a data controller, then each must submit a separate notification to cover that processing. It is not possible to submit one notification covering the personal data processing conducted by the entire group. Separate departments of a single company will be covered by the notification of the main company and should not be notified separately. However, if the departments are known publicly by different names (for example, as distinct trading divisions) then these different names should be listed in the entry for the main company.

Sole traders

In this scenario, the legal person will be the individual trader rather than the trading style of the unincorporated business. Where notification is required, the entry should therefore be made in the name of the trader rather than the business.

Pension trustees

Pension law (Pensions Act 1995, as amended by the Pensions Act 2004) provides that the trustees of occupational pension schemes retain ultimate control over the administration of pension schemes with the result that they are also responsible for determining how and why personal data are processed in the course of making decisions about how the scheme is run. The trustees of the pension scheme are required to collectively notify their role as trustees of the named pension scheme.

Insolvency practitioners

Insolvency practitioners, such as receivers or liquidators, can be data controllers in their own right for the processing of personal data arising from the legal appointment of the practitioner to take control of, manage or dispose of a business and its assets, which may include the personal data records of the business.

Other special arrangements

In some cases the complexities of shared legal responsibilities have resulted in special arrangements being made under the DPA for notifying certain types of entities.

- *Partnerships*: where two or more persons carry on business in partnership and are data controllers then, although each is in practice a separate legal person, only a single notification is required in the name of the firm rather than a separate notification being required in the name of each partner (Data Protection (Notification and Notification Fees) Regulations 2000, SI 2000/188, reg.5(1)).
- *Schools*: legal responsibility for the functioning of schools is in practice divided between the governing body and the head teacher (the school generally having no legal status of its own). Special arrangements for notification require only a single entry in the name of the school (DPA, s.6(1); Data Protection (Notification and Notification Fees) Regulations 2000).

4.4 EXEMPTIONS

4.4.1 Introduction

There are exemptions from the need for some data controllers to have to notify or from the need to notify certain types of processing of personal data. In all but a few limited cases, a data controller that is able to rely on an exemption from notification must still comply with the other provisions of the DPA, including the data protection Principles. Details of the exemptions relevant to notification and their scope are referred to below.

4.4.2 Personal, family, household affairs

Personal data processed by an individual purely for personal, family or household affairs (including recreational purposes) are exempt from the notification requirement.

Processing personal data for the purpose of personal, family or household affairs also provides a general exemption from other provisions of the DPA, although with the proviso that the Information Commissioner retains the power to investigate and take action when someone appears to be processing personal data outside the limits of the exemption.

4.4.3 Paper files

Where a data controller does not carry out any processing of personal data using a computer then notification is not required. The Information Commissioner considers that the term 'computer' applies quite widely to include any equipment capable of being described as a computer, such as mainframe, desktop, laptop and mobile palm devices. Other items of equipment not typically described as a computer but capable of automatically processing data are also included in the description of computer, such as automated retrieval systems for microfilm and microfiche, audio or visual systems and other recording mechanisms such as flexitime systems, telephone logging or CCTV systems.

Other provisions of the DPA still apply where the data exempt from notification are personal data processed in highly structured paper files (described by the DPA as relevant filing systems).

Where personal data are processed both on paper and on computer files then, when notifying the non-exempt personal data processing, it is also necessary to indicate whether or not the notification voluntarily includes the non-exempt paper files.

4.4.4   Not-for-profit organisations

Some not-for-profit organisations can benefit from an exemption from the requirement for notification where the organisation has not been created, or is not operated, for profit. In order to rely upon the exemption, the processing of personal data by the organisation must only be for the purposes of:

- establishing or maintaining membership or support for the organisation;
- providing and managing services to the membership or individuals who have regular contact with the organisation.

The personal data must also be limited to what is strictly necessary for the exempt purpose and must be disclosed only with the consent of the data subject or to third parties strictly necessary for the exempt purpose. The personal data must not be retained after the relationship with the data subject has come to an end unless, and for as long as, such data are still necessary for membership or supporter purposes.

These are quite strict limitations. The exemption would cease to apply in any case where the processing of personal data went beyond the limitations described.

4.4.5   Core business purposes

Personal data processing carried out by a data controller for only one or more of the following basic core business purposes is exempt from notification:

- staff administration (e.g. recruitment, termination, pay, performance, discipline and management of staff);
- advertising, marketing and public relations (e.g. promoting the data controller's own business, products or services);
- accounts and records (e.g. keeping accounts or records of transactions relating to the business in order to supply, bill or pay for services, or for management analysis and forecasting).

Each of these core purposes are, in practice, likely to be relevant only to smaller businesses or organisations whose processing of personal data in connection with any of the core purposes is limited to:

- only data about persons necessary for the core purpose;
- only classes of data necessary for the core purpose;
- only making disclosures to third parties with the consent of the data subject or to third parties necessary for the core purpose;
- only as long as the relationship with the data subjects lasts and that the personal data are not retained beyond this point or are only retained for so long as this is necessary for the core purpose.

The exemptions are restricted in scope and cease to apply in any case where personal data are processed in a way that goes beyond the limitations described. An example of circumstances in which a data controller is unlikely to be able to continue to be able to rely upon a core business purposes exemption from notification is where the personal data processed need to be transferred beyond the EEA to a country that does not offer adequate safeguards for the data (see Chapter 8 for more information on personal data exports).

In a more specific example, a data controller could not rely on the accounts and records core purpose exemption if it also used the services of a credit reference agency, with the result that it was responsible for data processed by the credit agency or it received personal data from a credit agency.

See Figure 4.1 for more examples of the scope of the exemptions.

4.4.6 Other miscellaneous exemptions

National security

Personal data required for the purpose of safeguarding national security are exempt from notification (in addition to being exempt from certain other provisions of the DPA).[2] Conclusive evidence that the personal data involved are required for national security purposes is accepted in the form of an exemption certificate signed by a Minister of the Crown. There is a right of appeal against such a certificate to an independent Information Tribunal.

Public registers

An exemption is available from notification if the sole purpose of the processing is the maintenance of a public register that the data controller is required to publish. The exemption only applies to the notification requirements of the DPA.

4.4.7 Duty to give details on request

Where a data controller relies on an exemption from the requirement to notify personal data processing, then it must still make certain information about the processing available free of charge to any person within 21 days of receiving a written request. Failure to do so is an offence under the DPA (the details to be provided to a person who makes a request in writing are paras (a) to (f) of the registrable particulars set out in **4.5.3**).

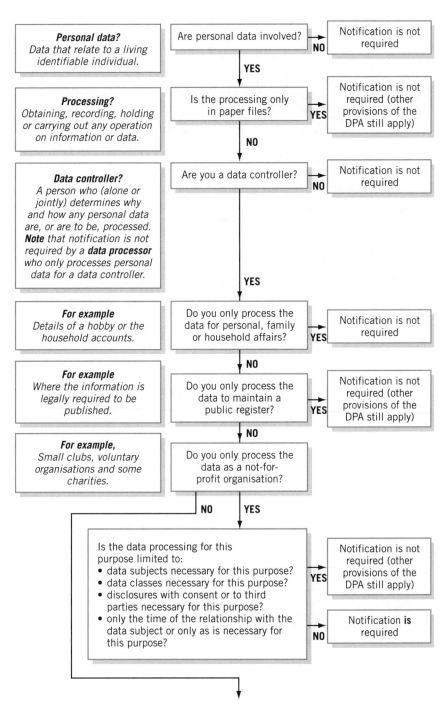

Figure 4.1 Does an exemption from notification apply?

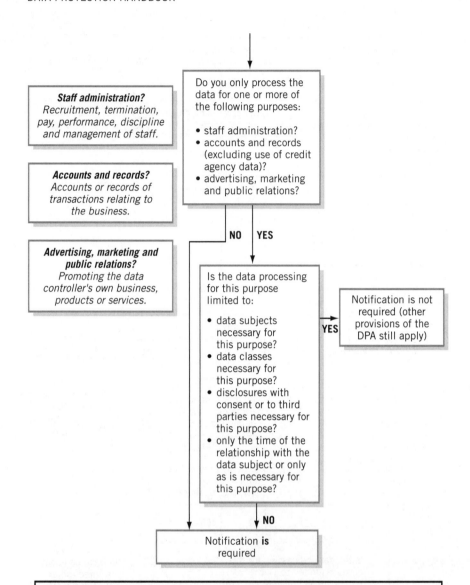

IMPORTANT NOTICE
In each case, it is important to remember that compliance with the notification requirement is only one aspect of compliance with the DPA as a whole. It is possible to notify properly and accurately but still to be in breach of the other provisions of the DPA including the data protection Principles.

4.4.8 Voluntary notification

An organisation that does not need to notify because it can rely on one of the exemptions described in **4.4.1–4.4.6** can still choose to notify voluntarily. There may be a number of reasons why an organisation chooses the route of a making a voluntary notification including:

- *Administrative convenience*: it can be considered easier in the long run to notify rather than stay on the alert for a direct request by a person for details of the personal data processing carried out, or continually to check that no processing of personal data inadvertently falls beyond the scope of the exemption.
- *To help comply with the other provisions of the DPA*: the process of reviewing the data held within the organisation as part of preparing a notification identifies any risks associated with the processing of personal data from which an organisation can structure a programme of corrective action.
- *Transparency*: an organisation may choose to notify as part of a wider corporate policy commitment to transparency and openness.

4.5 NOTIFICATION PROCESS

4.5.1 Initial research

In order to make sure that the notification is a full and accurate description of all the personal data processed within the organisation it is necessary first to identify the data controller(s) involved and then to understand the personal data. This is achieved by conducting an audit or review exercise with the objective of learning about the different types of personal data handled, and by whom and how they are treated. Data audits are also an important first step to assessing the level of compliance within an organisation as a whole with the DPA and in particular the data protection Principles.

When conducting any review or audit exercise it is important to make sure that this process takes into account all the personal data held within the organisation and the different ways in which they are used across the lifecycle of the data from creation through to destruction. In particular, the same data may be held in different forms within the organisation (such as e-mail, paper, database or CCTV images) and also used for a variety of different purposes.

A summary checklist for a notification review is provided in Box 4.1.

BOX 4.1 Preparing to notify checklist

STEP 1 Background

- Understand the issues.
- Gather further background information if needed.
- Establish whether the organisation already has a data protection officer.
- Agree the objectives and the scope of an information gathering exercise.
- Establish lines of responsibility and reporting.

STEP 2 Gather information

- Is more than one legal entity determining the data processing (e.g. is processing conducted within a group of companies or are there separate pension trustees)?
- Identify the legal and trading identities of the entities processing personal data.
- What specific data processing activities are carried out within each legal entity?
- About whom is the information processed?
- What types of information are processed?
- What sensitive personal data (if any) are processed about these individuals?
- What is this information used for or intended to be used for?
- How is this information held?
- Is this information processed on behalf of the business by others?
- Is this information processed by the business on behalf of other organisations?
- To whom is the information disclosed?
- To where are any transfers made?
- Are any new services or business processes envisaged that will involve processing personal data?
- What physical and technical security measures are in place?
- What policies, guidance and training are available to staff on security systems and procedures?
- Has a security policy been adopted within the organisation?
- Is there an established business continuity (disaster recovery) plan?
- Has the organisation adopted the British or equivalent International Standard on Information Security Management (BS 7799 or ISO/IEC27002:2005)?

STEP 3 Assess the information

- Establish the extent to which any data processing is exempt.
- Decide whether to notify exempt personal data or whether to declare exempt personal data processing when notifying non-exempt personal data.
- Identify who will be the contact for future correspondence with the ICO regarding the notification and compliance with the other provisions of the DPA.

4.5.2 How to notify

The fee (at time of writing) for notification is £35 and once filed the notification must be renewed after a period of one year. Applications for notification can be made in one of the following ways:

- *Telephone*: a member of the Information Commissioner's staff will draw up a part-completed draft notification form based upon the caller's description of the nature of the data controller's business. The draft notification form is then sent to the data controller in order to be checked for accuracy and completed before being returned to the ICO with the notification fee.

- *Post*: on receipt of a completed request for a notification form the Information Commissioner's staff will also pre-complete a draft notification for checking and completion by a data controller. Forms can be obtained from the ICO website.

- *Internet*: rather than request that the Information Commissioner produce an initial draft version of a notification, a data controller can complete a notification form on the ICO website. This can then be printed out and posted to the Information Commissioner along with the notification fee. The Information Commissioner provides an online notification process which takes the user through each of the different steps involved in putting together the notification form.

Contact details for each of the above methods of notification can be found in Appendix 4.

4.5.3 Information required – the registrable particulars

A notification entry must include certain details about the processing by the data controller of personal data. These details are described by the DPA as the 'registrable particulars' and cover:

- The data controller's name and address (the name provided should be the data controller's correct legal title and the address should be the registered office address for a limited company or, in other cases, the principal place of business).
- The Information Commissioner also asks for:
  - the name and address of a contact. The contact need not be an employee of the data controller or someone who operates from the principal place of business, however, the contact must be someone prepared to act as the point of communication for the data controller with the ICO. The contact could, for example, be the name and address of a legal adviser to the data controller;
  - the company registration number for the data controller (optional);
  - any trading names (excluding separate legal entities) by which the data controller is also known (optional).
- Where the data controller is not established in the UK, nor elsewhere in the EEA, but processes personal data using equipment in the UK for reasons other than merely transmitting the data through the UK, then the name and address of a nominated representative in the UK must also be given. This information is included in the publicly available register of data controllers published by the Information Commissioner.

- A description of the personal data being or to be processed, in particular:

  - a description of the type of people to which the personal data relate (the data subjects);
  - a description of the categories of data held about those data subjects (the data classes).

- A description of the purpose or purposes for which the data are being or are to be processed. The Information Commissioner has devised a number of standard descriptions of the typical purposes for which personal data are processed; a data controller can also devise a free-text description in the event that none of the standard purposes adequately describes the processing activity being carried out. See Box 4.2.

BOX 4.2 Available purpose descriptions

Standard business purposes

❑ Staff administration*

❑ Advertising, marketing and public relations*

❑ Accounts and records*

*If processing is only for the standard business purposes an exemption may apply (see Figure 4.1)

Other available purposes

❑ Accounting and auditing

❑ Administration of justice

❑ Administration of membership records

❑ Advertising, marketing and public relations for others

❑ Assessment and collection of taxes and other revenue

❑ Benefits, grants and loans administration

❑ Canvassing political support amongst the electorate

❑ Constituency casework

❑ Consultancy and advisory services

❑ Credit referencing

❑ Crime prevention and detection

❑ Debt administration and factoring

❑ Education

❑ Fundraising

❑ Health administration

❑ Information and databank administration

❑ Insurance administration

❑ Journalism and media

❑ Legal services

❑ Licensing and registration

❑ Pastoral care

❑ Pensions administration

❑ Policing

❑ Private investigation

❑ Processing for not-for-profit organisations

❑ Property management

❑ Provision of financial services and advice

❑ Realising the objectives of a charitable organisation or voluntary body

❑ Research

❑ Trading/sharing in personal information

- A description of the types of people or organisations to whom the data controller intends or may wish to disclose the personal data processed for each purpose (the recipients).
- The names or a description of any countries or territories outside the EEA to which the data controller transfers, or intends to transfer, or may wish to transfer, the data for each purpose. In particular data controllers are asked as part of the notification process to declare whether, in relation to a particular purpose for processing personal data, there will be:

  - no data transfers;
  - no data transfers outside the EEA;
  - worldwide data transfers;
  - transfers to individual countries (the individual countries must be specified).

- Where the personal data are exempt from notification and the notification does not extend to those data, it is also necessary to provide a statement as part of the notification form that that this is the case.

In order to simplify further the process of describing the processing of personal data, the Information Commissioner has developed a number of pre-completed descriptions of typical personal data processing activities carried out by different types of organisations. After selecting an appropriate off-the-shelf template, it is then just a matter of checking the template and updating or tailoring this where necessary, before forwarding it to the ICO along with the notification fee.

Organisations can also develop templates for approval by the Information Commissioner. Templates will typically be drawn up in cases where an organisation like a franchise network or an industry association is looking to make the notification process simpler for its independent representatives or members, while also ensuring that all the representatives or members apply a consistent standard of notification. See Box 4.3 for examples of available notification templates.

BOX 4.3 Examples of available notification templates

Education templates

❏ Further education/Sixth Form Colleges
❏ Learning and skills council
❏ Nursery school/play group/after-school club
❏ School (community)
❏ School (foundation and voluntary aided)
❏ School (private)
❏ School (voluntary controlled)
❏ Training company
❏ University

Finance templates

❏ Accountant
❏ Agents for NFU mutual
❏ Bank
❏ Building society
❏ Credit reference agency
❏ Credit union
❏ Debt administration and factoring
❏ Finance house/credit grantor
❏ Financial, mortgage and insurance services
❏ Independent financial adviser
❏ Insolvency practitioner
❏ Insurance company
❏ Insurance underwriter
❏ Nominee company
❏ Tied agent
❏ Trustees of a life assurance scheme
❏ Trustees of a pension scheme

General

❏ Airline
❏ Business specialising in direct marketing
❏ Catalogue mail order trade
❏ CCTV only
❏ Friendly society
❏ Genealogist
❏ Journalist
❏ List broking

❏ Mail order traders
❏ Manufacturer
❏ Motor trader
❏ Neighbourhood watch
❏ Petrol retailer
❏ Property management
❏ Publisher
❏ Retail/wholesale
❏ Software development
❏ Trade union

Health

❏ Ambulance service
❏ BUPA dentist
❏ Community Health Council
❏ Dentist
❏ Doctor
❏ Domiciliary care
❏ Forensic medical examiner
❏ NHS Trust/Health Authority
❏ Opticians
❏ Other healthcare professionals
❏ Pharmacist
❏ Primary Care Trust
❏ Residential care

Legal

❏ Individual barrister
❏ Magistrates' Court Committee
❏ Solicitor
❏ Will writers

Templates are also available in the following sectors

Leisure
Local and Central Government
Public Bodies
Religious/ Political / Charitable Services

4.5.4 Security measures

As part of the notification process it is also necessary to provide a general statement of the security measures that are in place within the organisation by answering either yes or no to a number of questions on the subject.

The security questions begin by asking whether any measures have been taken to guard against unauthorised or unlawful processing of personal data and against accidental loss, destruction or damage. If the answer to this question is 'yes', the data controller is then asked whether the methods adopted include in particular:

- adopting an information security policy;
- taking steps to control physical security;
- putting in place controls on access to information;
- establishing a business continuity plan;
- training staff on security systems and procedures;
- detecting and investigating breaches of security when they occur; or
- adopting the British Standard on Information Security Management BS 7799.

Answering 'no' to any of the security questions will not result in the Information Commissioner immediately penalising the data controller or refusing to accept a notification, nor will the answers given appear in the final public register. The Information Commissioner may choose, however, to revisit a data controller's security statement at a later date. This is most likely to occur in the context of investigating a complaint or as a result of the Information Commissioner undertaking a proactive compliance project and where there is reason to believe that a negative answer reveals an underlying weakness in the data controller's compliance with the Seventh (security) Principle of the DPA.

Further information about data security can be found in Chapter 7.

4.5.5 Other information required

Two final statements are required before the notification can be finalised and submitted with the fee. The first is to tell the Information Commissioner whether or not the notification covers all the personal data processed including exempt and non-exempt data. The second is to make a declaration as to whether the notification is being submitted voluntarily despite the fact that the personal data described are exempt from notification.

4.5.6 Acknowledgement of the entry

The notification period begins from the point the ICO receives a correctly completed form. An Acknowledgement of Notification letter is sent to the contact confirming that, subject to clearance of the fee, it is permitted to process the personal data described in the notification entry.

The form is then subjected to a second stage of processing by the Information Commissioner's notification staff. If a query arises during this process, the contact whose details are provided on the notification form will be approached. Queries can typically arise if, for example, a data controller has attempted to notify an excessive number of purposes or has notified a purpose that is inappropriate to the nature of its business.

Following the second stage processing of the form, a Confirmation of Entry in the Register letter will be sent to the contact for the data controller, along with a copy of the notification entry. The letter also confirms the date that the entry was made on the register of data controllers and the expiry date.

Both the acknowledgement and the confirmation letters include a registration number by which the entry is identified and an eight-digit security number for the entry. The security number should, in general, be provided in all future notification correspondence with the ICO (e.g. when renewing or making changes to an entry) and a record of the number should be kept safe.

The entire process from application to confirmation of the entry on the register usually takes between four and six weeks. See Box 4.4 for an overview of the notification process.

BOX 4.4 Notification process overview – summary

By telephone or post

1. Provide the data controller details.
2. Describe the nature of business.
3. Receive a draft notification form from the ICO.
4. Check the description of the processing in the draft notification, correcting or adding to the description where necessary.
5. Complete the security statement and declare any exempt processing.
6. Return the notification form with the fee.
7. Receive an acknowledgement that the notification form has received a preliminary screening.
8. Receive a confirmation of the entry on the register of the notification.
9. Check the entry for accuracy.
10. Keep a record of the security number.
11. Diarise regular reviews of the notification entry and in particular timetable for a review six weeks before the expiry date for the notification entry.

By Internet

1. Provide the data controller details.
2. Describe the data processing by selecting an appropriate online template notification; OR by selecting from the available purpose descriptions and update each purpose by selecting the appropriate categories of data subjects, classes, sources, recipients and transfers of personal data.
3. Complete the security statement and declare any exempt processing.
4. Print out the notification form and send this to the ICO along with the fee.
5. Receive the acknowledgement that the notification form has received a preliminary screening.
6. Receive the confirmation of the entry on the register.
7. Check the entry for accuracy.
8. Keep a record of the security number.
9. Diarise regular reviews of the notification entry and in particular timetable for a review six weeks before the expiry date for the notification entry.

4.6   ASSESSABLE PROCESSING

The DPA provides for the future possibility of more rigorous assessment of notifications covering certain categories of more sensitive areas of personal data processing (DPA, s.22). In particular, it is open to the Secretary of State to specify in an Order that processing appearing likely:

• to cause substantial damage or substantial distress to data subjects; or
• to otherwise significantly prejudice the rights and freedoms of data subjects

will be assessable processing.

Were such an Order to be made, then, on receiving a notification form, the Information Commissioner would first have to consider whether any of the processing covered by the notification related to assessable processing and, if so, he would then need to consider and inform the data controller within 28 days (capable of being extended up to 42 days in special cases) of receiving the notification, whether or not the processing would be likely or not to comply with the provisions of the DPA.

During the assessment period it would be an offence under the DPA to process the assessable data before the end of the assessment period or before an assessment finding had been made by the Information Commissioner. Although it would still be possible to proceed with processing the data in the light of an adverse assessment finding from the Information Commissioner, in practice this action would then be likely to prompt the Information Commissioner into taking formal enforcement action.

No Order for assessable processing has yet been made by the Secretary of State.

4.7   MAKING CHANGES TO A NOTIFICATION

The DPA requires that the Information Commissioner be told of any changes that will affect the accuracy of a notification entry. Failure to notify the Information Commissioner of any changes to a notification entry is a criminal offence under the DPA. An important first task is therefore to make sure that a person is tasked with the responsibility for maintaining the notification entry(ies) (this person may be the data protection officer). It should be the specific responsibility of this person to stay informed of changes taking place within the organisation, to consider the effects these may have on the notification entry and, where necessary, make changes to the entry.

The following list gives a few examples of scenarios likely to affect the accuracy or adequacy of an existing notification entry and trigger the need for changes to be made. The list is only a small selection of possible activities and is not intended to cover every conceivable scenario. Potential scenarios include the following:

- introduction of a new business process;
- creation of a new database;
- permitting other companies to market to the customer database;
- sharing data with other group companies;
- installing a CCTV system;
- changing the name of the data controller;
- making a change that has an impact on the security statement;
- transferring personal data to other countries;
- changing the registered office of the data controller;
- changing the contact for a data controller; and
- passing data to new recipients (perhaps a doctor, credit agency or private investigator).

4.7.1   How to make changes to a notification entry

The Information Commissioner will not generally handle requests for changes to a data protection entry over the telephone. Requests must be made to the Information Commissioner in writing using change request forms available from the ICO website or by otherwise making a clearly set out written request (on letter-headed paper). There is no fee payable when making changes to a notification entry.

The process for making changes to a notification entry differs slightly depending upon the nature of the change.

To add a new purpose to an existing entry, download a purpose form from the ICO website. The form asks for the name, registration and security number of the data controller, along with a full description of the new purpose. A separate purpose form must be completed for each new purpose to be added to the entry.

To request other alterations or seek to remove an existing entry, obtain the form to alter or remove an entry. It asks for the data controller name, along with the registration and security number of the data controller. The form is then divided up into sections and the nature of the change is described in the relevant section of the form.

After receiving an accurate alteration request, a confirmation and a copy of the updated entry is sent by the Information Commissioner to the contact for the entry.

4.8   RENEWING A NOTIFICATION ENTRY

Renewal of a data protection entry is necessary each year and the Information Commissioner should send out a renewal notice approximately six weeks before the existing entry is due to expire. It is important to ensure that the entry is renewed before the expiry date shown on the renewal notice. Entries automatically lapse and are removed from the register at the point when the renewal date has passed without the Information Commissioner having received a signed renewal notice along with the notification fee.

To continue processing personal data without having the benefit of a current notification entry is a criminal offence under the DPA. Following the receipt in good time of the signed renewal notice and the fee, the Information Commissioner will send to the contact a confirmation of the renewal and a copy of the renewed entry.

4.9   NOTIFICATION OFFENCES

There are a number of offences under the DPA associated with notification. In broad terms these are:

- processing personal data without an entry on the register of data controllers and where an exemption from the requirement to notify does not apply;
- failing to notify the Information Commissioner of any changes to the registrable particulars of an existing notification entry;
- failing to provide the details of the registrable particulars (the details set out in DPA, s.16(1)(a)–(f)) within 21 days of receiving a written request from any person (this offence only applies where the data controller is relying on an exemption from notification).

Processing personal data without a register entry is a strict liability offence. In other words, the absence of an intent to commit the offence or ignorance of the law is no defence. In the case of an offence of failing to notify the Information Commissioner of changes to an entry, or failure to provide details of the processing on request, it is a defence for the person charged to demonstrate having exercised all due diligence to comply.

4.9.1 Prosecutions

Prosecution action is generally taken against the legal entity itself, although in the case of a proven action against a corporate body, the Information Commissioner can also prosecute the managing director or another director, the company secretary or other officers for the same offence (DPA, s.61) and where the offence can be seen to be attributable to some action or neglect on the part of the individual.

In the UK the Information Commissioner is a prosecuting authority in his own right. Prosecutions in Scotland are brought by the Procurator Fiscal. Prosecutions are normally heard in the magistrates' court where maximum fines of up to £5,000 currently can be imposed. However, if a case is heard in the Crown Court, unlimited fines are then capable of being imposed.

Recent years have seen a drop in the level of prosecutions for non-notification offences under the DPA. The main reasons for this decline in prosecution activity are as follows:

1. Under the Data Protection Act 1984, the Information Commissioner (known at that time as the Data Protection Registrar) was unable to enforce compliance with the provisions of the 1984 Act against those who were not registered. Prosecution was the only practical enforcement option open to the Registrar in these cases. Under the DPA 1998, however, data controllers have to comply with the provisions of the Act even if they have not notified or if they are exempt from the requirement to notify.
2. There was a shift in priority away from pursuing non-notification offences during the transition to the DPA 1998. The purpose of this shift was to allow data controllers to become familiar with the provisions of the DPA. The Information Commissioner signalled the end to this policy in 2002, by stating that there was an intention to adopt a more proactive approach to investigating and prosecuting non-notification offences. In practice there has not been a significant increase since 2002 in the overall number of prosecutions for non-notification offences, although it is worth noting that the Information Commissioner has acted promptly to prosecute any solicitors' practice or law firm processing personal data without a notification entry.

See Chapter 3 for more information on the Information Commissioner's powers under the DPA.

4.10   NOTIFICATION IN THE CONTEXT OF CORPORATE TRANSACTIONS

Notification issues can also arise in relation to other business situations. This may be because personal data are processed as a by-product of a wider transaction, for example where employee or other records are acquired as part of the purchase of a business. Alternatively, the personal data could be the principal asset and the reason for the transaction, for example when selling a customer database.

In these situations, notification will only be one of a number of data protection issues for the data controller to consider in a business or data asset sale. In particular, any data transaction will also have to comply with the data protection Principles.

In terms of the specific notification considerations, both parties to a transaction should make sure that their notification adequately covers any personal data processed in connection with the transaction. This may include, for example:

- checking whether a vendor for personal data is notified;
- checking whether the notification entry of a vendor includes, where needed, a description of the processing for the purpose of trading or sharing of personal data;
- checking whether the notification entry of a vendor includes an adequate description of the appropriate recipient(s) for the personal data involved;
- checking whether a recipient for the personal data is adequately notified;
- checking whether a notification entry for the recipient of the data adequately describes the purposes of the processing, along with a correct description of the categories of data subjects, classes and recipients for the data and transfers of the data;
- making sure (for example, in the case of a business sale) that there is an appropriate notification entry for the new entity.

Data protection warranties included in corporate transactions can also be extended to cover compliance with, among other things, the specific notification requirements of the DPA. This is in addition to providing broader warranties of data protection compliance. For example:

[. . .] has complied with all relevant requirements of any applicable data protection [and privacy] legislation, including compliance with the following:

93

    (a) the data protection Principles;

    (b) requests from data subjects for access to data held by it; and

    (c) the requirements relating to the notification [or registration] by data controllers [under the Data Protection Act 1998].

It is not appropriate for a data controller to seek a notification warranty from a data processor for any personal data processed by the processor on the data controller's behalf. This is because notification is not required under the DPA by data processors. However, data controllers are required to obtain other contractual warranties from their data processors and these are explained in more detail in Chapter 7.

4.11 THE FUTURE FOR NOTIFICATION?

At the time of writing, it is likely that the current notification system will be the subject of future revision.

In the UK, the current notification fee of £35 has remained unchanged since it was introduced on 1 March 2000. However, on 27 July 2008 the Ministry of Justice published a consultation on the inspection powers and funding arrangements of the Information Commissioner. The consultation included proposed changes to the imposition and collection of notification fees that would generate increased income for the Information Commissioner, whilst not placing a disproportionate financial burden on the majority of data controllers. In particular, the consultation proposed introducing a tiered notification structure, exempting some smaller organisations from the obligation to pay a notification fee, whilst increasing the fee for larger organisations to up to £1,000. The proposals place the responsibility for assessing the correct notification fee band on the data controller, and suggested reinforcing this approach with the introduction of a new sanction that could be imposed on any data controller who knowingly or recklessly provided incorrect information as part of their notification fee self-assessment. The consultation closed on 27 August 2008 and it is anticipated that the Government will consider and respond to the outcomes of the consultation in the autumn of 2008.

In Europe there is an understanding that widely contrasting national approaches to notification requirements present data controllers with similar operations across a number of different countries with a significant administrative and financial burden. The independent European advisory body on data protection, the Article 29 Working Party, has started to work on a simplified single European notification process for similar processing operations; however, at the present time, there is no prospect that this exercise will be completed in the near future.

4.12 SOURCES OF FURTHER INFORMATION

4.12.1 Notification Handbook

The Information Commissioner has published a handbook containing guidance on notification under the DPA, which is available from the ICO website.

4.12.2 *Privacy & Data Protection* journal

This subscription-based journal publishes news on data protection developments, including information on prosecutions for notification offences and other updates. Contact details for the journal can be found in Appendix 4.

Endnotes

1 The ICO's Annual Report and Accounts for the year ending 31 March 2007 reported fee income of £10,204,761 from new notifications and notification renewals for the year 2005/2007.
2 Personal data required for safeguarding national security will be exempt from Parts II (individuals rights), III (notification) and V (enforcement) and DPA, s.55 (prohibiting the unlawful obtaining of personal data).

CHAPTER 5

Information requirements and fair processing

Louise Townsend[1]

5.1 FIRST PRINCIPLE

5.1.1 Introduction – fair and lawful processing

The DPA requires data controllers to comply with eight Principles (DPA, Sched.1, Part 1, para.1) in relation to all personal data that they process (DPA, s.4(4)). The First Principle states that:

> Personal data shall be processed fairly and lawfully and, in particular, shall not be processed unless:
> (a) at least one of the conditions in Schedule 2 is met, and
> (b) in the case of sensitive personal data, at least one of the conditions in Schedule 3 is also met.

In addition to this general statement of what the First Principle requires, Schedule 1 goes on to give, in Part II, a page and a half of interpretation of the Principle – this is discussed at **5.1.5**. Furthermore, in 'Data Protection Act 1998: Legal Guidance' (the Legal Guidance), the Information Commissioner dedicates 15 pages to discussing the complexities of this single Principle, while all the others are dealt with together in just 10 pages. It can be appreciated, then, that the First Principle is considerably more wide ranging and challenging to satisfy than the other seven.

The essence of the First Principle dictates that personal data should be processed 'fairly and lawfully'. The interpretation and the Guidance explain what is meant by 'fairly and lawfully' and how a data controller can achieve fair and lawful processing: see below.

The Schedule 2 and Schedule 3 conditions referred to in the First Principle are included as 'particular' elements of 'fairly and lawfully' and are a subset of the overall requirement for fair and lawful processing. The Guidance states that meeting these conditions is a 'requisite of fair and lawful processing', but

---

[1] Based on an original contribution by Shelagh Gaskill and Peter Wainman.

96

emphasises that 'meeting a Schedule 2 and Schedule 3 condition will not, on its own, guarantee that processing is fair and lawful. The general requirement that data be processed fairly and lawfully must be satisfied in addition to meeting the conditions' (Legal Guidance, p.19). It should be noted that the UK statute differs from the European Directive (see **5.1.4**).

In the Information Commissioner's view, it is not enough simply to comply with a Schedule 2 and 3 condition; 'fairness' and 'lawfulness' go beyond those conditions. A data controller which processes personal data merely in accordance with Schedules 2 and 3 risks nonetheless processing both unfairly and unlawfully.

This means that to be able to process any personal data, the data controller must process the data:

- fairly;
- lawfully; and
- with justification under one of the conditions in Schedule 2.

If the data are sensitive personal data, the data controller must, additionally, satisfy one of the conditions in Schedule 3.

The term 'processing' is given a wide definition under the DPA (s.1(1)), and encompasses anything that can be done with data. Most important from the point of view of the First Principle are obtaining and disclosing personal data, which along with using and destroying, cover the whole life-cycle of data use by a data controller. Even the action of anonymising personal data must, as a processing operation, be undertaken fairly and lawfully.

5.1.2   Schedule 2 conditions

There are six conditions for processing personal data listed in Schedule 2; only one is necessary for any processing operation (although sometimes several conditions may apply). They are:

1. The data subject has given his consent to the processing.
2. The processing is necessary:
    (a) for the performance of a contract to which the data subject is a party; or
    (b) for the taking of steps at the request of the data subject with a view to entering into a contract.
3. The processing is necessary for compliance with any legal obligation to which the data controller is subject, other than an obligation imposed by contract.
4. The processing is necessary in order to protect the vital interests of the data subject.
5. The processing is necessary:
    (a) for the administration of justice;
    (b) for the exercise of any functions of either House of Parliament;

    (c) for the exercise of any functions conferred on any person by or under any enactment;

    (d) for the exercise of any functions of the Crown, a Minister of the Crown or a government department; or

    (e) for the exercise of any other functions of a public nature exercised in the public interest by any person.

6. (1) The processing is necessary for the purposes of legitimate interests pursued by the data controller or by the third party or parties to whom the data are disclosed, except where the processing is unwarranted in any particular case by reason of prejudice to the rights and freedoms or legitimate interests of the data subject.

    (2) . . .

Consent of the data subject – paragraph 1

1. The data subject has given his consent to the processing.

The DPA does not define consent. Article 2 of the Directive defines the data subject's consent as 'any freely given, specific and informed indication of his wishes by which the data subject signifies his agreement to personal data relating to him being processed' (Data Protection Directive, Art.2(h)), and states that it should be given 'unambiguously' (Data Protection Directive, Art.7(b)). This definition can be split into four main components.

1. The requirement that the data subject is 'informed' means that he must be provided with sufficient information about the processing of the data to enable him to decide whether to allow the processing to go ahead. The fair processing requirements show the sort of information that should be provided.

2. The consent must be specific. This requirement works in conjunction with the requirement that the consent be informed. The data subject needs to be informed of the specific processing activities proposed in order to be in a position to consent to them.

3. The data subject must 'signify his agreement' and do so 'unambiguously' – that is, he must take a positive action to show his consent. Silence or inaction cannot suffice. The Legal Guidance states that 'data controllers cannot infer consent from non-response to a communication, for example from a customer's failure to return or respond to a leaflet' (p.29). On the other hand, if a data controller includes an opt-out box on the application form which clearly and fairly states all the purposes for processing, and the data subject then returns the form without ticking the box and continues to do business with the data controller, it could be argued that the data subject has signified his consent through a course of conduct.

4. The data subject must give consent 'freely'. Effective consent cannot be given under duress, and the data subject must have a real choice in the matter (i.e. the possibility of saying no). Unequal bargaining power may mean that a data subject is not in a position to consent freely. The Article 29 Working Party, in its Opinion relating to the use of consent in the employer/employee relationship, goes so far as to say that effective consent can never be given by an employee in these circumstances. The Information Commissioner's view is not quite as strong, saying that 'the extent to which consent can be relied upon in the context of employment is limited'. However, he does recognise that there may be situations where an employee can provide valid consent but 'the worker must have a real choice whether or not to consent and there must be no penalty imposed for refusing to give consent' (Employment Practices Code, Supplementary Guidance, p.75).

Given that the DPA does not contain a definition of consent, comparable principles may be drawn from case law. The data subject should be capable of understanding the action to which he is consenting (*R* v. *Lang* (1976) 62 Cr App R 50), and should understand the nature of any contract into which he enters (*Boughton* v. *Knight* (1873) LR 3PD 64). A data subject can withdraw his consent at any time.

The Information Commissioner's Guidance says that 'consent is not particularly easy to achieve and that data controllers should consider other conditions . . . before looking at consent' (p.29). The difficulty of obtaining consent will depend on the circumstances in which the data controller puts forward the option of consenting. One option is to make use of the data protection notice required under the fairness provisions to obtain the consent.

EXAMPLE

Someone completes an application form for membership of a cricket club, and the application form clearly includes a notice describing the purposes for which the data will be processed, including the administration of the club. The act of signing and returning the form, including the notice, amounts to consent on the part of the applicant/data subject to the processing of the data as described on the form.

Performance of a contract to which the data subject is a party

2. The processing is necessary:
   (a) for the performance of a contract to which the data subject is a party, or
   (b) for the taking of steps at the request of the data subject with a view to entering into a contract.

The word 'necessary' is used in five of the six conditions in Schedule 2, and in six of the ten Schedule 3 conditions. Common law and civil law jurisdictions tend to treat the term differently. In the UK, the word is generally interpreted narrowly. The *Oxford English Dictionary* defines necessary as 'that which is indispensable; an essential, a requisite'. Case law is diverse on the issue; it has been said that necessary means something between 'indispensable' and 'useful' (*Re an inquiry under the Companies Securities Insider Dealing Act 1985* [1988] 1 All ER 203, [1988] AC 660 (HL)). The Information Commissioner takes the view that data controllers will need to consider objectively whether:

- the purposes for which the data are being processed are valid;
- such purposes can only be achieved by the processing of personal data;
- the processing is proportionate to the aim pursued (Legal Guidance, p.30).

It is safe for a data controller in the UK to assume that 'necessary' means 'can only be achieved by'. The European civil jurisdictions have adopted a more relaxed interpretation, treating necessary as 'reasonably required'.

This condition would not cover processing beyond whatever is necessary for the contract, but it is not necessary for this condition that the requirement to process should be a term of the contract. Nor, on the other hand, will the fact that a processing requirement is a term of the contract be sufficient evidence that the processing is necessary for the contract, so just making it a term may not be enough. It all depends on the particular circumstances, such as where a contract could be performed by other means. Even where a data controller can use this condition initially, it may nonetheless seek to use a different Schedule 2 condition (such as consent) for processing for other purposes further down the line.

The second part of the condition, 'taking steps at the request of the data subject with a view to entering into a contract', covers processing which leads up to the formation of a contract. This might apply where a data controller undertakes a credit search against an individual before entering into a contract with that individual, or where a company processes the personal data of a job applicant with a view to offering a contract of employment.

EXAMPLE

A customer orders a number of CDs from an online retailer. She provides her contact details to allow the retailer to deliver them, and her credit card details to pay for the goods. It is necessary for the retailer to process these data to enter into the contract to supply the CDs, and also to perform the contract. The retailer will not be able to use the details for any further purposes (e.g. selling the individual's name and address to a list broker) under this condition.

Legal obligation of the data controller

3. The processing is necessary for compliance with any legal obligation to which the data controller is subject, other than an obligation imposed by contract.

See the earlier discussion of 'necessary'. This condition applies where the data controller is under a legal obligation to process the data, and will certainly be used by public sector bodies which have statutory obligations. Of course, all data controllers will have some obligations under statute – if only under the Taxes Management Act 1970, to keep HMRC informed of their earnings or profits, and of what they pay their staff. This condition may be compared with the fifth Schedule 2 condition considered below.

EXAMPLE

The housing department of a local authority receives an application for housing from someone who is homeless. The authority is under a statutory duty to process the personal data of the applicant/data subject, including the carrying out of checks on the applicant with other public authorities (such as the police).

In the vital interests of the data subject

4. The processing is necessary in order to protect the vital interests of the data subject.

The Information Commissioner states that 'reliance on this condition may only be claimed where the processing is necessary for matters of life and death' (Legal Guidance, p.20). The Recitals to the Directive state that processing should be lawful 'where it is carried out in order to protect an interest which is essential for the data subject's life' (Data Protection Directive, Recital 31). The Employment Practices Code (p.73) refers to a situation where an individual is 'at risk of serious harm', again suggesting that this is a strong test.

EXAMPLE

The Legal Guidance gives the example of 'the disclosure of a data subject's medical history to a hospital casualty department treating the data subject after a serious road accident' (Legal Guidance, p.20). The data controller making the disclosure, perhaps a different health trust, would be able to rely on this condition to be allowed to make the disclosure.

101

Public functions

 5. The processing is necessary:
    (a) for the administration of justice,
    (aa) for the exercise of any functions of either House of Parliament,
    (b) for the exercise of any functions conferred on any person by or under any enactment,
    (c) for the exercise of any functions of the Crown, a Minister of the Crown or a government department, or
    (d) for the exercise of any other functions of a public nature exercised in the public interest by any person.

Although there is some similarity between this condition and the legal obligation condition in condition 3, processing that is 'necessary . . . for the exercise of any functions' might include non-obligatory processing. A data controller might argue that the processing it is undertaking is not strictly defined in statute and therefore it is not under a legal obligation, but that it is necessary to process data in the way proposed in order to achieve the functions conferred by statute. Reporting crime, or taking steps to prevent it, is something any data controller might justify under condition 5(d).

EXAMPLES

Court proceedings would come under condition 5(a); bodies carrying out their statutory functions (which may fall short of specific obligations) under condition 5(c), such as a local education authority processing applications for funding from students, a function which is conferred on it by statute. The police process details of witnesses to a particular incident, or of suspects, pursuant to their common law powers under condition 5(d).

Legitimate interests of the data controller

 6. (1) The processing is necessary for the purposes of legitimate interests pursued by the data controller or by the third party or parties to whom the data are disclosed, except where the processing is unwarranted in any particular case by reason of prejudice to the rights and freedoms or legitimate interests of the data subject.
    (2) The Secretary of State may by order specify particular circumstances in which this condition is, or is not, to be taken to be satisfied.

This condition is particularly useful to a data controller, especially one operating in the private sector (who is not able to take advantage of some of the other conditions listed above), because legitimate interests is such a wide concept. It is also the condition commonly being used by public authorities when considering disclosure of personal data in response to a request under the Freedom of Information Act 2000.

The disadvantage of relying on this ground for processing is that it is vulnerable to challenge by a data subject who can show that processing is nevertheless prejudicial to his rights or freedoms or legitimate interests (and the individual can then also benefit from the wide meaning of legitimate interests). Note that even if nobody else has complained or feels prejudiced, the controller cannot justify carrying on under this ground if someone has established that it is unwarranted as far as he is concerned. (Although the fact that one person has justifiably complained does not mean that the processing in relation to everyone must be stopped.)

The Information Commissioner:

> [. . .] takes a wide view of the legitimate interests condition and recommends that two tests be applied to establish whether this condition may be appropriate in any particular case. The first is the establishment of the legitimacy of the interests pursued by the data controller or the third party to whom the data are to be disclosed and the second is whether the processing is unwarranted in any particular case by reason of prejudice to the rights and freedoms or legitimate interests of the data subject whose interests override those of the data controller. (Legal Guidance, p.20).

The data subject's interests will therefore always be paramount. The data controller has to show the following:

- that the processing is necessary for the purposes of the data controller's interests; and
- that there is no more than trivial prejudice to the rights and freedoms or legitimate interests of the individual.

This condition therefore involves a balancing exercise between the interests of the data controller and the data subject, and this is not always clear cut.

In the case of public authorities dealing with requests under the Freedom of Information Act 2000 this balancing act may lead them not to make a disclosure of personal data. For example, in *London Borough of Camden* v. *Information Commissioner* (Appeal EA/2007/0021) the Information Tribunal agreed with the London Borough of Camden that this condition was not met in relation to the disclosure of names of those who had been subject to an anti-social behaviour order.

No order has yet been made under part (2) of condition 6.

An organisation decides that it would be appropriate, given the particular services it wishes to advertise, to publicise photographs and other personal details of its key line managers in particular areas. Most are happy for this to take place, but one individual is concerned because she is estranged from her violent husband and fears that he may track her down to her new place of employment via this information. In her case, she can argue that the processing, while in the legitimate interests of the controller, is unwarranted in her case because of prejudice to her.

5.1.3 Schedule 3 conditions – sensitive personal data

Where a data controller intends to process sensitive personal data, it must satisfy one of the conditions under Schedule 3 in addition to satisfying one of the conditions under Schedule 2. The Schedule 3 conditions are narrower than the Schedule 2 conditions.

Categories of sensitive personal data

Sensitive personal data are defined (DPA, s.2) as personal data consisting of information as to:

- racial or ethnic origin;
- political opinions;
- religious beliefs or other beliefs of a similar nature;
- membership of a trade union (within the meaning of the Trade Union and Labour Relations (Consolidation) Act 1992);
- physical or mental health or condition;
- sexual life;
- commission or alleged commission of any offence;
- any proceedings for any offence committed or alleged to have been committed, the disposal of such proceedings or the sentence of any court in such proceedings.

Conditions for processing sensitive personal data

There are 10 conditions which allow data controllers to process sensitive personal data, summarised as follows:

1. Explicit consent of the data subject.
2. Legal right or obligation of the data controller in connection with employment.
3. Protection of the vital interests of the data subject or another person.

4. Legitimate interests of non-profit-making bodies.
5. Information made public by the data subject.
6. Legal proceedings, legal advice, legal rights.
7. Administration of justice, statutory functions, government department.
8. Medical purposes.
9. Equal opportunities monitoring.
10. Further conditions may be specified in a statutory instrument.

Explicit consent of the data subject

1. The data subject has given his explicit consent to the processing of the personal data.

Compare this condition with condition 1 of Schedule 2, which refers simply to 'consent'. The discussion of consent at **5.1.2** applies equally to explicit consent under Schedule 3. Explicit is generally interpreted to reinforce the meaning of informed and specific, and to require that the data subject be provided with a very detailed description of the purposes for which the data are being processed.

Furthermore, the positive indication of consent by the data subject will also need to be specific. Data controllers who wish to rely on consent by conduct by the data subject need to analyse the business process carefully to make sure that they can identify the positive action on the part of the data subject that signifies consent. In relation to explicit consent, the Legal Guidance states that:

> the consent of the data subject should be absolutely clear. In appropriate cases it should cover the specific detail of the processing, the particular type of data to be processed (or even the particular information), the purposes of the processing and any special aspects of the processing which may affect the individual, for example, disclosures which may be made of the data. (p.30)

EXAMPLE

An individual applies for a job that involves heavy lifting and other physical work. The application form asks the applicant to answer questions relating to his health (i.e. sensitive personal data). The application form states that the information will only be used to assess the applicant's suitability for the job, and will not be transferred to any other organisation. If the applicant gives details about his health on the form, signing and returning the form provides his explicit consent to the processing of those data (but only for the limited purpose specified).

Legal right or obligation of the data controller in connection with employment

> 2. (1) The processing is necessary for the purposes of exercising or performing any right or obligation which is conferred or imposed by law on the data controller in connection with employment.

In the Employment Practices Code, Supplementary Guidance (p.72) the Information Commissioner states that:

> this condition can have quite wide application in the context of employment . . . Thus, an employer may be able to collect and use sensitive personal data if this can be shown to be necessary to enable the employer to meet its legal obligations, for example in relation to the safety of its workers, in relation to others to whom it owes a duty of care, or to prevent unlawful discrimination.

Employers who read the words 'wide application' should, however, be wary. This condition is only wide in that it refers to a range of different statutory obligations; each obligation provides for a narrow range of processing which will be considered 'necessary'. It will not allow employers to undertake a trend analysis that is not related to a legal obligation, such as to discover how many employees were absent on the day of a World Cup football match; nor will it enable employers to undertake departmental comparisons.

Note that the data subject concerned does not have to be an employee. For example, if an employer needs to keep track of places such as residential addresses at which visiting staff, such as social workers, might be at risk of violence, then the employer's duties under health and safety law would justify keeping records of those who, because of past offences or convictions, or mental health problems, might pose a risk to staff.

This condition is qualified by allowing for Orders made by the Secretary of State to specify cases where this condition is excluded or narrowed by requiring further conditions. A data controller satisfying this condition will also satisfy the condition under Schedule 2 referring to 'any legal obligation' (para.2.3).

Employers monitoring racial or ethnic origin, religious beliefs or health of workers should also consider condition 9.

EXAMPLE

Employers of 15 or more employees are required to make reasonable changes to practices and procedures within the workplace to assist disabled people to do their jobs. It is necessary to monitor the proportion of disabled employees and their specific workplace requirements to fulfil this obligation.

Protection of the vital interests of the data subject or another person

3. The processing is necessary:
   (a) in order to protect the vital interests of the data subject or another person, in a case where:
      (i) consent cannot be given by or on behalf of the data subject, or
      (ii) the data controller cannot reasonably be expected to obtain the consent of the data subject, or
   (b) in order to protect the vital interests of another person, in a case where consent by or on behalf of the data subject has been unreasonably withheld.

This condition is closely related to the Schedule 2 vital interests condition discussed at **5.1.2**, and the same life and death meaning of 'vital' applies here. This condition is both narrower and wider than the Schedule 2 condition: narrower because it only applies where consent is impossible to obtain, or the data controller cannot reasonably be expected to obtain it, but wider in that it also applies to processing necessary to protect the vital interests of someone other than the data subject.

EXAMPLE

A student is taken ill with meningitis and is taken to a local hospital. The student loses consciousness, and has not consented to the hospital informing the university. Assuming that nobody else is able to consent on behalf of the student, the hospital can rely on this condition to allow the disclosure of this information to the university so that appropriate medication can be made available to other students who are at risk of infection.

Legitimate interests of non-profit-making bodies

4. The processing:
   (a) is carried out in the course of its legitimate activities by any body or association which:
      (i) is not established or conducted for profit, and
      (ii) exists for political, philosophical, religious or trade-union purposes,
   (b) is carried out with appropriate safeguards for the rights and freedoms of data subjects,
   (c) relates only to individuals who either are members of the body or association or have regular contact with it in connection with its purposes, and
   (d) does not involve disclosure of the personal data to a third party without the consent of the data subject.

Note that all of the strands of this condition, (a) to (d), must be met in order for the organisation to process sensitive personal data under this condition. On the other hand, the processing need not be necessary for any purpose – merely 'in the course of ... [the organisation's] legitimate activities'. Although the provision in (b) is intended to ensure that the data subject is not unfairly prejudiced, it is not entirely clear what the appropriate safeguards ought to be.

The meaning of (d) has been clarified by the Information Commissioner, who states that: 'data controllers who rely on this condition as a basis for processing may make subsequent non-consensual disclosures of sensitive personal data only if there is a basis for doing so under one of the other Schedule 3 conditions' (Legal Guidance, p.22).

Casual readers of the DPA might assume that this condition is a general get out for charities who process sensitive data, but clearly it is limited to the specific kinds of not-for-profit organisations mentioned. It is there to enable certain bodies who by their nature process sensitive data just by running a membership list, in order to run their organisations, for example political parties, church groups or trade unions. Such organisations necessarily deal in the kinds of sensitive information specified in categories (b) to (d).

EXAMPLE

A civil liberties charity processes data relating to the political opinions of its major donor members with appropriate safeguards, such as by keeping the data subject informed of the uses to which these data are to be put. No disclosure of the data to third parties would be possible without the member's consent.

Information which has been made public by the data subject

> 5. The information contained in the personal data has been made public as a result of steps deliberately taken by the data subject.

The problematic concepts in this condition are 'made public', and 'steps deliberately taken'. Clearly, a reader at a televised church service who discusses his faith can be seen to have planned and deliberated upon this disclosure of his religious beliefs to the public. The status of a disclosure to a closed group of individuals where it is not made clear that the disclosure is made in confidence is, however, debatable.

Note that only processing of the specific information that the data subject has chosen to make public is allowed under this condition. Similar or related information would remain protected or would require another sensitive data condition for disclosure.

A journalist announces during a radio broadcast that she is suffering from cancer, and will be seeking treatment. Under this condition, the hospital where she is being treated is at liberty to acknowledge this if the press makes enquiries. The hospital is not allowed to discuss any further details of the treatment than were made public in the broadcast.

Legal proceedings, legal advice, legal rights

    6. The processing:
- (a) is necessary for the purpose of, or in connection with, any legal proceedings (including prospective legal proceedings),
- (b) is necessary for the purpose of obtaining legal advice, or
- (c) is otherwise necessary for the purposes of establishing, exercising or defending legal rights.

This provision allows a data controller to reveal a data subject's sensitive personal data to a solicitor to obtain advice, without needing to seek the consent of the data subject, as long as the disclosure is necessary for that purpose.

In response to attempts to widen this condition along the lines of the Schedule 2 provision, the Information Commissioner stated that it is of limited scope and suggests that 'data controllers should adopt a narrow interpretation and rely upon another Schedule 3 condition if there is any doubt as to whether it applies' (Legal Guidance, p.23). However, in many situations, it will be very clear that the processing is necessary either to obtain legal advice, or in connection with legal proceedings, and it is only really possibility (c) which is open to wide interpretation.

EXAMPLE

An employee accuses his employer of racial discrimination. The employer is entitled to seek legal advice in relation to the accusation, and to reveal the details of the claim, including the ethnic background of the employee, to its legal adviser.

Administration of justice; statutory functions; government department

    7. (1) The processing is necessary:
- (a) for the administration of justice,
- (aa) for the exercise of any functions of either House of Parliament,

      (b)   for the exercise of any functions conferred on any person by or under an enactment, or

      (c)   for the exercise of any functions of the Crown, a Minister of the Crown or a government department.

This condition is narrower than (in that it does not allow for the exercise of any functions of a public nature exercised in the public interest) but otherwise the same as the fifth Schedule 2 condition discussed at **5.1.2**, so any data controller meeting this condition will also by implication satisfy the Schedule 2 condition. Note, however, that it will generally be more difficult to show that it is necessary to process sensitive personal data than it is to process non-sensitive personal data.

In addition, the Secretary of State can make an Order specifying cases where this condition is altogether excluded, or add further conditions that must also be satisfied. No such Order has been made to date.

EXAMPLE

Someone applies to a local authority's housing department for housing. The local authority will undertake certain enquiries of the police in relation to the individual's criminal record to determine what status to give the applicant. This processing is necessary to fulfil the function that is conferred on the housing department.

Medical purposes

8. (1) The processing is necessary for medical purposes and is undertaken by:
     (a) a health professional, or
     (b) a person who in the circumstances owes a duty of confidentiality which is equivalent to that which would arise if that person were a health professional.
  (2) In this paragraph 'medical purposes' includes the purposes of preventative medicine, medical diagnosis, medical research, the provision of care and treatment and the management of healthcare services.

The meaning of health professional is set out in the DPA, and includes registered doctors, dentists, opticians, nurses, as well as osteopaths, music therapists and psychologists (DPA, s.69(1)). Although there is a finite list under the first limb, subparagraph (b) extends the list to include those who owe an equivalent duty of confidentiality but fall outside the meaning of health professional.

This is a useful condition in the context of all administration of health records and patient information in the health sector, since all such processing will necessarily involve sensitive personal data concerning the health of the data subject. Clearly, most of this sort of processing will not be justifiable on the life or death ground of Schedule 3. This condition will cover activities such as exchanges of information between GPs and hospitals, and administrative matters. The sensitive data are most likely to be health data but the condition would also cover other categories of sensitive data, such as religious opinions, if processed for the specified purposes under the required conditions.

EXAMPLE

A hospital decides to share its database of patients suffering from senile dementia with a medical research body run by qualified researchers, only some of whom are doctors. Provided that the individuals having access to the data owe a similar duty of confidentiality to that owed by the doctors, and that the hospital is satisfied that the disclosure is necessary for the research, disclosure can be justified under this condition (although whether it would be fair to the data subjects under the fairness requirements of the First Principle is another matter).

Equal opportunities monitoring

9. (1) The processing:
  (a) is of sensitive personal data consisting of information as to racial or ethnic origin,
  (b) is necessary for the purpose of identifying or keeping under review the existence or absence of equality of opportunity or treatment between persons of different racial or ethnic origins, with a view to enabling such equality to be promoted or maintained, and
  (c) is carried out with appropriate safeguards for the rights and freedoms of data subjects.

In contrast to the preceding condition, the condition as defined in the DPA only applied to one category of sensitive personal data: information as to racial or ethnic origin. This was expanded to include information relating to religious or similar beliefs and physical or mental health or condition (Data Protection (Processing of Sensitive Personal Data) Order 2000, SI 2000/417, Sched., para.7). The condition is most notably useful to an employer who maintains a record for the monitoring of equality of opportunity in the workplace, but also applies outside the employment context.

The Secretary of State is allowed to provide for the meaning of 'safeguards for rights and freedoms' by use of an appropriate Order, but no such Order has yet been made.

EXAMPLE

A university maintains a record of the equality of treatment afforded to applicants of different racial or ethnic origins, and includes a form to complete as part of the application process. The processing of these data is necessary to monitor the success of the university's equal opportunity policy.

Circumstances specified in an order made by the Lord Chancellor

> 10. The personal data are processed in circumstances specified in an order made by the Secretary of State for the purposes of this paragraph.

The Data Protection (Processing of Sensitive Personal Data) Order 2000 is the main Order made under this provision. This allows sensitive personal data to be processed in the following circumstances:

- to prevent/detect unlawful acts;
- to discharge functions to protect the public from certain conduct;
- for journalistic, artistic, or literary purposes;
- for confidential counselling, advice or support;
- for insurance and occupational pension schemes;
- for insurance business-processing before 24 October 1998;
- to promote equality of opportunity;
- for political activities;
- for research purposes; and
- for policing.

Note, however, that these grounds are subject to limitations and qualifications as set out in the Order.
Further Orders are:

- Data Protection (Processing of Sensitive Personal Data) (Elected Representatives) Order 2002, SI 2002/2905 – this provides for the disclosure of sensitive personal data to and processing by elected representatives such as MPs and councillors in connection with these functions, and
- Data Protection (Processing of Sensitive Personal Data) Order 2006, SI 2006/2068 – this allows information about a criminal conviction or caution to be processed for the purpose of administering an account relating to the payment card or for cancelling the card used in the commission of certain listed offences relating to indecent images of children.

5.1.4 Lawful processing

The First Principle is derived from the Directive, which states that any processing must be lawful and fair to the individuals concerned (EC Directive 95/46/EC, Recital 28), and goes on to list the conditions a data controller must satisfy in order to be lawful (Recital 30). These conditions were implemented in the UK in Schedule 2 to the DPA (see para.3). Article 5 of the Directive states that 'Member States shall, within the limits of the Provisions of this Chapter, determine more precisely the conditions under which the processing of personal data is lawful'. This suggests that Member States are limited to the scope of the Chapter II provisions ('on the Lawfulness of the processing of personal data') when deciding what is lawful, but does not restrict them in defining further conditions under which the processing of personal data might be unlawful.

The DPA separates the requirement that personal data be processed lawfully from the requirement to process in accordance with one of the conditions in Schedule 2 (and Schedule 3, in the case of sensitive personal data). In fact, any processing of personal data that is not justified under Schedule 2 will therefore be unlawful processing. The requirement to process lawfully can usefully be seen as a requirement to:

- meet one of the conditions for processing in Schedule 2 (and Schedule 3, in the case of sensitive personal data); and
- observe any other statutory or common law obligations that relate to the processing of the data, such as copyright law, sex discrimination regulations, or the law of confidence.

The Schedule 2 conditions are considered in **5.1.2**. Below are some examples of other legal obligations to which a data controller must adhere in order to process data lawfully under the DPA.

Confidentiality

A data controller processing personal data in breach of confidence will thereby be processing data unlawfully under the First Principle. The duty of confidentiality applies:

- to information that is not generally available;
- where the information is disclosed in circumstances imposing an obligation on the confidant to respect the confidence (e.g. where it is imparted for a limited purpose); and
- where no other overriding public interest outweighs the public interest of upholding the law of confidence.

For instance, an employer may hold data relating to the health of its employees. That information is not generally available, and has been imparted for a limited purpose (e.g. to administer the attendance records of the employee in relation to timekeeping). If the employer discloses the information, for instance to a company providing health insurance, the disclosure will be in breach of confidence, and so the processing will be unlawful under the DPA. Where the obligation of confidence is owed to the data subject, the consequent restriction on, for example, a disclosure may be overcome if the data subject consents to the processing. Otherwise, a statutory obligation or a public interest justification will release a data controller from restrictions imposed by confidentiality.

Government departments and local authorities are restricted to the activities defined in statute. If they go beyond these powers, they are acting unlawfully under the First Principle. It is for each public authority to determine what its powers are and to stay within them. No amount of consent on the part of individuals will make public sector bodies' processing lawful if there is no statutory basis for it.

Copyright

A data controller processing in breach of copyright will be processing unlawfully. Any published information that is copyright protected may not be used other than in accordance with the terms specified, and breach of the conditions (e.g. by copying without obtaining permission of the copyright holder) will be unlawful.

5.1.5 Fair processing

The interpretation of the requirement for fair processing in the DPA states:

> In determining for the purposes of the first principle whether personal data are processed fairly, regard is to be had to the method by which they are obtained, including in particular whether any person from whom they are obtained is deceived or misled as to the purpose or purposes for which they are to be processed (DPA, Sched.1, Part II, para.1(1)).

The Legal Guidance states that 'in assessing fairness, the first and paramount consideration must be given to the consequences of the processing to the interests of the data subject' (p.31), and the Information Commissioner has written that:

> Standards of fairness and lawfulness must be objectively assessed and applied. To assess the proper standards the . . .. [Commissioner] will use the standpoint of

the 'common man'. Thus the . . . [Commissioner] may decide that a data user has contravened the [first] principle even though the data controller did not intend to be unfair and did not consider himself to be acting unfairly (Information Commissioner's Guidelines, 3rd Series, November 1994, p.59).

So, fairness will be determined by reference to the method of obtaining the data and the effect on the data subject's interests, and will be assessed objectively. Fortunately, the DPA gives some guidance on how to process fairly in the form of the fair processing requirements, or fair processing code, though the Information Commissioner states that it is important to note that compliance with the fair processing requirements will not of itself ensure fair processing (Legal Guidance, p.30). These requirements should be seen as a starting point for achieving compliance with the requirement to process fairly. A data controller who does not comply with the fair processing requirements will certainly be in breach of the First Principle; a data controller who *only* complies with the fair processing requirements nonetheless risks being in breach.

Statutory obtaining

Paragraph 1(2) of the interpretation of the First Principle in Part II of Schedule 1 states:

> Subject to paragraph 2, for the purposes of the first principle data are to be treated as obtained fairly if they consist of information obtained from a person who –
> (a) is authorised by or under any enactment to supply it, or
> (b) is required to supply it by or under any enactment or by any convention or other instrument imposing an international obligation on the United Kingdom.

Note that this provision does not excuse the data controller from giving the fair collection notice, discussed below, but it does mean that whenever the controller doing the disclosing is under any statutory obligation to do so, the receiving party obtains the data fairly. This means that any measures passed by Parliament to promote data sharing between public sector bodies will, if they authorise the supply of information, circumvent scrutiny of the obtaining process under general considerations of fairness. However, all other processing activities (other than mere obtaining) have to be justified under Schedule 2 (and 3 if appropriate).

The fair processing requirements

Paragraph 2 of the interpretation in Part II of Schedule 1 states that where personal data are received directly from the data subject, they:

> are not to be treated as processed fairly unless ... the data controller ensures so far as practicable that the data subject has, is provided with, or has made readily available to him, the information specified ... (DPA, Sched. 1, Part II, para. 2(1)).

When should the information be provided?

The Legal Guidance states:

> the Act makes no specific provision relating to timescale in the case of data obtained from a data subject, [therefore] it should be presumed that the fair processing information should be provided to the data subject at the time the data are obtained. (p.35)

Where the data have been received from a source other than the data subject, the information should generally be provided before or as soon as practicable after the data controller first obtains the data (DPA, Sched.1, Part II, para.2(2)). There is one exception to this rule, giving more time for the controller to give the required information, which is where the data controller has received data from a source other than the data subject, and envisages disclosing the data to a third party. In that case, the information need not be provided to the data subject immediately, but should be provided when the data are indeed subsequently disclosed. If the data controller becomes aware (or ought to become aware) that the disclosure to the third party will not take place at all within a reasonable period then the information should be provided immediately the data controller becomes aware of that fact.

What information must be provided?

The required information is specified at DPA, Sched.1, Part II, para.2(3):

(a) the identity of the data controller;
(b) if he has nominated a representative for the purposes of this Act, the identity of that representative;
(c) the purpose or purposes for which the data are intended to be processed; and
(d) any further information which is necessary, having regard to the specific circumstances in which the data are or are to be processed, to enable processing in respect of the data subject to be fair.

Note that although the requirement that the data controller should notify the purposes of the processing to the data subject seems to duplicate the Second Principle, as will be seen in the discussion of that principle later in this chapter, that the Second Principle obligation can be satisfied by notification of purposes to the Information Commissioner. This still leaves the controller to comply with the fair obtaining requirements by telling the data subject of the purposes for processing.

Category (d) of para.2(3) can be summarised as: anything else necessary to guarantee fair processing, and it will depend very much on the circumstances what this information ought to be. The Legal Guidance (p.32) states that data controllers considering what further information is necessary should consider:

> what processing of personal data they will be carrying out once the data have been obtained and consider whether or not data subjects are likely to understand the following:
> (a) the purposes for which their personal data are going to be processed;
> (b) the likely consequences of such processing such that the data subject is able to make a judgement as to the nature and extent of the processing; and
> (c) whether particular disclosures can reasonably be envisaged.

It should be noted in relation to the consent conditions in Schedules 2 and 3 that compliance with that element of consent which requires that consent be 'informed' will often be satisfied by complying with the requirement to provide this information.

When obtaining personal data from other sources, Art.11 of the Directive suggests telling the data subject of:

- the categories of data concerned;
- the proposed recipients or categories of recipients; and
- rights of access and rectification.

Other suggested possibilities for 'anything else', whether data are obtained from the data subject or elsewhere, are: what the proposed recipients intend to use the data for; how long the controller and any recipient will retain the data; any risky transfers outside the EEA; major security risks known to the data controller; and any automated decision taking.

Exemption

Where data are obtained other than from the data subject, there is, at para.3(2), an exemption to the obligation to give the required information in the following circumstances:

(a) where the provision of the information would involve a disproportionate effort; or

(b) where the recording or disclosure of the data by the data controller is necessary to comply with any legal obligation on the data controller other than a contractual obligation.

Subparagraph (b) ties up with the provisions of para.1(2) which say that statutory obtaining is always fair (see above); this will take processing required under statute completely outside the fairness provisions where the data are not obtained directly from the data subject. The Legal Guidance provides clarification of the meaning of 'disproportionate effort':

> the Commissioner will take into account a number of factors including the nature of the data, the length of time and the cost involved to the data controller in providing the information,

and points out that:

> the above factors will always be balanced against the prejudicial . . . effect to the data subject. (p.34)

Data controllers should not therefore see this as an easy get out and should document their reasons if they do rely on disproportionate effort.

The Secretary of State has prescribed further conditions that must also be met (Data Protection (Conditions Under Paragraph 3 of Part II of Schedule 1) Order 2000, SI 2000/185). These include the requirements that the data controller should provide the information to any data subject who requests it, and that a data controller relying on the disproportionate effort exemption should keep a record of why it believes that the disapplication of the fair processing requirements is necessary.

The data protection notice

The subject information requirement of fairness does not have to be satisfied by any formal notice to the data subject where the identity and purposes of the controller are obvious in the circumstances, as when visiting a doctor for a consultation about a health problem. Other circumstances, for example processing for non-obvious purposes, or when it may be necessary to evidence compliance with the requirement, or when consent needs to be obtained, will always give rise to the need for a specific communication to the data subject.

A convenient method for ensuring that the data controller complies with the fair processing requirements is to use a data protection notice, sometimes referred to as a fair collection notice, privacy policy or data protection statement. The notice may be given in writing, or orally over the telephone, but in either case, it must be reasonably intelligible and appropriately visible or audible. A data protection notice given in an inappropriate format may itself be unfair because it is not visible (*Linguaphone Institute Ltd* v. *Data Protection Registrar* (Case DA/94/31/49/1)).

The data protection notice can also be used as a handy means of obtaining the consent of the data subject to certain processing (as specified in para.1 of both Schedules 2 and 3) – but note that this use of a fair collection notice does not indicate that any consents sought must be obtained in order for processing to take place; it is merely a convenience to the data controller. If the data subject is required to return an application form containing a data protection notice with consent wording (e.g. by returning this form, you signify your consent to . . .), then a returned form will amount to consent from the data subject to the processing described.

Data controllers should consider the most practical means of providing this information at the point of collection of the data, by whatever format. For example, the Information Commissioner has issued guidance on 'Collecting personal information using websites' which makes clear that 'it is not enough simply to say 'click here to see our privacy statement'. You need to show some basic description of your use of individuals' information wherever personal information is collected, even where more detailed information is provided elsewhere.'

5.2   SECOND PRINCIPLE

> Personal data shall be obtained only for one or more specified and lawful purposes, and shall not be further processed in any manner incompatible with that purpose or those purposes.

In paras.5 and 6 of Part II of Schedule 1, the statutory interpretation of the Second Principle states:

> 5. The purpose or purposes for which personal data are obtained may in particular be specified:
>   (a) in a notice given for the purposes of paragraph 2 by the data controller to the data subject; or
>   (b) in a notification given to the Commissioner under Part III of this Act.
> 6. In determining whether any disclosure of personal data is compatible with the purpose or purposes for which the data were obtained, regard is to be had to the purpose or purposes for which the personal data are intended to be processed by any person to whom they are disclosed.

The Second Principle is known as the 'purpose limitation Principle'. This Principle may be the best protection that individuals possess against data controllers that wish to process their personal data in very extensive ways. For example, the purpose limitation Principle is the Principle which currently prevents central and local government departments from using for other purposes personal data which they originally collected for a specific purpose. The word 'incompatible' in the DPA is the same word as is used in Art.6(*b*) of Directive 95/46/EC. It is intended to denote that the use of the information throughout its whole processing life must be consistent with the purposes which were communicated to the individual at the time the personal data were collected, or if no purposes were communicated at that time then the use of the personal data must remain consistent with the obvious purposes which were in the mind of the individual at the time when he gave the information.

The requirement of a data controller that it must inform the data subject about the purposes for processing is set out in Art.10 of the Directive and reproduced in Schedule 1 to the DPA. Additionally, data controllers must process fairly. In order to do so they must either give data subjects a data protection notice at the time when their information is collected in order to convey to the data subject all the purposes for processing, or ensure that the data subject already has that information in his head at the time of giving personal data to the data controller – this is an additional requirement to that presented by the First Principle's fairness obligations (see above).

This state of knowledge of the data subject may arise from a previous course of dealings between the data controller and the data subject or from the surrounding circumstances from which the data subject can derive the requisite state of knowledge. It will never be an obvious purpose for an individual to have personal data passed to a third party without being informed.

Since the collection and storage of personal data is an expensive activity, most data controllers will want to ensure that the personal data are usable in the widest possible ways so that they can get the best return on their investment of time and capital. This is why a wise data controller does not rely on any knowledge it may suppose to be in the mind of the data subject at the time of giving personal data. Nor do most data controllers want to be put to the difficulty of proving what that state of mind was. Instead, the safest and most cost-effective way of ensuring that the personal data are capable of being exploited to extract their maximum value is to use a data protection notice which does lend itself to proving the state of knowledge of the data subject at the time when his information was collected. There may, however, be circumstances in which the data have already been collected, or are collected in a commercial setting which does not easily allow for the use of notices, for example, in a retail outlet. These are the cases that the Second Principle was drafted to accommodate.

It could be argued that there is no requirement for the Second Principle at all, since any processing which is incompatible with the originally stated purposes would be unfair and would therefore breach the First Principle, but this argument misses the point of the Second Principle, which is: how does a data controller state its purposes to a data subject?

Processing must be compatible with the originally stated purposes, but there are certain circumstances in which a data controller does not have to give a data protection notice. The first of these is where the purposes for the processing are obvious to the data subject at the time when the information is collected.

The second circumstance in which a data controller does not have to give a data protection notice is if the controller can benefit from the disproportionate effort qualification to the obligation to give a data protection notice set out in the interpretation of the fairness obligation of the First Principle.

The third circumstance is where the data controller may benefit from an exemption from giving a notice such as the exemption contained in s.34. This applies in cases where, for example, a data controller is a public body which is obliged by law to gather personal data and to make it available to the public. Electoral Registration Officers are obliged to compile and make available databases of those who are eligible to vote, and under s.34 they are exempt from the subject information provisions of the DPA which means that they do not have to give a data protection notice to all the individuals concerned.

Notification of an organisation's purposes to the ICO is the second method set out in the interpretation provisions of the Second Principle under which the data controller can specify its purposes. This is obligatory for most data controllers in respect of most processing. However, certain data controllers are exempt from notification because their processing is so innocuous that the DPA allows them to process without notification. Section 17(3) introduces the concept of innocuous processing and the notification regulations made by the Secretary of State under that section provide the details.

A further method for making purposes known is set out in s.24, which allows a data controller to specify its purposes by providing a statement of processing (within 21 days and free of charge) to any person who has made a written request to the data controller. A data controller who fails to provide such a statement of processing within the requisite time will be guilty of a criminal offence, but s.24 only applies to data controllers who fall under the exemption from notification set out in s.17 and who have not chosen to notify voluntarily under s.18. The concept of the statement of processing is derived from Art.21(3) of the Directive and the list of information required to be provided to the applicant is the same as that required for notification to the ICO (relevant particulars).

Great care must be taken in the drafting of data protection notices in order not to fall foul of the purpose limitation Principle. It is suggested that before any data protection notices are drafted, a data protection audit of an organisation should be carried out in order that a comprehensive list of purposes for processing can be compiled. In addition, those responsible for drafting the data protection notices should certainly have discussions with planning sections or future business development departments within organisations to try to establish whether those purposes are likely to change radically within the next two or three years, this being the expected shelf life of a data protection notice.

The reason for this recommendation is that if any purposes have been deliberately or accidentally left out of the data protection notice, it will be very difficult to process the personal data for those purposes unless they were so obvious that they were already known to the data subject at the time of collection. The very fact that a data protection notice has been given which omits a purpose or purposes will militate against the fact that the forgotten purpose is obvious. It could be argued that such a data protection notice would be misleading to the data subject and therefore unfair under the First Principle (see **5.1**). In practice, this means that data controllers who forget to include a purpose or who resolve, at a later date, to process personal data for a new purpose have to carry out an exercise under which they re-collect the personal data from the individuals on their database under the terms of a new data protection notice which includes the new or additional purposes.

These re-collection exercises are slow and extremely expensive and following the *Innovations* case before the Data Protection Tribunal (Case DA/92/31/49/1), consent is required from each individual for the use of personal data for the new purpose. Although consent is discussed in **5.1**, it is worthwhile to mention here that consent in these circumstances will require a positive action on the part of the individual to indicate agreement to the new purpose. Unless a suitable business process can be found to encourage this consent (e.g. waiting until renewal of an insurance policy), the level of response from the database of individuals subject to a re-collection exercise is likely to be low.

Data protection notices often state that information may be disclosed to or shared with 'other carefully selected organisations', 'our business partners', 'other organisations with whom we have a business relationship', 'other group companies' and then set out the purposes for which these third parties may use the information, for example: 'contacting you by mail with offers of goods or services in which you may be interested'. All of these are examples of data controllers complying with the final paragraph of the interpretation to the Second Principle. This requires data controllers to have regard to the purpose or purposes for which the personal data are intended to be processed by any person to whom they are disclosed.

Such disclosure will be from one data controller to another data controller and will be for commercial purposes. There will generally therefore be a contract in place which contains the commercial arrangements between the parties. In order not to be in breach of the Second Principle, the original data controller will provide in the contract terms that the second data controller must only use the information for the purposes specified in the original data protection notice and will take an indemnity from the second data controller to ensure that if any breach occurs, the original data controller is protected.

CHAPTER 6

Data quality – Third, Fourth and Fifth Principles

Sue Cullen

6.1 INTRODUCTION – SOME COMMON THEMES

6.1.1 Data quality

The Third, Fourth and Fifth Principles concern the quality of personal data which are being processed by the data controller. The Third Principle provides that personal data must be adequate, relevant and not excessive; the Fourth Principle requires that data be accurate and up to date; and the Fifth Principle prohibits unnecessary retention of personal data. Since few people will try to argue that they are justified in holding data which are, for example, out of date or irrelevant, these common sense Principles, particularly the Third and Fourth, are relatively easy for data controllers to understand and accept. This is reflected in the fact that unlike all the other Principles, the Third and Fifth have no interpretation provisions allocated to them in Part II of Schedule 1 to the DPA.

6.1.2 Relative to purpose

Another common theme running through the Third to the Fifth Principles is that they relate to the concept of processing relative to purpose. In this respect, the Third, Fourth and Fifth Principles follow through the important maxim laid down in the Second Principle: that the data controller should have a specific purpose whenever personal data are being processed. On the other hand, the need for a purpose is sometimes the aspect which causes inexperienced data controllers most difficulty. Some organisations remain convinced that having large quantities of personal data is a good idea in principle, on the basis that they never know what information they may need in the future. They need to understand that they have to have a purpose for holding personal data, and that if they do not have a good reason to hold the data then they must get rid of them (Fifth Principle – retention; Third Principle – excessive processing).

6.1.3 Data subject consent not relevant

A third common feature of these three Principles is the irrelevance of data subject consent. There is often considerable overlap between some of the eight Principles, but nevertheless each Principle is self-standing. The fact that the data subject has specifically consented to the processing will be very important for the purposes of satisfying a Schedule 2 or Schedule 3 condition under the First Principle, and may also be relevant for the purposes of the Sixth and Eighth Principles. The data controller must, however, comply with all eight Principles in respect of every processing operation.

A data subject may, for example, consent to the processing of data concerning ethnic origin but, if this processing is nevertheless irrelevant or excessive in relation to the data controller's stated purpose, then it breaches the Third Principle. The only difference made by the data subject's consent is that in those circumstances it is unlikely to be the data subject who makes a complaint. If, on the other hand, the Information Commissioner is investigating the data controller, then such consent will not influence any determination of whether the Third Principle has been breached. Similar considerations apply if the data subject consents to the processing of inaccurate data (Fourth Principle) or to indefinite retention (Fifth Principle).

6.2 THIRD PRINCIPLE

Personal data shall be adequate, relevant and not excessive in relation to the purpose or purposes for which they are processed.

6.2.1 Information appropriate to purpose

The Third Principle is specifically aimed at ensuring that data controllers process the correct amount of information about data subjects. There must be not too much, nor too little data. As will be seen at **6.2.6,** quite a lot of what is covered by the Third Principle is also entailed by the application of some of the other Principles, but the stipulation that data must be adequate, relevant and not excessive in a self-standing Principle emphasises the importance of these elements of data subjects' rights under Directive 95/46/EC. Just because a data controller has a legitimate reason to process certain information about an individual, that does not mean that it can process whatever information it likes about that individual.

There is no interpretation given of the Third Principle in Part II of Schedule 1, but in the Legal Guidance, the Information Commissioner says of the Third Principle:

> In complying with this Principle, data controllers should seek to identify the minimum amount of information that is required in order properly to fulfil their purpose and this will be a question of fact in each case. If it is necessary to hold additional information about certain individuals, such information should only be collected and recorded in those cases. (p.36)

The Information Commissioner focuses on the common circumstance in which a data controller is routinely processing the same classes of data in relation to a large number of data subjects for a particular purpose. Clearly, it will be convenient for the data controller to process the same information in respect of each data subject for that purpose, but considerations of the controller's convenience do not outweigh the individual entitlement of each data subject to have personal data processed in accordance with all the Principles. The Information Commissioner illustrates this point by quoting a case decided under the earlier DPA 1984 (such cases are generally still good law):

> This guidance has been endorsed by the Data Protection Tribunal in the context of the 1984 Act in the case of Runnymede Borough Council CCRO and Others v The Data Protection Registrar (November 1990). Where a data controller holds an item of information on all individuals which will be used or useful only in relation to some of them, the information is likely to be excessive and irrelevant in relation to those individuals in respect of whom it will not be used or useful and should not be held in those cases. (p.36)

6.2.2 Adequacy

Interestingly, the Third Principle requirement that the data controller should process adequate personal data is the only obligation under the Principles which comes close to requiring the data controller to do some processing. The tenor of this legislation is to restrict and regulate the processing of personal data, and advice generally is not to do any processing unless it is clearly needed, in order to avoid unnecessary liability under the DPA. In the context of the exemptions, the fact that the DPA does not compel anybody to do any processing is often misunderstood, and third parties requiring personal information from a data controller have been known to couch their enquiries as demands pursuant to a stated exemption, as if they were exercising an entitlement to information conferred under the DPA. The police still have a tendency to demand disclosure of personal data 'under section 29(3)', and even solicitors have had to be gently disabused of the idea that, for example, the possibility of the controller choosing to apply the s.35(2) exemption (disclosure necessary for legal proceedings) actually obliges a data controller to give them some information.

By the Third Principle, however, the data controller must, if it chooses to process information about somebody, process adequate information.

Adequacy is by reference to the purpose for which the data are being processed; clearly, information which may be adequate for one purpose may not be sufficient for a different purpose – something which needs to be borne in mind whenever data-sharing or data-matching exercises are being undertaken. For example, information about someone collected for a general marketing purpose may not be adequate if that individual becomes a customer of the data controller for, by way of example, healthcare products.

The main area in which this element bites is where personal data are inadequate to identify the data subject. If you are processing information about a lot of Joneses, who live in South Wales, then you may need more than a middle name and an address to identify which is which. In that case a date of birth may also be required, but if the surname is more unusual, such as 'Saxe-Coburg Gotha', and processing of such additional information would not be required to identify the individual, then including a middle name could be excessive processing. The Third Principle requires the data controller to process enough information for the purpose, but not too much.

Credit reference agencies were, under the 1984 Act, held up as the biggest offenders when it came to adequacy, regularly misidentifying individuals because their records did not contain sufficient information to distinguish individuals with the same surname, or who lived at the same address. Sometimes this was due to limitations of technology (not enough space to record a middle name) and often it was because they were at the mercy of credit grantors who failed to gather enough information about the individuals to be checked.

6.2.3 Relevance

Data controllers who offend against the relevance element of the Third Principle tend to be those who think that the more information they hold, the better off they will be. Because this Principle is tied to the purpose of the processing (and as will be seen when the Fifth Principle is considered below, the data controller must always maintain a purpose for processing), the question of what information is relevant is determined by the data controller's particular purpose. The Information Commissioner says:

> It is not acceptable to hold information on the basis that it might possibly be useful in the future without a view of how it will be used. This is to be distinguished from holding information in the case of a particular foreseeable contingency which may never occur, for example, where an employer holds details of blood groups of employees engaged in hazardous occupations. (p.37)

Examples of irrelevant information are the requirement, often found on forms which individuals are required to fill in when applying for goods or services, to give a date of birth where the age of the consumer has no bearing on eligibility for the product or service; information about similar products or services already used by the consumer (usually requested for purposes of marketing or consumer research which are not clearly stated to the data subject); and information about other data subjects close to the data subject, such as family members, which although possibly of great interest to the data controller, has nothing to do with the particular transaction in hand.

6.2.4 Excessive data

Excessive data are those data that are not necessary for the particular purpose. Irrelevant information and excessive information will often amount to the same thing. An example of excessive processing could be the recording of information as to racial or ethnic origin of data subjects where that information has no apparent bearing on the stated purpose for processing (which is often the case for these data). It might be relevant for the purpose of equal opportunities monitoring (in accordance with the special dispensation given for such processing under para.9 of Part II of Schedule 3) but if the data controller's purpose could be achieved by anonymising the data, which would be in accordance with the Information Commissioner's recommendations, then the processing might well be excessive.

6.2.5 Information Commissioner's advice

The Information Commissioner makes the following recommendations in the Legal Guidance:

> Data controllers should continually monitor compliance with this Principle, which has obvious links with the Fourth and Fifth Principles. Changes in circumstances or failure to keep the information up to date may mean that information that was originally adequate becomes inadequate. If the data are kept for longer than necessary then they may well be both irrelevant and excessive. In most cases, data controllers should be able to remedy possible breaches of the Principle by the erasure or addition of particular items of personal data so that the information is no longer excessive, inadequate, or irrelevant.
>
> The data controller should consider for all data:
>
> * the number of individuals on whom information is held;
> * the number of individuals for whom it is used;
> * the nature of the personal data;
> * the length of time it is held;
> * the way it was obtained;
> * the possible consequences for individuals of the holding or erasure of the data;

- the way in which it is used;
- the purpose for which it is held. (p.37)

6.2.6 Links to other Principles

The Third Principle is strongly linked to the First Principle. First, there is an obvious argument that the processing of personal data which are inadequate, irrelevant or excessive is unfair to the data subject – the First Principle requires fairness in processing. Second, it will be difficult to justify the processing of any such data by reference to the conditions in Schedules 2 or 3, on the basis that it can never be necessary to process such data regardless of the particular purpose. Where, however, the data controller can show that the data subject gave an effective consent to the processing, then any arguments under those two Schedules become irrelevant.

Similarly, the processing of irrelevant or excessive data will by definition not be justifiable by reference to a purpose specified pursuant to the Second Principle. If personal data are inadequate or irrelevant then there may also be a problem of accuracy under the Fourth Principle since, as will be seen, data are inaccurate if they are misleading as to matters of fact. Inadequate or irrelevant data may provide misleading information about the data subject.

Under the Fifth Principle, since irrelevant or excessive data cannot be justified by reference to the purpose for processing, it follows that those data are not necessary for that purpose and, therefore, the data controller has an obligation to get rid of them.

6.2.7 Links to data subject rights

A data subject who suspects a data controller of processing inadequate, irrelevant or excessive personal data should check what personal data of his the data controller actually holds (unless he already has sufficient information about the processing). He can do this by making a subject access request under s.7 (see Chapter 9) and requesting a copy in permanent form of all his data held by the data controller.

Under s.10, the data subject has the right to object to processing that causes unwarranted damage or distress to the data subject (or to someone else). This is useful where, for example, the data subject's file reveals information not relevant to the data controller's particular processing operation, and which the data subject feels is prejudicial to him, and he wants to put a stop to the processing. The severe limitations of this right are that the damage or distress which must be demonstrated need to be substantial, and in any event the right is not available where the data controller is justifying the processing under grounds 1 to 4 of Schedule 2 (consent, contract, legal obligation and vital interests of the data subject).

129

The s.14 right to rectification, blocking, erasure or destruction (see **6.3.6** for detail) may also be relevant. Since its application is confined to inaccurate personal data, it will be brought into play under the Third Principle only if the inadequacy, irrelevance or excessive data are consequently misleading as to matters of fact so as to amount to inaccuracy.

It is also open to a data subject who has suffered damage because of breach of the Third Principle to claim compensation from the data controller under s.13.

6.3 FOURTH PRINCIPLE

Personal data shall be accurate, and where necessary, kept up to date.

6.3.1 Importance of accuracy

Accuracy is, in many ways, the most fundamental obligation of any data controller. Once a data controller has overcome the hurdles imposed by the First and Second Principles, which determine whether or not it can lawfully process the personal data in the first place, the next consideration must always be data quality, of which accuracy is the most important component.

Some of the early attempts to legislate for data protection were motivated to a great degree by concerns that data controllers held inaccurate information which could not be checked, and that important decisions taken about people were based on inaccurate data. There was a perception that data controllers were faceless organisations owing no duty of accountability to those individuals whose information they compiled.

Indeed, this emphasis on the importance of accuracy of personal data is so strongly rooted in data protection law that a learned judge went so far as to state, of the DPA, that:

> the purpose of the legislation, it seems to me, is to ensure that records of an inaccurate nature are not kept about an individual. A citizen needs to know what the record says in order to have an opportunity of remedying an error or false information.
>
> *Durant* v. *FSA* [2003] EWCA Civ 1746

Although this was an overstatement which ignored the many other purposes of the DPA, it says a lot about one of the chief aims of the legislation.

Examples of the problems caused to individuals by the recording of inaccurate data abound, particularly in the field of access to financial services controlled by means of a credit reference agency. If a credit reference agency maintains (inaccurately) that a person has three county court judgments for debt outstanding against him, then his chances of getting a loan from a bank are significantly reduced. In the field of medical records, inaccuracies, such as incorrect classification of a person's blood group, could prove life threatening. Inaccuracy may lead to misidentification of a data subject, and among other things, could cause a disclosure of personal data to be made to or about the wrong data subject.

6.3.2   What is accuracy? What about opinions?

The Information Commissioner says in the Legal Guidance: 'data are inaccurate if they are incorrect or misleading as to any matter of fact'.

Clearly, incomplete information will be inaccurate if it is misleading as a consequence, even if what is actually said happens to be true. Personal data which are so inadequate as to mislead the data controller or others as to the identity of the data subject will therefore breach the Fourth Principle, as well as the Third. Factual inaccuracies need no further explanation; in any particular case, it is just a matter of evidence. Information consisting of an opinion is, however, another matter.

You could argue that the above extract from the Guidance does itself err in the direction of being inaccurate since it could mislead an unsuspecting reader to the conclusion that Fourth Principle accuracy is confined to matters of fact. But it does not say that accuracy is confined to factual accuracy, and the definition of 'personal data' specifically includes expressions of opinion, so these personal data are also required to be accurate. This interpretation of accuracy is also supported by s.14 which, in conferring the right to rectification, blocking or erasure of inaccurate data, stipulates that this right extends to expressions of opinion based on inaccurate data. So what about opinion data?

The trouble with opinions is that they lack the precision of facts; they are judgements or evaluations which can be the subject of debate and differing views. For example, an opinion might be formed about the age of a particular individual. A true statement of his age as 40 years old is, of course, a fact. If, however, someone else judges this individual's age to be about 50 – that is an opinion. If, like Guy Fawkes night, the day and month (but not, of course, the year) of the individual's birth are maddeningly memorable, then the person who has judged the age of the individual to be 50 might conclude that the individual is about to become eligible for the products and services offered by a commercial organisation specialising in holidays for the over-50s. As a consequence, the individual's details may, for example, be passed to the holiday company as a birthday present by his well-meaning friend.

The opinion about the individual's age is clearly inaccurate, even though it may be justified by appearances. On the other hand, a description of the individual as 'balding, 50-ish, wearing a 1970s suit and kipper tie' could be an objectively accurate description. Records of that description taken, for example, by the police following an incident, will, as far as that description goes, be perfectly accurate.

By contrast, the records maintained by the holiday company on the basis of the information supplied to them will be inaccurate if they record the individual's age as 50. And as will be seen, the holiday company will have to do more to demonstrate compliance with the Fourth Principle than just to accept what it has been told – the interpretation provisions relating to the Fourth Principle require the company to take reasonable steps to verify the accuracy of the information. In this case that means checking either with the individual concerned or by some other method.

The real difficulties with accuracy in opinion data arise where the data subject and the data controller disagree about an opinion recorded by the data controller, where the information is some kind of assessment or evaluation which is essentially a matter of informed or expert opinion rather than an independently verifiable matter of fact. Areas of disagreement commonly arise in the evaluation of the ability or performance of an employee by an employer, or certain medical diagnoses or psychological assessments. The data controller must be prepared to justify any opinions recorded about the data subject, and it follows that the training of human resources personnel, and others, such as partners, who deal with employment issues, is particularly important for law firms.

It should be remembered, however, that even if a disputed opinion can be shown to be justified, and not vulnerable to challenge under the Fourth Principle, it might still be challenged under one or more of the other Principles (e.g. First Principle fairness or Third Principle relevance) and may be the occasion for the exercise of data subject rights.

A particular problem can be caused when inaccurate information is accurately recorded. In one example of a case of a wrong diagnosis of Munchausen's syndrome by proxy, the data subject wanted the hospital to erase the record, as she would clearly otherwise be stigmatised as a danger to children. The hospital claimed that it was justified in maintaining the record as an accurate record of a wrong diagnosis. Similarly, credit reference agencies have in the past argued that they were entitled to maintain, on a data subject's file, records of county court judgments which were nothing to do with the particular data subject because they were accurate records of the inaccurate information supplied by the court.

In terms of the accuracy of the data subject's personal data, the above will usually be specious arguments, although in some cases it might conceivably be necessary to maintain some record, e.g. of a wrong diagnosis, to account for any treatment given. But in any event any well-advised data subject would attack the processing on the additional grounds of unfairness, and challenge the data controller to demonstrate a Schedule 2 condition (bear in mind that condition 6 falls away if unwarrantable prejudice is caused to the data subject); in addition they could exercise the rights to object and to rectification.

6.3.3   Interpretation of the Fourth Principle

Paragraph 7 of Part II of Schedule 1 to the DPA states:

The fourth principle
7.   The fourth principle is not to be regarded as being contravened by reason of any inaccuracy in personal data which accurately record information obtained by the data controller from the data subject or a third party in a case where:
   (a)   having regard to the purpose or purposes for which the data were obtained and further processed, the data controller has taken reasonable steps to ensure the accuracy of the data, and
   (b)   if the data subject has notified the data controller of the data subject's view that the data are inaccurate, the data indicate that fact.

This is a very useful 'get out of jail free card' for any data controller who holds information the accuracy of which is disputed by the data subject. Provided that the data accurately record the information which the controller originally obtained, and bearing in mind the controller's purposes for processing, then so long as the controller has done whatever is appropriate to ensure accuracy, it will not be in breach of the Fourth Principle where the data record the fact of the data subject's disagreement as to their accuracy.

Of course, this is not a satisfactory resolution of any such dispute, and in most cases it is to be expected that agreement would be reached and that the data controller would correct any inaccuracies revealed by the data subject's complaint. Indeed, controllers should encourage data subjects to review data held and should facilitate complaints, since it is not in the interest of any controller to hold inaccurate data, and in practice they must place extensive reliance on data subjects to ensure that what they hold is correct. The payoff, for data controllers, of compliance with the transparency requirements of the DPA is enhanced data quality.

In any event, the Information Commissioner states in the Legal Guidance that:

> It is not enough for a data controller to say that, because the information was obtained from either the data subject or a third party, they had done all they could to ensure the accuracy of the data at the time. Now data controllers have to go further and take reasonable steps to ensure the accuracy of the data themselves and mark the data with any objections. The extent to which such steps are necessary will be a matter of fact in each individual case and will depend on the nature of the data and the consequences of the inaccuracy for the data subject. (p.38)

This is a risk-based approach to checking accuracy, comparable with the approach to Seventh Principle security. Further detail on the Commissioner's approach can be found in his 'Data Protection Technical Guidance – Filing defaults with credit reference agencies' (August 2007):

Accuracy of a lender's default records

39 Records

Any default record should be accurate. We normally expect a lender to keep records that are necessary to show an agreement exists and to support filing a default. We would also expect a lender to be able to produce evidence to justify a default record they had placed on a credit reference file. Not having any supporting records may indicate a breach of the data protection principle requiring personal data to be adequate, relevant and not excessive for the purpose for which it is processed. A record that a notice of an intention to file a default was sent, if not a copy of the notice itself, will help lenders to comply with this requirement.

40 Factors to be taken into account in enforcement

Any decisions on enforcement action will be taken in accordance with our Regulatory Action Strategy. When we consider enforcement action in cases where there is inconclusive evidence of whether a default did or did not occur, or the amount of a default, we must make a judgment on whether we consider that the Information Tribunal would support a view that a default record filed with an agency is incorrect or misleading. To reach a judgment we will consider, among other factors:

- any evidence that exists, even if it is inconclusive;
- the credibility of the data subject;
- the credibility of the lender;
- the reliability of the lender's internal procedures;
- the existence of other similar complaints about the lender; and
- the use which the customer, or lender has made of other mechanisms to determine the accuracy of the record, for instance the courts or a relevant ombudsman scheme.

The Fourth Principle obligation and the strictures in the interpretation provisions constitute another reason why data controllers might want to retain details concerning the source of their information. Unlike records of disclosures, there is no obligation to retain information as to source (although if the information about the source is available, then it must be revealed to data subjects on a subject access request), but it will be difficult to demonstrate the element of accurate recording from source required in para.7 without maintaining evidence of the source.

Quite often the source will be the data subject himself, which is likely to be relevant in any dispute where the data merely record what the data subject told the data controller. Good records management, which links sources information (e.g. by a marker cross-referencing to the source database) to databases of personal data at a keystroke, will save considerably on the time and costs incurred in collating this information.

6.3.4 Keeping up to date

The second limb of the Fourth Principle requires that personal data must be kept up to date. This is limited to circumstances where the keeping of the data up to date is necessary. As the Information Commissioner points out in the Legal Guidance to this Principle, the purpose for which the data are held will be relevant in deciding whether updating is necessary. Obviously, where the purpose of maintaining the information is for a historical record of, for example, a particular transaction, then updating would be inappropriate, and would in such a case lead to an inaccurate record.

The Information Commissioner goes on to say:

> sometimes it is important for the purpose that the data reflect the data subject's current circumstances, for example, if the data are used to decide whether to grant credit or confer or withhold some other benefit. (p.38)

The Information Commissioner recommends that the data controller considers the following factors:

1. Is there a record of when the data were recorded or last updated?
2. Are all those involved with the data – including people to whom they are disclosed as well as employees of the data controller – aware that the data do not necessarily reflect the current position?
3. Are steps taken to update the personal data – for example, by checking back at intervals with the original source or with the data subject? If so, how effective are these steps?
4. Is the fact that the personal data are out of date likely to cause damage or distress to the data subject? (p.38)

6.3.5 Links to other Principles

The examples given above have already indicated the strong link between accuracy and fairness, under the First Principle. If a data controller maintains inaccurate personal data and takes decisions about the data subject based on those data, then it is likely that it is being unfair to the data subject, and the processing will be open to challenge on those grounds alone.

Still under the First Principle, where inaccurate or out-of-date data are being processed, the data controller may have difficulty in maintaining a Schedule 2 ground for processing. Assuming that the data subject has not consented to the processing of inaccurate data (out-of-date information may have had consent when it was originally obtained, but consent for processing data which were originally accurate will not justify continued processing when it becomes out-of-date) it will be hard for the data controller to demonstrate the necessity of the processing for any of the other conditions (can I seriously maintain, for example, that it is in your vital interests that I process inaccurate information about you, or that I have a legal obligation to process inaccurate information?).

Where there is a dispute about accuracy, and the data subject complains of resulting prejudice, then it will be very difficult for the data controller to justify the processing on ground 6 – that the processing is necessary in the legitimate interests of the data controller, except where it is unwarranted in any particular case owing to prejudice to the data subject.

Where the wrong information is being processed in relation to a data subject the data controller will not be able to demonstrate that that processing is for the purpose it has specified, so inaccuracy may sometimes be open to challenge under the Second Principle.

The Third Principle is, however, the one most closely linked to accuracy – inaccurate or out-of-date information about somebody is not likely to be relevant to the purpose for which the data are processed, so there will often be a breach of the Third Principle whenever there is a breach of the Fourth Principle. Out-of-date information might also be excessive in relation to the current purpose. There is also a close link between Third Principle adequacy, and Fourth Principle accuracy, particularly where inadequate information causes misidentification of a data subject.

Under the Fifth Principle, the data controller is unlikely to be able to demonstrate a purpose for processing inaccurate or out-of-date information, and the data controller would in those circumstances be in breach of the Fifth Principle if it continued to keep it.

Of course, under the Fourth Principle interpretation, a data controller who disagrees with a data subject's complaint of inaccuracy can, so long as it has taken reasonable steps to verify accuracy, mark any disputed information with the fact of the data subject's disagreement and still be in compliance with the Fourth Principle. The disappointed data subject can nevertheless pursue the argument, albeit not on grounds of inaccuracy, under the other Principles mentioned above and may still have a chance of success. Failing that, there are always the data subject's rights, discussed next.

6.3.6   Link to data subject rights

A data subject who suspects that information held about him by a particular data controller may be inaccurate or out of date will first of all want to see what personal data of his the data controller actually holds. Therefore, unless the data subject already has sufficient evidence of inaccuracy, his first step should be to make a subject access request under s.7, and ask for a copy of all his personal data currently held by the data controller.

The right, under s.10, to object to processing that causes unwarranted damage or distress to the data subject will also be relevant in the case of inaccurate personal data – see **6.2.7** for discussion of the limitations of that right.

The option specifically designed for a data subject complaining of inaccuracy, in the face of an intransigent data controller who refuses to correct its records, is the right conferred under s.14. If the data subject can satisfy the court that his personal data are inaccurate then the court may order the data controller to rectify, block, erase or destroy those data, including any opinion data based on the inaccurate data. The Information Commissioner points out in the Legal Guidance that this right applies whether or not the data accurately record information received from the data subject or a third party.

A clear case of the processing of inaccurate personal data will, if the processing has caused damage to the data subject, found a claim to compensation under s.13.

6.4   FIFTH PRINCIPLE

> Personal data processed for any purpose or purposes shall not be kept for longer than is necessary for that purpose or those purposes.

6.4.1   Need to show a purpose

This strong link to purposes for processing means that for as long as a data controller retains personal data it must show a purpose for having them. The purpose may or may not be the same as that for which they were originally obtained or that for which data may have been disclosed – those elements of purposes for processing are addressed, not by the Fifth Principle, but by the First and Second Principles. The point here in the Fifth Principle is not whether the processing can be justified in a particular way, or whether the purposes have been adequately notified, or are compatible with the purpose for which data were first obtained. Nor indeed does it matter whether an exemption from any of those obligations can be applied.

Under the Fifth Principle the essential element to show is that personal data are being held, i.e. processed, for a purpose. There must always be a reason why the data controller retains personal data. If a sufficient reason cannot be shown (the possibility that they may come in useful some day does not amount to a purpose) then the Fifth Principle imposes an obligation upon the data controller to get rid of the data, or of those data in respect of which the purpose for processing has been exhausted. Under the Fifth Principle, it does not matter what the reason for retention is, nor that it may not be a very good reason – those elements of the justification for processing are addressed by the requirements of Schedules 2 and 3 under the First Principle. What the Fifth requires is a current purpose for processing.

The Fifth Principle is always brought into play whenever a data controller appears to be merely retaining some personal data (i.e. the only processing operation is holding data) without any apparent reason. Usually, there will have been some reason why the controller originally obtained the data, but that reason no longer applies. Data intentionally acquired will invariably have been acquired for a particular purpose but data unintentionally acquired will pose a problem from the outset. An example of unintentional acquisition by the data controller is where an over-zealous employee gathers more informa-tion than the controller has specified for the particular purpose – this could also amount to the employee obtaining personal data without the consent of the data controller, which would constitute an offence under s.55. These cases should be uncovered by a data protection audit, when all the processing of personal data should be brought to light, and with it, the reasons why each database is maintained.

While it may always be possible for a data controller to come up with a purpose if questions are asked about the processing, it should be borne in mind that all purposes for processing must be notified to the Information Commissioner and should appear in the entry for the data controller in the Register, unless an exemption applies or the processing is of manual data only. Therefore, the stated purposes for processing which demonstrate that the data controller is complying with the Fifth Principle must be consistent with the controller's public statement on the Register of Data Controllers (see Chapter 4). In practice this is not an onerous requirement as the purposes and related information appearing on the Register are so general that they do little to pin down the specifics of any processing operation; the emphasis will always be on the controller to justify particular processing by reference to a specified purpose regardless of the generalities published in the Register.

Data controllers sometimes have the idea that they 'own' information which consists of personal data, and that such ownership justifies their holding on to the information, possibly indefinitely, without having to show any reason. That view is incorrect. Concepts of ownership are foreign to data protection law, which is not concerned with intellectual property rights, but rather with the rights of individuals. These rights override any consid-eration of ownership of a particular database, and the DPA makes it quite clear that unless all the obligations laid upon data controllers under the eight Principles are fully complied with, the data controller must not process personal data.

The Fifth Principle spells this out by stipulating that a data controller must not keep personal data for any longer than is necessary in relation to the purposes for which the controller has justified the processing. This means that if the data controller cannot justify keeping personal data then it must get rid of them, and the fact that the data controller may consider that it owns the information is irrelevant.

6.4.2 Data retention criteria

The key element of compliance with the Fifth Principle is a data retention policy which will set out data retention criteria. Each data controller needs to work out, in relation to all personal data which it holds, how long it needs to keep it. This exercise, which often follows from an audit showing what information is held, and why, involves considering the purpose or purposes for which each bit of information is held. There is no interpretation given for the Fifth Principle in Part 2 of Schedule 1 to the DPA, but there is some published guidance on retention periods.

When considering appropriate periods for the retention of personal data, bear in mind that different periods may apply to different personal data of the same data subject. For example, the vast majority of data controller organisations are employers who will hold personal data of staff in personnel files. This information will usually include items such as the offer of employment, references taken up, the employment contract, appraisals, records of promotions and pay reviews, and sickness and absence records. In addition, the payroll department will have records of wages or salary paid, and tax, pension and National Insurance deducted.

Not all this information needs to be retained for the same length of time. Information obtained for assessing the eligibility and bona fides of a prospective employee does not need to be retained in respect of unsuccessful applicants, and not all of it will need to be retained in respect of successful recruits – for example, the information as to any criminal convictions. For specific guidance, see the Information Commissioner's Employment Practices Code, also available in the form of a quick guide and alternatively with supplementary detailed guidance, which gives good practice recommendations. For example, in the context of the concern that allegations of unlawful discrimination might be made, the Commissioner advises that the obligation to delete does not rule out keeping information to protect against legal action. Continuing with the example of employee data, how long should the employer keep the information after the employee leaves? For example, information which could relate solely to a claim for unfair dismissal need be retained only during the period in which a claim can be brought, which is three months, but information relating to salary and payments must, under the Taxes Management Act 1970 be held for six years. The Code makes it clear that, for example, a statutory obligation to retain certain information will satisfy the Fifth Principle.

It can be seen that the well-organised firm should have no difficulty with the Fifth Principle because compliance is part of archiving and good records management. This is often carried out effectively in law firms in relation to client files which are regularly archived, but the same principles are not always applied to personnel files and other HR information. When it comes to regular housekeeping applied to other databases, such as lists of business contacts or supplier information, the picture is less clear – as has been indicated, data controllers are sometimes unaware that they still maintain certain databanks. Therefore, any firm which has not already done so should conduct a data protection audit to check what personal data it holds, and the reason for continuing to do so.

6.4.3 Getting rid of personal data

Although the obligation to get rid of personal data for which a processing purpose cannot be shown is straightforward enough, the process by which a data controller divests itself of information is not always straightforward. The use of the term 'process' here is apposite; getting rid of personal data is a processing operation which must itself comply with the Principles, so far as they apply to the operation in question – the definition of the term 'processing' in the DPA specifically mentions erasure and destruction.

The main concern is the security of the process under the Seventh Principle (see Chapter 7). There have been well-publicised horror stories of patient medical records contained in manual files being found dumped on a canal towpath or a council tip, and read by members of the public. Controllers who hire specialists to remove and destroy manual files are, of course, outsourcing a processing operation to a data processor, and in these circumstances, the security checks and guarantees which are in any event required under the Seventh Principle interpretation must be stringently carried out and enforced. At least in the case of manual files, physical destruction, for example by incineration, is a possibility which can give a guaranteed end result.

Not so in the case of deletion of electronic information. The layers of back-up offered by all IT systems mean that we do not succeed in expunging an item from the system just by pressing the 'delete' button. The vast majority of lawyers operate on a networked IT system, and these systems are designed to ensure that information is always retrievable. Furthermore, for the purposes of disaster recovery security, backup tapes will be made, and usually held off site, going back a number of years. Nevertheless, although information on backup systems, being 'held', is still subject to all the

Principles, its retention is unlikely to breach the Fifth if it has been effectively deleted from the active record.

Therefore, law firms and others need to work out procedures with their IT departments and other IT advisers which ensure an effective and secure process by which personal information can be erased, as far as possible, from the system, and relevant staff need to be trained to use it. When old computer equipment is disposed of, information recorded on the hard drive needs to be cleaned off – disclosures of personal data have been known to occur as a result of retrieval of information from second-hand computer equipment.

6.4.4   Links to other Principles

Although the Fifth Principle is not concerned with aspects of purpose such as specification, or satisfying one of the required conditions, looking at it another way, if the First and Second Principles are complied with in respect of processing which is currently being carried out then there is unlikely to be a problem under the Fifth Principle. So if, for example, a Schedule 2 or 3 condition (other than data subject consent) can be met in respect of holding the data, then the Fifth Principle is automatically satisfied because a current purpose will have been demonstrated. This will be the case whenever the processing consists of an event which can be justified under the First and Second Principles (such as doing some data collection, or making a specific disclosure). The Fifth Principle is most likely to be engaged in cases where personal data have been passively held for some time for no apparent reason.

Retaining personal data beyond the period during which they are required is not just a problem under the Fifth Principle. Once it is considered that such information may soon pass its sell-by date, it becomes obvious that keeping old information risks triggering the Fourth Principle, which requires that personal data shall be accurate and, where necessary, kept up to date. Quite apart from the problem of inaccuracy creeping in over time, demonstrating that it is not necessary to keep the information up to date would, unless it is held for the purposes of a historical record, immediately raise the question as to what is the current purpose for which those data continue to be held.

The Fifth Principle can, however, be triggered in circumstances other than cases where the controller fails to dispose of old databases. Consider cases in which the controller is processing in breach of the requirement not to process irrelevant or excessive data under the Third Principle. Relevant and excessive are stipulated to be in relation to the purpose for processing. This means that if processing specific items of personal data is not justified by reference to the stated purpose, then they are not necessary for that purpose, so it follows that unless some other purpose can be demonstrated, the Fifth Principle prohibits keeping those data.

These links to purpose show the Fifth Principle as the logical extension of the preceding Principles, but the practical consideration which might persuade reluctant data controllers to get rid of redundant information is the Seventh Principle. For as long as the data controller keeps the data it must comply fully with all the security requirements of the Seventh Principle. Holding personal data is, of course, a liability which might prove expensive both in terms of the measures required to keep it safe (see Chapter 7), and in terms of the cost of being held responsible for any security breach, or the loss of credibility of a firm which is subjected to enforcement action by the Information Commissioner. Furthermore, server capacity is both costly and finite in any electronic storage system. There seems to be little point in taking on this liability and these costs in respect of personal data for which the data controller does not even have any apparent use.

6.4.5   Link to data subject rights

There are two aspects of the interaction between the Fifth Principle and data subject rights. On the one hand there is the need for the data controller to avoid unnecessary liability towards data subjects by keeping information which it does not need – the negative aspect – and on the other hand, where there is a requirement to hold adequate information (pursuant to any existing obligation, and bearing in mind the Third Principle), the Fifth Principle must not be used as a reason to delete it – the positive requirement.

The negative aspect – the downside of holding on to data unnecessarily – is that this continuation of processing exposes the data controller to action from the data subject. The most likely event is a subject access request pursuant to s.7, which when satisfied, may lead to further action, such as an objection to processing pursuant to s.10, or possibly a requirement to rectify the data pursuant to s.14. Proof of a breach of the Fifth Principle would, if damage could be shown as a result, found a claim to compensation from the data controller under s.13.

Responding to a subject access request is time consuming and expensive for any business, but this is especially burdensome in respect of old information which should have been got rid of, and which may also be difficult to locate and copy. Furthermore, the data controller may be required to state the purpose for which it holds the information, and if it is in breach of the Fifth Principle it will be unable to do so. Such a confession could prompt the data subject to complain to the Information Commissioner and request an assessment pursuant to s.42.

6.5   RELEVANT EXEMPTIONS FROM THE THIRD, FOURTH AND FIFTH PRINCIPLES

There are a number of blanket exemptions in the DPA which embrace, among others, the Third, Fourth and Fifth Principles.

The first is the exemption from the non-disclosure provisions, defined at s.27(4) to include the Third, Fourth and Fifth Principles. Note that this exemption applies only to the extent to which the particular Principle would be inconsistent with the disclosure in question. Examples of the processing purposes for which the non-disclosure exemption may be claimed are: crime prevention and detection, and taxation purposes (s.29(3)); information required to be made public (s.34(c)); and disclosures required by law or necessary for legal proceedings (s.35).

Other blanket exemptions from these Principles are at s.28 – national security; s.32 – processing for the special purposes (journalism, literature and art), and s.36 – processing for social, recreational or domestic purposes. In addition, there are two one-off exemptions addressed to specific Principles. At s.33(3) (exemption for processing for research, history and statistics), there is an express provision to enable data processed for research purposes, in accordance with the relevant conditions, to be kept indefinitely notwith-standing the Fifth Principle. At s.34(b) (information required to be made public), the Fourth Principle gets specific mention, despite being included in the non-disclosure provisions invoked at s.34(c). This is because the non-disclosure exemption applies only in so far as the application of the relevant provision would be inconsistent with the disclosure in question, whereas the separate mention of the Fourth Principle in s.34(b) (along with parts of s.14) means that there is no such qualification of the Fourth in relation to this particular purpose.

CHAPTER 7

Security – the Seventh Principle

Daniel Pavin

Recent security breaches – permitting the wrong people to access confidential information – provide a powerful illustration of the need to ensure that safeguards are achieved in practice. The roll call of banks, retailers, government departments, public bodies and other organisations which have admitted serious security lapses is frankly horrifying.

(from the Information Commissioner's foreword to the 2006/7 ICO Annual Report)

7.1 AT A GLANCE

Appropriate technical and organisational measures shall be taken against unauthorised or unlawful processing of personal data and against accidental loss or destruction of, or damage to, personal data.

(DPA, Sched.1, Part I, para.7)

- The Seventh Principle, often called the Security Principle, requires data controllers to take appropriate technical and organisational measures against:
    - unauthorised processing of personal data;
    - unlawful processing of personal data; and
    - accidental loss or destruction of, or damage to, personal data (**7.2**).
- Data controllers should adopt a risk-based approach to determine what are 'appropriate' measures (**7.3**).
- Examples of technical measures include the use of passwords, encryption and anti-virus software (**7.4.2**).
- Examples of organisational measures include:

- taking steps to ensure the reliability of staff who work with personal data, for example through training (**7.4.3**); and
- having in place a comprehensive security policy (**7.5**).

- If a data controller has implemented ISO/IEC 27001, the data controller is likely to have satisfied the Information Commissioner that it has appropriate technical and organisational measures in place (**7.6**).
- Data controllers must provide a description of their security arrangements in relation to personal data as part of the notification process (**7.7**).
- The Seventh Principle requires that the data controller must have a written contract in place with any data processors acting on behalf of the data controller (**7.8** and **7.9**).
- A data controller that breaches the Seventh Principle risks substantial adverse publicity, legal liability and enforcement action from the Information Commissioner and other regulators that may have jurisdiction, such as the Financial Services Authority (**7.14.1**). While there is currently no law in the UK requiring data controllers to report data security breaches, proposals for such a law are under discussion (**7.14.3**) and best practice is evolving rapidly. A data controller should have in place a data security breach management plan that covers notification of affected individuals and relevant authorities (**7.14.4**).
- Following the wide reporting of a series of major data security incidents in 2007 and 2008 (**7.14.6**), the topic of data security now has a high public profile. This high profile, increased regulator activity and enhanced regulator powers are acting as incentives for data security to become a board-level priority within prudent data controllers.

7.2 SCOPE OF THE SEVENTH PRINCIPLE

7.2.1 Introduction

The Seventh Principle is broad in its scope, as can be seen by considering:

- the language of the Seventh Principle itself;
- key definitions under the DPA; and
- guidance from the Information Commissioner.

7.2.2 The language of the Seventh Principle itself

The Seventh Principle requires data controllers to take measures to guard against:

- unauthorised processing of personal data;
- unlawful processing of personal data; and
- accidental loss or destruction of, or damage to, personal data.

Measures against unauthorised processing include, for example, taking steps to prevent employees from processing personal data without proper authority through a combination of training, compliance and monitoring procedures, and restricting physical access to personal data.

Unlawful processing could occur through, for example, a breach of contract or breach of a common law obligation of confidence. Accordingly, measures must be in place to guard against such breaches.

Guarding against accidental loss or destruction of, or damage to, personal data involves putting in place technical measures such as controls that verify delete commands, organisational measures such as training staff how to use software properly and combined measures such as a disaster recovery system.

7.2.3 Key definitions under the DPA

- *Processing*: the definition of processing (DPA, s.1(1)) covers operations in relation to data ranging from initial collection through to destruction. Therefore, the Seventh Principle imposes an obligation on data controllers to take security measures throughout the data lifecycle.
- *Data*: the definition of data (DPA, s.1(1)) includes 'information which . . . is recorded with the intention that it should be processed by means of [equipment operating automatically in response to instructions given for that purpose]'.

Therefore, if a market research company is collecting information about individuals on paper survey forms, with a view to entering that information on to a computer, then irrespective of whether the forms are kept within a relevant filing system pending data entry, the Seventh Principle covers the personal data contained in them.

7.2.4 Guidance from the Information Commissioner

The Legal Guidance states:

> It is important to note that the Seventh Data Protection Principle relates to the security of the processing as a whole and the measures to be taken by data controllers to provide security against any breaches of the [DPA] rather than just breaches of security. (para.3.7)

7.2.5 Security and other DPA Principles

For many data controllers, one of the most effective ways of improving data security will be to minimise the amount of personal data that they process in the first place, by not collecting more personal data, or retaining personal data for longer, than they need to. Data minimisation can also be the most cost-effective way of improving security, obviating the need to implement certain security measures.

When designing and implementing their security systems, data controllers should therefore have regard not only to the Seventh Principle, but also the First, Second, Third and Fifth Principles, and keep the question 'do we need this data?' high on their list of considerations.

7.3 WHAT IS APPROPRIATE?

7.3.1 Guidance within the DPA

The DPA does not contain a definition of the term 'appropriate', but some guidance is set out in para.9 of Part II of Schedule 1 to the DPA (the interpretation of the Principles in Part I):

> Having regard to the state of technological development and the cost of imple-
> menting any measures, the measures must ensure a level of security appropriate to:
> (a) the harm that might result from such unauthorised or unlawful processing
>   or accidental loss, destruction or damage as are mentioned in the seventh
>   principle, and
> (b) the nature of the data to be protected.

In essence, a data controller must carry out a risk assessment in order to establish what are appropriate measures to take. This approach is set out in the security statement section of the notification form (see **7.7** and Chapter 4).

It is important for a data controller to consider all the implications of a breach of security, such as inadvertent disclosure, with respect to any personal data that it may be processing. Personal data need not be sensitive (as defined in the DPA) or otherwise normally confidential (for example, bank account details) for unauthorised or unlawful processing to cause considerable harm.

EXAMPLE

A member of staff at a travel agency prints out a summary report of all holiday bookings made in the last month, which lists customer name, address, destination, tour operator and dates of travel. The summary report is absent-mindedly left on the comer of a desk on the shop floor and is picked up by an opportunistic thief who uses the report to target unoccupied homes.

Further guidance is set out in para.10 of Part II of Schedule 1 to the DPA:

> The data controller must take reasonable steps to ensure the reliability of any employees of his who have access to the personal data.

This is discussed further at **7.4.3**.

7.3.2 The Information Commissioner's Legal Guidance

The Legal Guidance states:

> With regard to the technical and organisational measures to be taken by data controllers, the Directive states that such measures should be taken 'both at the time of the design of the processing system and at the time of the processing itself, particularly in order to maintain security and thereby to prevent any unauthorised processing.' Data controllers are, therefore, encouraged to consider the use of privacy enhancing techniques as part of their obligations under the Seventh Principle.
>
> [T]here can be no standard set of security measures that is required for compliance with the Seventh Principle. The Commissioner's view is that what is appropriate will depend on the circumstances, in particular, on the harm that might result from, for example, an unauthorised disclosure of personal data, which in itself might depend on the nature of the data. The data controller, therefore, needs to adopt a risk-based approach to determining what measures are appropriate. (In fact, the Directive refers to 'a level of security appropriate to the risks represented by the processing'). (para.3.7)

7.3.3 Other considerations when determining what is 'appropriate'

When determining what is 'appropriate', data controllers should also have regard to standards imposed on them by other laws, regulatory obligations and applicable industry codes, examples of which are discussed at **7.14.1**, in the context of additional liability that may arise as a result of breaching the Seventh Principle. An analysis of decisions issued and undertakings obtained by the Information Commissioner in relation to breaches of the Seventh Principle may also assist data controllers in determining what is considered appropriate, through their illustrations of what technical and organisational measures have been considered by the Information Commissioner not to meet the required standards in a given context.

7.3.4   Consequences – the state of technological development

As can be seen above, the interpretative provisions to the Seventh Principle state that security measures must be taken '[h]aving regard to the state of technological development' (DPA, Sched.1, Part II, para.9). Accordingly, compliance with this Principle is something of a moving target, given the ever-increasing sophistication of data processing technology.

Examples of recent developments that give rise to security issues include the following.

The use of laptops and other portable devices

Increasingly, employers are issuing employees with laptops rather than desktop computers, enabling employees to work off site. In addition, increasing numbers of employees are using personal digital assistants (PDAs) and other portable electronic devices to enable them to access and update copies of their electronic diaries and contacts databases anywhere, and use USB or memory sticks to transport increasingly large amounts of data between locations.

These trends create potentially serious security risks. Leaving a laptop, PDA or memory stick on a train could cause a far more severe breach of the Seventh Principle than, for example, the penetration by a hacker of a data controller's firewall. The following issues should be considered by a data controller:

- Are the contents of the laptop or other device protected, for example by using passwords (both to access the machine per se and to access the individual documents) or by encrypting the contents? By way of illustration:

  - On 9 January 2008 a Ministry of Defence laptop containing approximately 600,000 unencrypted personal records of Royal Navy/Royal Air Force recruits and potential recruits, was stolen from a Royal Navy recruiter. (See further at **7.14.6**.)
  - It was reported in February 2008 that the UK Government had imposed a ban on staff taking mobile devices outside Whitehall premises unless any personal information on them is encrypted to a suitable standard; see 'Ban on taking electronic devices outside the workplace', *Privacy & Data Protection*, Volume 8, issue 4, p.1).
  - The Financial Services Authority (FSA) warned regulated financial services businesses in its report of 24 April 2008 'Data Security in Financial Services':

    Firms should note that we support the Information Commissioner's position that it is not appropriate for customer data to be taken offsite on laptops or other portable devices which are not encrypted. We may take enforcement action against firms that fail to encrypt customer data offsite.

(See **7.15.3** for more information about the FSA's report.)

- Is training given to users of portable devices on how to guard against unauthorised access to their contents and on taking steps to ensure that personal data cannot be viewed on screen by strangers when the laptop/device is being used out of the office?
- Does the data controller know what personal data are being taken out of the confines of its secure network?
- Has the data controller assessed whether a worker needs to be able to copy data from his computer onto a memory stick? If the worker does not, steps may be taken to prevent copying, for example by installing security software and/or disabling the computer's USB ports.

An example 'Laptop Security Policy' may be found on the NHS Information Governance website (see **www.igt.connectingforhealth.nhs.uk**).

Client and customer access to intranets/extranets

Some data controllers offer their clients and customers access to limited parts of their network; for example, some firms of solicitors allow clients access to knowhow resources. Access must be carefully controlled, to prevent clients intentionally or innocently straying into areas of the data controller's network and obtaining access to personal data that they have no right to access.

Web interfaces permitting customers to check and update their own details

By automating as much customer administration as possible, data controllers conducting business through the Internet are able to keep running costs down.

An interface enabling customers to view their details on-screen and to update or amend them without reference to the data controller's staff is one such way of automating customer administration. Typically, access to such interfaces is restricted by means of a username and password to authenticate the identity of the customer wanting to view and change details. However, this empowerment of customers brings with it the risk of a security breach in the form of compromise of the security of the authentication process.

Wireless local area networks (LANs) and network access points

Wireless LANs are proving to be a popular alternative to fixed LANs for many businesses and organisations. Wireless LANs offer a number of advantages, such as flexibility of positioning equipment (and consequently, staff) and avoiding the relatively costly process of laying network cables.

Wireless network access points (or hot spots) at places such as hotels, airports, train stations and coffee shops permit remote workers to dip in remotely to their corporate networks and pick up and respond to e-mails, view documents and so on.

However, while wireless networks and access points offer convenience, strong concerns have been expressed about the inherent insecurity of the standards that govern wireless communication. Further, while a fixed LAN will be protected by physical boundaries (a locked room, for example), without special (and therefore expensive) shielding in place, an office wall will not confine the radio signals used for communication within a wireless LAN. Therefore, with the appropriate equipment, someone outside the building in which the wireless LAN is operating, but within the coverage of the wireless LAN's signals, could gain access.

Social networking sites

In recent years, the popularity of social networking sites has exploded. However, many users remain unaware of, or do not appreciate, the data security risks (for example, as to identity fraud) created by posting substantial amounts of personal data about themselves on these sites. Many workers access and communicate via social networking sites from their workplace. Indeed, the popularity and utility of social networking sites has led to some organisations actively incorporating use of them into their ways of doing business. However, social networking sites can create serious security risks. For example, a user may inadvertently post to a networking site personal data relating to colleagues, or a site may be inherently technologically insecure, permitting unauthorised third parties to access content that a user has marked as private. For further information see, for example:

- the Information Commissioner's press release of 23 November 2007 regarding social networking sites (available on the ICO website);
- the Information Commissioner's guidance on social networking sites (available on the ICO website);
- the UK Home Office's 'Good practice guidance for the moderation of interactive services for children' dated December 2005 (available at **www.crimereduction.homeoffice.gov.uk/internet05.htm**);

- European Network and Information Security Agency (ENISA) Position Paper No.1: 'Security Issues and Recommendations for Online Social Networks' dated October 2007 (available at **www.enisa.europa.eu/doc/pdf/deliverables/enisa_pp_social_networks.pdf**).

Radio Frequency Identification (RFID)

Section 4 of the Information Commissioner's technical guidance note with respect to Radio Frequency Identification highlights various security risks associated with this technology, including 'skimming' (the reading of RFID tags by unauthorised readers, accessing personal information stored on them) and 'cloning' (the copying of personal information stored on the RFID chip of an identity card). The guidance note recommends that 'security and privacy safeguards should be built into the architecture of RFID systems, rather than added on later' and provides brief guidance on possible technical solutions to reduce these risks. A copy of the guidance note is available on the ICO website.

On 24 June 2008, the OECD published an extensive report on RFID technology, sub-titled *OECD Policy Guidance: A focus on information security and privacy applications, impacts and initiatives*. The report includes commentary and guidance on security and privacy issues associated with RFID technology (available at **www.oecd.org/dataoecd/19/42/40892347.pdf**).

Conclusion

Data controllers must ensure that their security arrangements are reviewed regularly. As part of their reviews, data controllers should consider the impact of the introduction of new technologies on their security arrangements and adapt them accordingly.

7.4 TECHNICAL AND ORGANISATIONAL MEASURES

7.4.1 Introduction

The Seventh Principle requires technical and organisational measures to be taken. This contrasts with the Eighth Principle under the Data Protection Act 1984 (repealed by the DPA), which required that '[a]ppropriate security measures shall be taken ...' (Data Protection Act 1984, Sched.1, Part I, para.8).

The change from 'security measures' to 'technical and organisational measures' helps to reinforce the message that data controllers' responsibilities with respect to security are not confined to technical safeguards. In this respect, the

Legal Guidance notes: 'Management and organisational measures are as important as technical ones' (para.3.7).

The organisational (and technical) measures that a data controller has in place are manifestations of its culture with respect to data security. The importance of a data controller's culture can be seen in the findings of the reports commissioned following the HMRC and other data security incidents (see **7.14.6**). In particular, if there is no accountability for data security (or for, using the terminology of the Poynter Report, 'data guardianship'), specific measures aimed at data security will be seriously, if not completely, undermined.

7.4.2   Examples of technical measures

Examples of technical measures include (as appropriate) the use of passwords, firewalls, anti-virus software, secure Internet payment systems, encryption (in which respect, see **7.3.4** in relation to laptops and other portable devices) and other privacy enhancing technologies (PETs). In each case, implementation and use of these measures should be the subject of a defined security policy (see **7.5**).

The ICO has issued guidance with respect to encryption (see the Guidance Note 'Our approach to encryption') and PETs (see the Technical Guidance Note on Privacy Enhancing Technologies, 11 April 2006), both of which are available on the ICO website.

7.4.3   Examples of organisational measures

Reliability of staff

Security is commonly thought of as guarding against external threats. However, in reality, more breaches arise through mistakes or deliberate misuse of personal data by a data controller's own staff. The interpretation provisions of the DPA state that: 'The data controller must take reasonable steps to ensure the reliability of any employees of his who have access to the personal data' (DPA, Sched.1, Part II, para.10).

Example steps to take in order to meet this obligation may include:

- making appropriate checks and taking appropriate references in respect of staff who will have access to personal data;
- putting in place an employee education programme;
- setting out guidance as to the use of personal data in a data protection policy and incorporating this into the staff handbook;
- taking disciplinary action in the event of a breach by an employee of the data protection policy;

- acting on breaches of security committed by employees; and
- placing appropriate controls on who may access personal data.

The following example of a security breach with respect to staff reliability was given in the Information Commissioner's 2003 Annual Report (available on the ICO website):

> An individual made a complaint against a debt collection company which, in the process of trying to collect the debt, disclosed information about the complainant's account to members of his family. The information disclosed included details of how much the individual owed. It appeared unlikely that the processing concerned had been in compliance with the Act and in particular appeared to contravene the seventh data protection principle. Although the debt collecting company stated that staff undergo induction training on data protection when they first join the company, the recommendation was made that debt collectors should undertake regular annual training to ensure future compliance. (p.11)

Temporary staff (for example, students hired to carry out data entry in the evenings or at weekends) should not be overlooked with respect to the need to ensure their reliability.

Other examples of organisational measures include monitoring to ensure compliance with security standards, putting in place effective contractual measures when sharing personal data or appointing a data processor (see **7.8** and **7.9**) and controlling physical access to IT systems.

Security in the context of data is commonly, but erroneously, thought of as the sole province of the data controller's IT department. However, as stated in the Supplementary Guidance to Part 3 of the Information Commissioner's Employment Practices Code (on monitoring at work) (available on the ICO website):

> It is important to remember that data protection compliance is a multidisci-plinary matter. For example, a company's IT staff may be primarily responsible for keeping computerised personal data secure, whilst a human resources department may be responsible for ensuring that the information requested on a job application form is not excessive, irrelevant or inadequate. All workers, including line managers, have a part to play in securing compliance, for example by ensuring that waste paper bearing personal data is properly disposed of. (paragraph 0.2, p.6)

It is prudent for a data controller to appoint a data protection officer – someone responsible for data protection compliance in general. The data protection officer may take on the following roles in the context of security:

- liaising with all staff within the data controller's organisation who are responsible for security matters, such as the head of IT and head of human resources;
- maintaining the data controller's notification in the event of a change in circumstances that affects the data controller's security statement;
- staff training; and
- reviewing agreements with data processors to ensure that the terms of the agreements comply with the requirements of the DPA (see **7.8** and **7.9**).

Security policy

Security policies are considered in **7.5**.

7.4.4   Technical and organisational measures – examples from an employment context

Job application data

Part 1 of the Information Commissioner's Employment Practices Code (on recruitment and selection) contains a number of examples of technical and organisational measures that data controllers are recommended to take with respect to job applications:

- Ensure that a secure method of transmission is used for sending applications online (e.g. encryption-based software).
- Ensure that once electronic applications are received, they are saved in a directory or drive which has access limited to those involved in the recruitment process.
- Ensure that postal applications are given directly to the person or people processing the applications and that these are stored in a locked drawer.
- Ensure that faxed applications are given directly to the person or people processing the applications and that these are stored in a locked drawer.
- If applications are processed by line managers, make sure line managers are aware of how to gather and store applications.

Employment records

Part 2 of the Information Commissioner's Employment Practices Code (on employment records) sets out six security benchmarks with respect to employment records:

1. Apply security standards that take account of the risks of unauthorised access to, accidental loss or destruction of, or damage to, employment records.
2. Institute a system of secure cabinets, access controls and passwords to ensure that staff can only gain access to employment records where they have a legitimate business need to do so.
3. Use the audit trail capabilities of automated systems to track who accesses and amends personal data.
4. Take steps to ensure the reliability of staff that have access to workers' records.
5. Ensure that if employment records are taken off-site, e.g. on laptop computers, this is controlled. Make sure that only the necessary information is taken and there are security rules for staff to follow.
6. Take account of the risks of transmitting confidential worker information by fax or e-mail. Only transmit such information between locations if a secure network or comparable arrangements are in place

(para.2.2; pp.31 to 33).

These six benchmarks are accompanied by a set of notes and examples that amplify the benchmarks and provide further security guidance, applicable beyond the context of employment records.

An example of a breach of security with respect to employee records was given in the Information Commissioner's Annual Report for 2003 (available on the ICO website):

The Criminal Records Bureau (CRB) produces Disclosure Certificates for Registered Bodies in England and Wales seeking criminal records checks on individuals in connection with their prospective employment. A member of staff at one Registered Body who was Counter Signing Officer for such checks received a number of disclosure certificates at his home address rather than at his place of work. Copies revealing the officer's home address were also sent to potential recruits. The officer raised this matter several times with CRB without the matter being resolved. He then complained to the Commissioner. Following contact with the CRB they undertook to revise their procedures to prevent similar disclosures happening again. (p.17)

Monitoring

Monitoring is an essential part of maintaining security. However, the act of monitoring brings with it its own data protection issues.

Part 3 of the Information Commissioner's Employment Practices Code (on monitoring at work) states that:

Many employers carry out monitoring to safeguard workers, as well as to protect their own interests or those of their customers. For example, monitoring may take place to ensure that those in hazardous environments are not being put at risk through the adoption of unsafe working practices. Monitoring arrangements may equally be part of the security mechanisms used to protect personal information. In other cases, for example in the context of some financial services, the employer may be under legal or regulatory obligations which it can only realistically fulfil if it undertakes some monitoring. However where monitoring goes beyond one individual simply watching another and involves the manual recording or any automated processing of personal information, it must be done in a way that is both lawful and fair to workers. (p.54)

The Supplementary Guidance adds:

Monitoring may involve others having access to personal information about workers ... They must be subject to rules to ensure the information is kept securely, not misused or improperly disclosed. Those carrying out any monitoring should be clear on procedures and fully trained. They have responsibilities to ensure that information obtained through monitoring is kept secure, only used for the purpose for which it was obtained and is deleted once the purpose for carrying out the monitoring is complete. (para.3.1.6; p.46)

The Code advises that, if routine monitoring is carried out for the purpose of checking the security of a system, the data controller should 'consider – preferably using an impact assessment – whether any monitoring of electronic communications can be limited to that necessary to ensure the security of the system and whether it can be automated' (Part 3 of the Information Commissioner's Employment Practices Code on monitoring at work, section 3.2.3).

7.4.5 Technical and organisational measures – examples with respect to CCTV

The Information Commissioner's CCTV Code of Practice (revised edition 2008) (available on the ICO website) contains guidance as to the application of the Seventh Principle in the context of CCTV systems and the processing, access to, disclosure and use of CCTV images. This Code of Practice replaces an earlier Code of Practice issued by the ICO in 2000 and the guidance for small users.

Guidance as to security measures includes the following.

On ensuring efffective administration (section 5):

If someone outside your organisation provides you with any processing services, for example, editing the images, is a written contract in place with clearly defined

157

responsibilities? This should ensure that the images are only processed in accordance with your instructions. The content should also include guarantees about security, such as storage and the use of properly trained staff.

On using the CCTV equipment (section 7):

If a wireless transmission system is used, are sufficient safeguards in place to protect it from being intercepted?

On storing and viewing images (section 8.1):

Viewing of the images on monitors should usually be restricted to the operator unless the monitor displays a scene which is also in plain sight from the monitor location.

Recorded images should also be viewed in a restricted area, such as a designated secure office.

On disclosing images (section 8.2):

Do you record the date of the disclosure along with details of who the images have been provided to (the name of the person and the organisation they represent) and why they are required?

7.4.6 Further examples of technical and organisational measures

ICO publications

Further examples of technical and organisational measures may be found within various documents available on the ICO website, including:

- the Legal Guidance (at para.3.7);
- 'Data security tips';
- Good Practice Note on security of personal information (v1.0, 22 November 2007);
- Framework Code of Practice for sharing personal information (at section 5).

Financial services industry

On 24 April 2008 the FSA published a report entitled 'Data Security in Financial Services: Firm's controls to prevent data loss by their employees and third-party suppliers'. The report followed an FSA review, conducted between April and December 2007, of systems and controls for data security at 39 firms including banks, building societies, insurance companies and financial advisers. The review was prompted by the FSA's strong concerns about poor data security in the financial services sector, notwithstanding warnings and guidance issued previously by the FSA with respect to data security, and notwithstanding increased public awareness of the risks of identity theft and its impact.

This significant report contains a substantial amount of valuable guidance on how to prevent data loss, including many examples of good and poor practice. Although the report is addressed to the financial services industry, the guidance within it is of general applicability, across sectors.

While the FSA states that the report does not constitute formal guidance, the FSA

> [expects] firms to use our findings, to translate them into a more effective assessment of this risk [of fraudulent activity], and to install more effective controls as a result ... As in any other area of their business, firms should take a proportionate, risk-based approach to data security, taking into account their customer base, business and risk profile. Failure to do so may result in us taking enforcement action. (p. 6)

The report and other FSA documents of relevance to data security (including earlier information security reports and the FSA's Financial Crime newsletter) are available from the FSA website (**www.fsa.gov.uk**).

The NHS/healthcare sector

The 'Information Governance' section of the NHS 'Connecting for Health' website contains extensive information relating to security in the context of NHS services. It can be accessed at **www.connectingforhealth.nhs.uk/ systemsandservices/infogov**.

The Poynter Report and other public sector reports

The reports commissioned following the HMRC and Ministry of Defence data security incidents (see **7.14.6**) contain detailed analysis of the flawed measures in place within HMRC and the Ministry of Defence that led to data loss. Many of the conclusions drawn and recommendations made in the reports are not confined to the specific facts of the incidents under investigation, and as such they provide useful guidance to data controllers as to examples of good and poor practice with respect to technical and organisational measures.

7.5 SECURITY POLICIES

7.5.1 Introduction

In order effectively to comply with the Seventh Principle, a data controller must have in place a sound security policy.

Steps for the creation and administration of a simple security policy are set out in **7.5.2** to **7.5.4**. The security policy may overlap with, or form part of, a data protection policy that addresses other aspects of data protection compliance, such as lawful marketing using personal data and transfers of personal data. It may also overlap with a document or data retention and management policy. More complex and comprehensive methodologies exist, for example ISO 27001 (which is discussed in **7.6**), but the checklists below provide a basic framework.

The importance of information security policies for listed companies is discussed briefly in **7.5.5**, in connection with their corporate governance obligations.

7.5.2 Preparation for the policy

1. Obtain management approval and ongoing support for the policy.
2. Appoint an individual and/or establish a team to take responsibility for the policy.
3. Budget resources for the administration of the policy.
4. Carry out an audit and a risk assessment to determine what steps are to be taken in order to comply with the Seventh Principle and in particular what are the appropriate technical and organisational measures to be adopted.

7.5.3 Security policy content

1. A general explanation of the need for security.
2. IT security procedures relating to matters such as:

   (a) passwords and usernames – allocation, changing, guidance on what is and is not a good password;
   (b) policies for procuring or designing new IT systems;
   (c) use of software;
   (d) automatic locking out of idle terminals;
   (e) installation of new software;
   (f) virus checking;
   (g) the use of encryption;
   (h) e-mail and Internet use;
   (i) monitoring;[1] and

(j) use of portable equipment/removal of data from the premises (for working from home or otherwise).

3. Physical and organisational security procedures relating to matters such as:

(a) locking of rooms and storage cabinets;
(b) staffing of reception area and other access points;
(c) visitor access to the premises;
(d) positioning of equipment and screens;
(e) marking documents confidential where appropriate;
(f) regulating and, where appropriate, recording access to paper-based files of personal data;
(g) clear desk policy;
(h) procedures for storage and safety of manual files;
(i) hardware and printout disposal – secure wiping of fixed media and shredding of paper copies; and
(j) procedures to be adopted when outsourcing the processing of personal data.

4. Back-ups, disaster recovery and business continuity (to cover both IT and non-IT elements).
5. An explanation that audits and checks will be conducted to ensure adherence to the policy.[2]
6. Procedures to be followed (including forms to be used and reporting procedures) in the event of a breach or suspected breach of security, including:

(a) notifying relevant personnel within the organisation;
(b) assessing the risks of the breach posed to affected individuals (staff, customers and others), notifying those individuals and providing them with advice to help limit or eliminate the risks;
(c) notifying relevant third parties, for example, regulatory bodies, the organisation's insurer and, possibly, the media (as part of a proactive reputation management campaign); and
(d) taking steps to prevent further breaches.

(For further information regarding security breach notification, see **7.14.4.**)

7. Address personnel-related matters, such as:

(a) training for new arrivals;
(b) training for staff intending to work from home as to security measures to be adopted in their homes in respect of personal data;
(c) ongoing education; and

(d) the procedure to be followed in the event a member of staff leaves, for example for the return of employer's materials in the employee's possession, confirmation from the employee that he does not retain any of the employer's materials and cancellation of system passwords and username.

8. Set out the disciplinary consequences of failing to comply with the security policy.
9. Identify the staff member(s) responsible for the creation and administration of the security policy, in the event of staff enquiries.

7.5.4 Actions following introduction of the policy

1. Publicise the security policy (e.g. on the intranet and as part of the staff handbook) and provide training as appropriate. As part of the publicity and training, organisations should emphasise and reinforce key points in the policy (such as a prohibition on sending by post unencrypted discs containing personal data).
2. Periodically conduct adequacy and compliance audits and spot-checks with respect to the policy and its implementation, including testing of the security breach response procedures.[3]
3. Act on breaches of the security policy, for example:

    (a) follow an in-house data security breach management and notification plan (see above) and/or the Information Commissioner's Guidance on Data Security Breach Management (see **7.14.4**); and
    (b) if the breach arises through staff negligence/wilful act then take the appropriate disciplinary procedures.

4. Review the security policy from time to time, and as necessary update it and associated procedures, in the event of changes in:

    (a) business operations (including acquisition or disposal of businesses or business units);
    (b) IT systems or location;
    (c) key staff; and
    (d) legislation.

7.5.5 Corporate governance and information security – responsibilities of listed companies

Effective corporate governance involves the management of business risks. A failure to manage information security risks is a failure in a company's system of internal control.

In the UK, standards of corporate governance for companies listed on the Stock Exchange (rather than companies listed on other markets, such as the Alternative Investment Market) are set out in the Combined Code. The Combined Code consists of Principles and Provisions. Principle C.2 of the Combined Code states that: 'The board should maintain a sound system of internal control to safeguard shareholders' investment and the company's assets.'

The Code also requires the directors to conduct reviews of the effectiveness of the company's internal control systems and to report to shareholders in light of those reviews (Code Provision C.2.1). Stock Exchange-listed companies are not legally required to comply with the Combined Code. However, Paragraph 9.8.6 of the London Stock Exchange Listing Rules (available from the FSA website at **www.fsa.gov.uk**) requires companies incorporated in the United Kingdom to explain in their annual reports and accounts how they have applied the Principles set out in Section 1 of the Combined Code, and a statement as to whether or not they have complied with the Code Provisions set out in Section 1. The text of the updated Combined Code, published by the Financial Reporting Council, is available at **www.frc.org.uk/corporate/combinedcode.cfm**.

The Internal Control Working Party of the Institute of Chartered Accountants in England and Wales has published Guidance for Directors on the Combined Code, also known as the Turnbull Guidance (available at **www.frc.org.uk/corporate/internalcontrol.cfm**). It sets out best practice on internal control for UK listed companies, and assists them to implement section C.2 of the Combined Code.

The Appendix to the Turnbull Guidance sets out example questions for consideration by the board when reviewing reports on internal control and carrying out its annual assessment.

The section headed 'control environment and control activities' contains the question (emphasis added):

> Does the company communicate to its employees what is expected of them and the scope of their freedom to act? This may apply to areas such as customer relations; service levels for both internal and outsourced activities; health, safety and environmental protection; *security of* tangible and intangible assets; business continuity issues; expenditure matters; accounting; and financial and other reporting.

Therefore, focusing specifically on information security:

1. The Combined Code, as amplified by the Turnbull Guidance, requires the boards of companies listed on the Stock Exchange to:

   (a) adopt a risk-management approach to information security; and
   (b) explain to employees what is required of them with respect to information security.

163

2. Best practice dictates that:

   (a) as part of their internal control systems, listed companies must have a sound information security policy in place; and

   (b) as part of their reporting requirements, listed companies must note failures in the effectiveness of their internal control systems with respect to information security.

Suppliers to Stock Exchange-listed companies will in practice have to ensure that their goods and services are designed to enable their customers to meet their regulatory obligations (in order to win business, to meet contractual standards etc.), and in this way the standards described above are replicated through the supply chain.

7.5.6 Further information on security policies

ISO/IEC 27001 is discussed at **7.6**. The BERR website contains a large amount of information about security policies in the section on Information Security (**www.berr.gov.uk/sectors/infosec/index.html**).

7.6 ISO/IEC 27001: 2005 ('ISO 27001')

7.6.1 Introduction

ISO 27001 is an international standard, based on British Standard BS7799-2. Its formal title is 'Information technology – Security techniques – Information security management systems – Requirements'. ISO 27001 sets out a model for implementing and maintaining an Information Security Management System (ISMS), against which an organisation's ISMS can be audited by an independent certification body (which is in turn accredited by an accreditation body). An ISMS is defined as 'that part of the overall management system, based on a business risk approach, to establish, implement, operate, monitor, review, maintain and improve information security' (ISO 27001 Terms and conditions, section 3.7). It includes 'organizational structure, policies, planning activities, responsibilities, practices, procedures, processes and resources' (ISO 27001 Terms and conditions, section 3.7, Note). ISO 27001 is accompanied by ISO/IEC 27002 Information Technology – Security techniques – Code of Practice for information security management (formerly called ISO/IEC 17799). ISO 27001, as a standard, sets out requirements that must be followed if an organisation is to meet it (though compliance with ISO/IEC 27001 is not a statutory requirement). ISO 27002 provides guidance on how to implement an ISMS capable of certification.

Central to ISO 27001 is the Plan-Do-Check-Act (PDCA) model:

- Plan: establish the ISMS.
- Do: implement and operate the ISMS.
- Check: monitor and review the ISMS.
- Act: maintain and improve the ISMS.

7.6.2 The scope of ISO 27001

ISO/IEC 27001 sets out 11 (non-exhaustive) security categories. Each security category specifies a 'control objective' and one or more controls that operate to achieve that objective. The categories are:

1. Information security.
2. Organisation of information security.
3. Asset management.
4. Human resources security.
5. Physical and environmental security.
6. Communications and operations management.
7. Access control.
8. Information systems acquisition, development and maintenance.
9. Information security incident management.
10. Business continuity management.
11. Compliance.

ISO 27001 is a detailed methodology and, as a result, prohibitively expensive for many businesses and organisations to implement fully and achieve certification. Comparatively few businesses and organisations in the UK are certified to ISO 27001. Nonetheless, the standard itself provides a template for use by anyone looking to implement an ISMS. In particular, the 11 points above contain useful guidance and illustrations of technical and organisational measures that may be adopted by a data controller. They may also be useful in forming a due diligence checklist for use in relation to a potential data processor – see **7.8.3** below.

7.6.3 Why is ISO 27001 relevant to the Seventh Principle?

Compliance with ISO 27001 provides a solid foundation for compliance with the Seventh Principle. The status of ISO 27001 as a benchmark for compliance is illustrated by the inclusion of a specific question within the security statement of the notification form (see **7.7**) asking whether the data controller has adopted the British Standard on Information Security Management ISO 27001, and by the various references to ISO 27001 (or BS

7799) in publications from the Information Commissioner, such as the Legal Guidance.

7.6.4 Other standards and frameworks

ISO/IEC 27001 cross-refers to other potentially relevant standards, such as ISO 9001 (Quality management systems – Requirements) and ISO/IEC TR 18044: 2004 (Information technology – Security techniques – Information security incident management). In addition, the following standards and guides may be helpful when developing an information security or governance system.

Control Objectives for Information and related Technology (CobiT)

CobiT is a set of best practices for information technology management created by the Information Systems Audit and Control Association (ISACA) and the IT Governance Institute (ITGI) in 1992. The latest version is 4.1. Further information is available from the ISACA website (**www.isaca.org**).

The IT Infrastructure Library (ITIL)

ITIL is a set of best practices for IT service management, providing guidance on the management of IT infrastructure. It includes a manual called 'Best Practice for Security Management'. Further information is available from the official ITIL website (**www.itil-officialsite.com**).

Payment Card Industry (PCI) Data Security Standard

The PCI Data Security Standard sets out detailed requirements with respect to payment account data security. A copy is available, subject to licence, from the PCI Security Standards Council website (at **www.pcisecuritystandards.org/ pdfs/pci_dss_v1–1.pdf**).

7.6.5 Further information on ISO 27001 and other standards

A copy of BS ISO/IEC 27001, BS ISO/IEC 27002 and other standards may be purchased from:

BSI British Standards
389 Chiswick High Road
London W4 4AL
England

Tel: (44) (0) 20 8996 9001
Fax: (44) (0) 20 8996 7001

or via the BSI website (**www.bsi-global.com**).

The DTI (as was) published a short guidance note entitled Information security: BS7799 and the 1998 Data Protection Act. A copy may be downloaded from the BERR website.

7.7 NOTIFICATION REQUIREMENTS

Data controllers are required as part of the notification process to provide a general description of the measures they take to comply with the Seventh Principle (a security statement). The description does not appear in the public register.

Further information about the security statement is given in Chapter 4.

By s.20 of the DPA, data controllers are under a legal duty to keep their notifications up to date. Therefore, if the data controller's security measures change in such a way that has a bearing on the data controller's security statement, the data controller must update its notification. This needs to be done as soon as practicable, and in any event within 28 days (Data Protection (Notification and Notification Fees) Regulations 2000, SI 2000/188, reg.12(2)) from the date the security statement became inaccurate. If a data controller fails to do this, it is committing a criminal offence (DPA, s.21(2)).

7.8 USING A DATA PROCESSOR

7.8.1 Introduction

The DPA defines a data processor as, in relation to personal data: 'any person (other than an employee of the data controller) who processes the data on behalf of the data controller' (DPA, s.1(1)).

Examples of controller–processor relationships include:

- insurance company and call centre;
- retail outlet and website host and operator;
- company and payroll bureau;
- group of related companies and subsidiary responsible for administration of group-wide marketing campaigns; and
- law firm and secure data disposal agency.

7.8.2 What must a data controller do under the DPA if it uses a data processor?

1. *Requirements of the DPA:* Under Part II of Schedule 1 to the DPA:

    11. Where processing of personal data is carried out by a data processor on behalf of a data controller, the data controller must in order to comply with the seventh principle –
        (a) choose a data processor providing sufficient guarantees in respect of the technical and organisational security measures governing the processing to be carried out, and
        (b) take reasonable steps to ensure compliance with those measures.
    12. Where processing of personal data is carried out by a data processor on behalf of a data controller, the data controller is not to be regarded as complying with the seventh principle unless –
        (a) the processing is carried out under a contract –
            (i) which is made or evidenced in writing, and
            (ii) under which the data processor is to act only on instructions from the data controller, and
        (b) the contract requires the data processor to comply with obligations equivalent to those imposed on a data controller by the seventh principle.

2. *Summary of steps for compliance*: In light of the DPA's requirements described above, a data controller:

    (a) must identify any existing controller–processor relationships and make sure that written agreements conforming with the DPA are in place with each processor;
    (b) should conduct appropriate due diligence before appointing a data processor (an example checklist is set out at **7.8.3**); and
    (c) must put in place with each new processor (and any processors identified at (a) above – see **7.9.3**) a written agreement that complies with the requirements of the DPA (an example checklist is set out at **7.9.2**).

7.8.3 Checklist for the selection and appointment of a data processor

The following is a (non-exhaustive) checklist of points to consider when selecting and appointing a data processor.

1. What technical and organisational security measures does the processor have in place that are relevant to the intended processing? For example:

    (a) Does the processor have a data protection or information officer?
    (b) How secure are the processor's premises?

(c) What back-up and disaster recovery procedures does the processor have in place?

(d) Does the processor have a documented data protection/security policy in place?

- Does the processor adhere to ISO 27001 or standards that are equivalent? Can the processor demonstrate adherence to that standard, for example, by being certified by an accredited certification body?
- Does the processor have a security breach management plan (as part of compliance with ISO 27001 or otherwise)? If so:

  – Has it used the plan in response to a security incident and how effective was it?
  – Has the plan been independently tested and approved?

(e) Does the processor conduct compliance and adequacy audits in respect of its data processing?

(f) Has the processor suffered any security incidents?

2. What steps does the processor take to ensure the reliability of its employees?

(a) What checks are made during the recruitment stage? If applicable, does the processor work to BS7858 (Security screening of individuals employed in a security environment)?

(b) What training do the processor's employees receive in data protection (and other relevant) law and practice?

3. Do the processor's staff work from telephone scripts? If so, what do the scripts say?

4. Does the processor have a standard set of terms and conditions? If so, do they cover the processing of personal data?

5. What is the financial status of the processor? Can this be determined from accounts filed at Companies House?

6. Does the processor have appropriate insurance cover in place?

7. Does the processor provide similar services for third parties? If so:

(a) Can the processor provide you with references from other clients for whom it has performed those services?

(b) Are any of those third parties competitors of yours? If so, what steps does the processor take to avoid conflicts and breaches of confidentiality?

8. Does the processor subcontract any aspect of its processing? If so, what is subcontracted, to whom and under what terms?

9. Are there sector-specific laws, regulations or guidance applicable to the appointment of the data processor? For example, in the financial services sector, the Supervision chapter of the Regulatory Process section of the FSA Handbook contains guidance on the conditions that must be met before an authorised representative (which may be a data processor) is appointed. (See **http://fsahandbook.info/FSA/html/handbook/SUP/12/ Annex1.**)

A data controller may find the following useful as sources of further due diligence questions:

- Annex A of ISO 27001 (Control objectives and controls) (see **7.6**); and
- Section G.7 (the Seventh Principle) of the Information Commissioner's Data Protection Audit Manual (available from the ICO website).

7.9 AGREEMENTS WITH DATA PROCESSORS

7.9.1 Introduction

The following checklist is intended to assist in the preparation and drafting of an agreement with a contractor who will carry out processing of personal data on behalf of a data controller. The checklist covers both terms specific to personal data processing contracts and the sort of provisions that appear in general contracts for services, such as service levels and liability clauses.

7.9.2 Checklist of issues to consider and terms to include in a controller–processor agreement

1. Who are the parties?
2. What are the obligations of the processor?

    (a) To process personal data only in accordance with the controller's instructions. In connection with this: What is the purpose of the transfer to the processor? To whom may the processor transfer personal data? How will instructions be communicated?

    (b) To implement and maintain appropriate technical and organisational security measures with respect to processing personal data.

3. What are the applicable service levels? For example:

    (a) To what standards must the processor provide the services?

    (b) Are there any applicable industry standards or codes?

    (c) Within what time limits must the processor carry out its obligations?

4. How much will the controller pay for the services and when will payments be made?
5. What are the controller's obligations (other than payment)?
6. What are the controller's remedies if the processor doesn't comply with its obligations?
7. What guarantees (warranties) will the processor give the controller in respect of the services it is providing? The processor may be required to warrant or undertake:

    (a) that it will use appropriately trained staff to carry out its obligations;
    (b) that it will promptly notify the controller of any:

    - request for disclosure of or access to the personal data; and
    - accidental or unauthorised access or other security breach;

    (c) to deal promptly with reasonable enquiries from the controller or the data subjects;
    (d) to comply with any instructions from, or otherwise facilitate compliance with requests or requirements of, the relevant data protection supervising body (in the UK, the Information Commissioner) and any other regulatory body of competent jurisdiction;
    (e) to provide the data subject with a copy of the processor contract if requested (Commission-approved controller–processor clauses: see **7.9.4**); and
    (f) that its own national laws do not prevent compliance with the standard terms (relevant to international processing contracts).

8. Can the controller audit or otherwise carry out checks on the processor's processing facilities (either itself or using an independent third party)? As part of the audit or checks, can the controller carry out penetration testing of the processor's systems?
9. What is the liability of the processor?

    (a) What is excluded from liability (for example, is the processor liable for the controller's loss of profits in the event that it does not do what it is contractually required to do)?
    (b) Under what circumstances will one party indemnify the other for failure to perform an obligation?
    (c) Is the processor required to keep a minimum level of appropriate insurance cover in place?

10. Rights of individuals (Commission-approved controller–processor clauses: see **7.9.4**):

    (a) Can individuals exercise their rights directly against the controller?
    (b) Can individuals exercise their rights directly against the processor?
    (c) Are individuals entitled to a copy of the contract terms on request?

11. What information is to be kept confidential?
12. Who owns the intellectual property rights in the data generated during the performance of the services?
13. What events entitle the controller and/or the processor to terminate the agreement and when does the agreement expire?
14. What happens on termination/expiry?

   (a) Will copies of personal data and other data provided by the controller to the processor be returned or destroyed?
   (b) Will there need to be a run-off period in which orders already placed etc. will be dealt with by the processor even though the contract has otherwise come to an end?
   (c) Does the processor need to be bound by ongoing confidentiality restrictions?

15. Boilerplate terms:

   (a) Who is authorised to make changes to the agreement?
   (b) What is the process for one party to serve a notice on the other?
   (c) Can the agreement be assigned or the obligations subcontracted?
   (d) What is the governing law of the agreement (probably English law if two UK businesses; the Commission-approved clauses state that the governing law of the agreement will be that of the country in which the exporter is established)?
   (e) Where and how will disputes be resolved: in court; by arbitration; or by mediation or other dispute resolution mechanism?
   (f) Does the processor agree to submit to the jurisdiction in which the controller and the data subjects are based (this is relevant to international processing contracts)?

16. Are there sector-specific laws or regulations that impose particular obligations on either or both of the parties in the context of outsourcing of personal data processing?

7.9.3 What if existing contracts with data processors do not include clauses covering data protection matters?

It may be that a data controller already uses the services of data processors, but it does not have an appropriate written agreement in place with each of them. The data controller should contact these data processors and explain that under the DPA it is under a legal obligation to have in place a written agreement covering the processing of personal data. This can be in the form of a short letter agreement just covering data protection issues if there is already a written agreement in place covering other matters. Provided that the contractual clauses are reasonable, then an existing data processor should not refuse to sign up to the new terms.

7.9.4 Using a data processor outside the European Economic Area

The European Economic Area (EEA) is made up of the countries of the European Union together with Iceland, Liechtenstein and Norway.

The Eighth Principle

If a data controller intends to use a data processor based outside the EEA then, in addition to complying with the general requirements for a processor contract, the data controller must ensure compliance with the Eighth Principle. Therefore, unless (a) the data processor is established in a country or territory that benefits from a decision of adequacy from the European Commission; or (b) another exemption from the Eighth Principle applies, the data controller is required by the DPA to take additional precautions and include further terms in its data processing contract.

The European Commission's approved clauses for processor contracts

In its Decision of 27 December 2001,[4] the European Commission approved a set of contractual clauses for use between a data controller established in the EEA and a data processor established outside the EEA in a country not recognised as offering an adequate level of data protection.

It is not compulsory to use the Commission-approved clauses but a clear advantage of doing so is that the Information Commissioner (and every other EEA supervisory authority) may not refuse to recognise them as providing adequate data protection safeguards (Recital 5 of the Decision). The Commission-approved clauses may be supplemented by other contractual terms, provided that those terms do not contradict them (Recital 4 of the Decision).

7.9.5 Using a data processor outside the UK but based in the EEA

If entering into a controller–processor agreement with a data processor based in an EEA country other than the UK, local law advice should be obtained with respect to any particular contractual provisions that may be required by the non-UK data protection supervisory authority with jurisdiction over the data processing in question. This also applies to an agreement with a processor based in any other country recognised as offering an adequate level of data protection.

7.10   SECURITY AND INTERNATIONAL DATA TRANSFERS

7.10.1   The Eighth Principle

Data security is highly relevant when assessing whether a data transfer to a country or territory outside the EEA is permissible.

By the Eighth Principle:

> Personal data shall not be transferred to a country or territory outside the European Economic Area unless that country or territory ensures an adequate level of protection for the rights and freedoms of data subjects in relation to the processing of personal data.
>
> (DPA, Sched.1, Part 1, para.8)

By para.13, Part II of Schedule 1 to the DPA:

> [a]n adequate level of protection is one which is adequate in all the circumstances of the case, having regard in particular to . . .
>
> (h) any security measures taken in respect of the data in that country or territory.

The Information Commissioner's guidance note on transfers, The Eighth Principle and Transborder Dataflows,[5] states that:

> Exporting controllers may be able to ensure that the personal data are secure from any outside interference by means of, for example, technical measures such as encryption or the adoption of information security management practices analogous to those in ISO17799/BS 7799. In practice, security is often a key factor in the commercial considerations of the parties. (para.2.4.1.4)

7.10.2   Exceptions to the Eighth Principle where security is relevant

Schedule 4 to the DPA sets out nine cases where the Eighth Principle does not apply.

Looking at the last two cases listed in Schedule 4, a transfer is permissible if it:

- is made on terms which are of a kind approved by the Information Commissioner as ensuring adequate safeguards for the rights and freedoms of data subjects (DPA, Sched.4, para.8); or
- has been authorised by the Information Commissioner as being made in such a manner as to ensure adequate safeguards for the rights and freedoms of data subjects (DPA, Sched.4, para.9).

174

In both of these cases, data security will be a relevant factor in determining whether adequate safeguards are in place.

7.10.3   The Safe Harbor Principles

The Safe Harbor Principles impose obligations with respect to security and the appointment of data processors that are broadly equivalent to those set out in the DPA.

The Principle that governs security states:

> Organisations creating, maintaining, using or disseminating personal information must take reasonable precautions to protect it from loss, misuse and unauthorised access, disclosure, alteration and destruction.[6]

The appointment of data processors (described in the context of the Safe Harbor Principles as agents) is governed by the onward transfer Principle, which states:

> Where an organization wishes to transfer information to a third party that is acting as an agent . . . it may do so if it first either ascertains that the third party subscribes to the Principles or is subject to the Directive or another adequacy finding or enters into a written agreement with such third party requiring that the third party provide at least the same level of privacy protection as is required by the relevant Principles. If the organization complies with these requirements, it shall not be held responsible (unless the organization agrees otherwise) when a third party to which it transfers such information processes it in a way contrary to any restrictions or representations, unless the organization knew or should have known the third party would process it in such a contrary way and the organization has not taken reasonable steps to prevent or stop such processing.'[7]

International transfers and the Safe Harbor Principles are dealt with in more detail in Chapter 8.

7.10.4   National implementations of Art.17(1) of the Data Protection Directive

To the extent that a data controller is concerned with processing that is subject to the data protection laws of more than one European jurisdiction, the data controller should obtain advice as to the local implementations of Art.17(1) of the Data Protection Directive, which differ between Member States.

7.11   SECURITY AND THE RIGHT OF SUBJECT ACCESS

7.11.1   Breaches of security in responding to a subject access request

Failure properly to verify the identity of an individual making a subject access request, or incorrectly providing information about third parties in response to a subject access request, could amount to a breach of the Seventh Principle.

Staff who are, or who may be, involved in processing personal data should receive training with respect to the right of subject access and specifically:

- staff should be able to recognise a request for subject access; and
- if members of staff receive subject access requests, they should either know how to deal with it (if it falls within the scope of their duties) or should know to whom to refer the request.

Outside the context of subject access requests proper, where enquiries or transactions including personal data are being handled by telephone, staff should be trained in the security checks to be made before any personal data are disclosed to the caller.

7.11.2   Disclosing breaches of security in response to a subject access request

Under the DPA, in response to a subject access request, an individual is entitled to be told about (among other things) 'the recipients or classes of recipients to whom [the individual's personal data] are or may be disclosed' (DPA, s.7(1)(b)). If the data controller is aware at the time of receiving the request of a security breach that had resulted (or may result) in the disclosure of the individual's personal data to a third party, the data controller should provide details of the actual or possible disclosure. (Notification of security breaches is discussed in more detail at **7.14.3** and **7.14.4**.)

7.12   SECURITY AND IT SYSTEM DESIGN

7.12.1   Introduction

By virtue of the Seventh Principle, any IT system used for the processing of personal data by a data controller must be capable of providing an appropriate level of security in respect of that personal data. If a data controller's IT systems are inherently insecure then the data controller could be in breach of the Seventh Principle.

7.12.2   Issues to consider when procuring/developing a new IT system

The obligations imposed by the Seventh Principle on a data controller extend to the design of an IT system. Recital 46 of the Data Protection Directive states this expressly (emphasis added):

> Whereas the protection of the rights and freedoms of data subjects with regard to the processing of personal data requires that appropriate technical and organizational measures be taken, *both at the time of the design of the processing system and at the time of the processing itself*, particularly in order to maintain security and thereby to prevent any unauthorized processing; whereas it is incumbent on the Member States to ensure that controllers comply with these measures; whereas these measures must ensure an appropriate level of security, taking into account the state of the art and the costs of their implementation in relation to the risks inherent in the processing and the nature of the data to be protected.

If an IT system for use with personal data is being designed, developed, implemented and/or tested by contractors, the principal should ask the following questions:

- Are the contractors aware of the implications of the Seventh Principle for system design? How have they demonstrated this?
- Who is taking responsibility for specifying security requirements:
    - What do the tender documents say about security?
    - What does the contract say about security?

If development work is being carried out in-house then the first question should be considered by reference to the in-house development team, and although there will not be a tender document or a contract, responsibility for specifying security requirements must still be allocated.

7.12.3   Developers and maintenance providers

In developing or maintaining an IT system, a contractor may require access to personal data of which the principal is the data controller. As such, the developer would be a data processor under the DPA and the development contract should contain, or be supplemented by, terms governing the controller–processor relationship.

7.12.4   UMIST Guidance

In May 2002, the University of Manchester Institute of Science and Technology (UMIST) published its Best Practice Guidance on Data Protection for Systems Designers.

The UMIST Guidance contains very useful information on data protection compliance for those commissioning IT systems and those who design and implement those systems.

On the subject of security, the UMIST Guidance notes that:

> Security is not only about stopping outsiders getting in to your systems, or intercepting messages between legitimate users of the personal data under your control. It is just as much about restricting access to data within your organisation. It is also about making sure of the integrity of the personal data in your care, so that [accuracy] is not compromised by, for example, accidental corruption. [Security] follows on from a clear definition and delineation of [specific] purposes and also from good data management practices. (p.7)

A copy of the Guidance is available from the HiSPEC website (**www.hispec. org.uk/public_documents/BPDMay02.pdf**).

7.13 SECURITY OF NETWORKS

7.13.1 Introduction

Article 17(1) of the Data Protection Directive, from which the Seventh Principle derives, states:

> Member States shall provide that the controller must implement appropriate technical and organizational measures to protect personal data against accidental or unlawful destruction or accidental loss, alteration, unauthorized disclosure or access, in particular where the processing involves the transmission of data over a network, and against all other unlawful forms of processing.

The express inclusion of a reference to the risks of transmitting data over a network reflects the importance attributed within the European legislation to this particular aspect of data security. Although the Seventh Principle does not make any express mention of networks, processing involving the transmission of data over a network is just another form of processing with attendant risks in respect of which data controllers must have in place appropriate technical and organisational measures to guard against. Such measures may include the use of firewalls, encryption, secure payment systems, digital certificates and virus detection and eradication.

7.13.2 The Privacy and Electronic Communications (EC Directive) Regulations 2003

The Privacy and Electronic Communications (EC Directive) Regulations 2003, SI 2003/2426 (PEC Regulations) came into force in the UK on 11 December 2003. They implement Directive 2002/58/EC of the European Parliament and of the Council of 12 July 2002 concerning the processing of personal data and the protection of privacy in the electronic communications sector. The Directive contains Recitals and Articles that expressly address network security and the security of electronic communications services (see Recitals 20 and 21 and Art.4).

The security provisions of Art.4 are implemented in reg.5 of the PEC Regulations.

By reg.5, a provider of a public electronic communications services (the service provider) is under an obligation:

(a) to take appropriate[8] technical and organisational measures to safeguard the security of that service[9] (reg. 5(1)); and
(b) if, despite taking measures as required above, any 'significant' risk to the security of the electronic communications service remains, to inform subscribers concerned of:

  (i)   the nature of that risk;
  (ii) any appropriate measures that the subscriber may take to safeguard against that risk; and
  (iii) the likely costs to the subscriber involved in the taking of such measures (reg.5(3)).

This information must be provided free of any charge other than the cost incurred by the subscriber in respect of the receipt or collection of the information by him (reg.5(5)). The obligation is limited to notification of the subscribers concerned. There is no obligation to notify the Information Commissioner or other regulatory authority.

Arguably, the inherent insecurity of Internet traffic is a significant risk, and accordingly service providers should inform their subscribers about the risks of interception and measures they may take, such as encrypting communications.

This notification obligation is discussed further at **7.14.3**, in the context of data security breaches generally.

7.13.3 Data Retention (EC Directive) Regulations 2007

On 1 October 2007, the Data Retention (EC Directive) Regulations 2007, SI 2007/2199 (Retention Regulations) came into force in the United Kingdom. The United Kingdom is implementing the EU Data Retention Directive in two stages. The first stage was implemented by the Retention Regulations, which relate solely to fixed and mobile telephony data. As is permitted by the EU Data Retention Directive (2002/58/EC), the UK Government elected to delay until March 2009 implementation of the regime for retention of e-mail and Internet communications (including Internet telephony).

Under the Retention Regulations, if a 'public communications provider' (as defined in reg.2(d)) generates certain communications data in the course of providing its services, those data must be retained for 12 months from the date of the communication (reg.4(1) and (2)). Regulation 6 (data security) states:

(a) the retained data shall be of the same quality and subject to the same security and protection as those data on the public electronic communications network;

(b) the data shall be subject to appropriate technical and organisational measures to protect the data against accidental or unlawful destruction, accidental loss or alteration, or unauthorised or unlawful storage, processing, access or disclosure;

(c) the data shall be subject to appropriate technical and organisational measures to ensure that they can be accessed by specially authorised personnel only; and

(d) in the case of data retained solely in accordance with regulation 4(1), the data shall be destroyed by the public communications provider at the end of the period of retention.

7.13.4 Further information on data protection and networks

Information Commissioner's Guidance

The following Guidance Notes are available on the ICO website:

- Internet: Protection of privacy – Data subjects (Jan 2000, version 4).
- Guidance on the Privacy and Electronic Communication (EC Directive) Regulations 2003, Part 2: Security, confidentiality, traffic and location data, itemised billing, CLI and directories.

Parliamentary publications

- The House of Lords Science and Technology Committee Fifth Report of Session 2006–07: Personal Internet Security, published 10 August 2007 and the Government reply, Command Paper Cm 7234 (both available from **www.parliament.uk/parliamentary_committees/lords_s_t_select/ internet.cfm**).

European instruments relating to security and networks

- Article 29 Data Protection Working Party Opinion 9/2001 on the Commission Communication on Creating a safer information society by improving the security of information infrastructures and combating computer-related crime, adopted on 5 November 2001 (5074/01/EN/final WP 51) (see **http://ec.europa.eu/justice_home/fsj/privacy/workinggroup/ wpdocs/2001_en.htm**).
- Network and Information Security: Proposal for a European Policy Approach (COM (2001) 298, 6 June 2001) (**http://eur-lex.europa.eu /LexUriServ/site/en/com/2001/com2001_0298en01.pdf**).
- Regulation (EC) No 460/2004 of the European Parliament and of the Council of 10 March 2004 establishing the European Network and Information Security Agency (ENISA) (**http://europa.eu/scadplus/leg/en/ lvb/l24153.htm**), and see generally the 'Information Society' section of the Europa website (**http://europa.eu/scadplus/leg/en/s21012.htm**).

Documents issued by European organisations relating to security and networks

- ENISA: 'Overview of Current Developments in Network and Information Security Technologies'(ENISA/TD/ST/D(2007)0006)(**www.enisa.europa.eu/ doc/pdf/deliverables/enisa_overview_of_nis_developments.pdf**).
- ICT Standards Board Network and Information Security Standards Report (Issue 6.2, 4 June 2007 'Final Version') (**www.ictsb.org/NISSG/ nis-final-report_2007.pdf**).

International

- OECD Guidelines for the Security of Information Systems and Networks: Towards a Culture of Security (**http://www.oecd.org/dataoecd/ 16/22/15582260.pdf**).

The documents identified above contain background information, opinion and discussion in relation to security and networks. Their contents may be helpful to a data controller in forming a view as to, or seeking to demonstrate (for example, to a tribunal), what are generally acceptable standards and practices in relation to network security.

7.14   SECURITY BREACHES

7.14.1   Liability arising out of the circumstances of a breach of the Seventh Principle

A breach of the Seventh Principle may result in enforcement action by the Information Commissioner under the DPA – see Chapter 9. However, even where enforcement action does not result, the circumstances giving rise to the breach may amount to one or more of the following (for example):

- breach of one or more other Principles (for example, accuracy);
- breach of a common law or contractual obligation of confidence;
- breach of a statutory provision imposing obligations with respect to internal controls, for example, the Financial Services and Markets Act 2000 (FSMA 2000), the Companies Act 2006, or (for those UK companies in groups subject to its regime) the US Sarbanes-Oxley Act;
- infringement of copyright;
- breach of contract; and
- breach of applicable industry or professional codes, for example:
  - the Banking Code;
  - the General Medical Council Code of Professional Conduct; or
  - the Combined Code (for listed companies) (see **7.5.5**).

Examples from the financial services sector

Firms' responsibilities to the FSA with respect to data security are defined in the FSA's Principles for Business, which require firms to 'conduct [their] business with due skill, care and diligence' (Principle 2) and 'take reasonable care to organise and control [their] affairs responsibly and effectively, with adequate risk management systems' (Principle 3). Under Rule 3.2.6R in the FSA's Senior Management Arrangements, Systems and Controls sourcebook (SYSC), firms are required to 'take reasonable care to establish and maintain effective systems and controls for compliance with applicable requirements and standards under the regulatory system and for countering the risk that the firm might be used to further financial crime'. Under FSMA 2000, the FSA can impose various sanctions for breach of the Principles, including imposing financial penalties, withdrawing a firm's authorisation and prosecuting various offences.

On 14 February 2007 the FSA fined the Nationwide Building Society £980,000 for 'failing to have effective systems and controls to manage its information security risks', in breach of Principle 3 of the FSA's Principles for Businesses. The failings came to light following the theft of a laptop from a Nationwide employee's home in 2006. See FSA press release

FSA/PN/021/2007 (**www.fsa.gov.uk/pages/Library/Communication/PR/2007/ 021.shtml**). See also 'Banks put on notice by ICO', *Privacy & Data Protection*, Volume 7, Issue 5, p.6.

On 17 December 2007, the FSA fined Norwich Union Life and Pensions Limited and its associated companies ('Norwich Union') £1.26 million, for 'not having effective systems and controls in place to protect customers' confidential information and manage its financial crime risks'. As reported in the FSA's press release, 'the weaknesses in Norwich Union Life's systems and controls allowed fraudsters to use publicly available information including names and dates of birth to impersonate customers and obtain sensitive customer details from its call centres. The fraudsters were also, in some cases, able to ask for confidential customer records such as addresses and bank account details to be altered. The fraudsters then used the information to request the surrender of 74 customers' policies totalling £3.3 million in 2006'. See FSA press release FSA/PN/130/2007, 17 December 2007 (**www.fsa.gov.uk/pages/Library/Communication/PR/2007/130.shtml**).

It is important to note that the FSA does not only take action if data are lost or stolen. For example, on 17 June 2008 the FSA fined the stockbroking firm Merchant Securities Group Limited for not adequately protecting its customers from the risk of identity fraud. Merchant Securities was found to have inadequate procedures for verifying identities of customers contacting the firm by telephone, included personal account numbers in routine letters when it was not necessary to do so and stored back-up tapes containing unencrypted personal information of customers in a bag at a staff member's home. The fine was imposed notwithstanding the fact that the FSA did not find any evidence that customer details had been lost or stolen. See FSA press release FSA/PN/058/2008, 17 June 2008 (**www.fsa.gov.uk/pages/Library/ Communication/PR/2008/058.shtml**).

7.14.2 Liability in respect of unlawfully obtaining, or procuring a disclosure of, personal data

If a person circumvents a data controller's security measures and obtains or discloses personal data (or the information contained in personal data), or procures the disclosure to another person of information contained in personal data, in each case without the consent of the data controller, that person may be liable in respect of one or more of the following (for example):

- an offence under s.55(1) of the DPA;
- an offence under the Computer Misuse Act 1990;
- a theft offence;
- breach of a common law or contractual obligation of confidence;
- infringement of copyright; and

- if the person is an employee of the data controller, breach of express and/or implied terms of their contract of employment.

Directors and other officers can have personal liability for offences under the DPA committed by bodies corporate where those offences are proved to have been committed with their consent or connivance, or are attributable to their neglect (DPA, s.61(1)).

7.14.3 Legal obligations on a data controller to notify in the event of a security breach

The existing position in the UK and Europe

At the time of writing, there is no UK law that creates an obligation on data controllers to notify individuals or regulators in the event of a data security breach (though a data controller may be under a notification obligation by virtue of the fact that it is subject to sector-specific law or regulation requiring it). However, the UK is moving closer to adopting such a law as a result of domestic and European pressure (see *'Calls for a breach notification law'* below).

The PEC Regulations and the DPA each contain obligations to provide individuals with data security information in certain circumstances, but these obligations are not equivalent to the breach notification regime being called for by the Information Commissioner and others or created by various US state laws (see *'The position in the United States'* below).

Regulation 5(3) of the PEC Regulations, discussed above at **7.13.2**, applies only to 'communications providers', requiring them to inform affected subscribers of security risks rather than security breaches. It is submitted that in many instances a security breach will also be a security risk, but even in such instances, the notification required is limited in scope and extent.

The provisions of reg.5 of the PEC Regulations are in addition to the requirement on data controllers, imposed by the First Principle of the DPA, to provide to the data subject (among certain other information) 'any further information which is necessary, having regard to the specific circumstances in which the data are or are to be processed, to enable processing in respect of the data subject to be fair' (DPA, Sched.1, Part II, para.2(3)(d)). As noted elsewhere in this book (see Chapter 5), any major security risks known to the data controller may be an example of such 'further information'. It would seem that this information only needs to be provided once, for example, at the time of collection of the personal data, rather than there being an ongoing obligation to provide it. On that basis, a data controller would not be required under the First Principle to notify a data subject of a subsequent security breach. See also the discussion at **7.11.2** in relation to the disclosure of security breaches in response to subject access requests.

Similarly, there is no European data security breach notification law (in the form of a Directive or other instrument), although some other European countries, such as Norway (which is not an EU member), have implemented laws that create notification obligations.

Calls for a breach notification law

In the UK there have been calls for a breach notification law from, among others, the Information Commissioner and the House of Lords Science and Technology Committee (see paras.5.55–5.56 of its Personal Internet Security report, referenced at **7.13.4**). At a European level, there have been calls for breach notification laws (of varying extent) from the European Commission and the European Data Protection Supervisor. For further information, see:

- European Commission Communication (Commission Staff Working Document on the Review of the EU Regulatory Framework for Electronic Communications Networks and Services, 28 June 2006 (SEC(2006) 816)), 28 June 2006 (available at **http://ec.europa.eu/information_society/ policy/ecomm/doc/info_centre/public_consult/review/staffworking document_ final.pdf**).
- Commission Proposal for a Directive amending, among others, Directive 2002/58/EC concerning the processing of personal data and the protection of privacy in the electronic communication sector, 13 November 2007 (available at **http://ec.europa.eu/information_society/policy/ecomm/ doc/library/proposals/dir_citizens_rights_en.pdf**).
- European Data Protection Supervisor (EDPS) Opinion on the Proposal for a Directive amending (among others) the Directive on privacy and electronic communications, 10 April 2008 (available at **www.edps.europa.eu/EDPSWEB/webdav/site/mySite/shared/Documents/ Consultation/Opinions/2008/08–04–10_e-privacy_EN.pdf**).

The position in the United States

In 2003, the Californian Computer Security Breach Notification Act (SB1386) came into force. It requires businesses to notify California residents if the security of certain classes of personal information about them is breached. As at the date of publication, over 40 states have passed security breach laws. However, there are differences across states as to what constitutes a security breach, differing requirements with respect to demonstrating potential harm and in reporting requirements (for example, some states require only that affected individuals be notified, others require also that relevant regulatory bodies be notified). These differences act to weaken the effectiveness of the breach notification regime, prompting moves towards a federal law that aims to (among other things) create uniformity in standards.

7.14.4 Guidance with respect to notifying breaches

Introduction

If a data controller suffers a data security breach, should it notify the breach to the Information Commissioner and/or any other regulators, and should it notify individuals who have been, or may be, affected?

In the absence of a legal or other obligation compelling notification, these are not trivial questions for a data controller to consider. On the one hand, by notifying individuals of the breach, the data controller can help to make sure that those individuals are particularly vigilant against misuse of their data, and assists them to take steps to reduce or eliminate associated risks. On the other, publicising the breach may simply heighten the risk of someone capitalising on it, or may unnecessarily cause anxiety with customers if in fact there is no real risk of misuse of their data following the breach in question.

In any event, what is of crucial importance to data controllers is to have a data security breach management and notification plan in place, to help them react quickly and efficiently to a breach or suspected breach. If a data controller does not have appropriately skilled in-house resources, then external resources should be engaged to help create, implement and test the plan.

To provide assistance to data controllers with respect to the management and reporting of data security breaches, on 1 April 2008 the ICO published two Good Practice Notes. Copies of these notes are available on the ICO website.

Guidance on data security breach management

This note provides guidance to data controllers on points to consider in the event of a security breach. It describes a four-step 'breach management plan', consisting of:

1. Containment and recovery (the initial response, investigation, containment and recovery plan including damage limitation).
2. Assessing the risks.
3. Notification of breaches (whether the breach of security should be notified, who should be notified, what information should be provided in the notification).

4.   Evaluation and response (evaluation of the causes of the breach and the effectiveness of the organisation's response to it).

Notification of data security breaches to the ICO

This note provides guidance to data controllers as to:

- whether to bring breaches of security to the attention of the ICO. The note sets out factors for a data controller to consider, such as:
  - the potential harm to data subjects;
  - the volume of personal data lost/released/corrupted;
  - the sensitivity of the data lost/released/unlawfully corrupted;
- how to report the breach and what information to include;
- what will the Information Commissioner do when a breach is reported.

Further guidance on data security breach notification

At the time of publication, there is no specific standard applicable to data security breach management (including notification), but ISO 27001 (see **7.6**) does include controls in relation to 'information security management'.

Sector-specific guidance is also available. An example is the guidance on 'Security Incident Management', available from the Information Governance section of the NHS's 'Connecting for Health' website (**www.connectingforhealth.nhs.uk**).

Undoubtedly, following the recent (and continuing) data security breaches (see **7.14.6**), additional general and sector-specific guidance will become available.

7.14.5   Action by the Information Commissioner in response to security breaches

The Information Commissioner has been implementing a name and shame policy in relation to organisations that have breached the Seventh Principle and other provisions of the DPA. The standard approach taken by the Information Commissioner has been to:

- investigate the potential breach reported to him;
- on a finding of a breach, negotiate legally binding undertakings from the organisation in breach; and
- publish the undertakings on the ICO website and issue a press release.

Typical undertakings include:

* an obligation to admit a breach; and
* agreement to implement remedial action as specified by the Information Commissioner, including agreement to be audited by the Information Commissioner.

7.14.6 The HMRC data security incident and its aftermath

On 20 November 2007 the UK Government admitted that HM Revenue and Customs (HMRC) had lost two CDs containing what was thought to be personal data relating to approximately 25 million people in the UK. The data was reported as including the names, addresses and dates of birth of children, together with the National Insurance numbers and bank details of their parents.

The HMRC incident was followed by reports of several other major, high profile, data security incidents within the public and private sectors, involving (among others) the Driving Standards Agency, several Primary Healthcare Trusts of the NHS, the Ministry of Defence, Marks & Spencer, Skipton Financial Services and Norwich Union. (The Ministry of Defence incident is discussed further at **7.3.4**, and the Norwich Union incident at **7.14.1**.)

On 22 April 2008, the Information Commissioner issued a press release announcing that since the HMRC incident, the ICO had been notified of almost 100 data breaches by public, private and third-sector organisations. (See ICO press release 'Roll call of data breaches grows', 22 April 2008 (available from the ICO website).)

In the wake of the HMRC and other data security incidents, a number of studies and reports were commissioned by the Government and other bodies.

* *The Poynter Report.* The Government commissioned a study by the senior partner and chair of PricewaterhouseCoopers, Mr Kieran Poynter, into what went wrong. The terms of reference of Mr Poynter's review were:

    to establish the circumstances that led to the significant loss of confidential personal data on child benefit recipients, other recent losses of confidential data and the lessons to be learned in the light of those circumstances; to examine HMRC practices and procedures in the handling and transfer of confidential data on taxpayers on benefit and credit recipients; the processes for ensuring that such procedures are communicated to staff and the safe-guards in place to ensure that they are adhered to; the reasons those failed to prevent the loss of confidential data; and whether those procedures and processes are sufficient to ensure the confidentiality of personal data.

(Rt Hon Alistair Darling MP, HC Deb, 28 November 2007, col 308)

The final report, generally known as the Poynter Report, was published on 25 June 2008, together with the three other reports referenced immediately below. It is available on the HMRC website (**www.hm-treasury. gov.uk./independent_reviews/poynter_review/poynter_review_index.cfm**). The Poynter Report is in two parts. The first part sets out a detailed account of the circumstances giving rise to the loss of the two CDs. The second part contains principal findings of lessons to be learnt and 45 high level recommendations. The Poynter Report concludes that:

The data loss incident arose following a sequence of communications failures between junior HMRC officials and between them and the National Audit Office . . . The loss was entirely avoidable and the fact that it could happen points to serious institutional deficiencies at HMRC.

The two major institutional deficiencies from which many of the more detailed issues flow were:
• Information security simply wasn't a management priority as it should have been, and
• HMRC had an organisational design which was unnecessarily complex and crucially, did not clearly focus on management accountability.

Both of these issues have now been addressed, but a great deal of work will be required to bring HMRC up to and to sustain the world class standard for information security to which it now properly aspires.

These institutional deficiencies are by no means confined to HMRC, and many of the specific criticisms made of HMRC in the Poynter Report could also be made of numerous other data controllers. As such, the Poynter Report serves as a useful general security resource, particularly with respect to organisational measures.
• *The IPCC Report.* The Independent Police Complaints Commission (IPCC) also carried out an investigation into the HMRC's loss of data, focusing on the cause of the incident and whether relevant local and national policies and guidelines were complied with. The IPCC's investigation found that the processes for data handling were 'woefully inadequate', but that 'individual members of staff were not to blame'. The IPCC's report is available on the IPCC website (**http://www. ipcc.gov.uk/final_hmrc_report_25062008.pdf**).
• *The Burton Report.* Following the Ministry of Defence laptop loss, Sir Edmund Burton was invited to conduct a full investigation into the circumstances that led to the loss of the data and examine the adequacy

of the steps taken to prevent recurrence, and to consider the broader Ministry of Defence approach to data protection. The resulting report identified significant failings within the Ministry of Defence with respect to data security, and set out 51 recommendations as to improvements in the handling of personal data . The Ministry of Defence published an 'action plan' in response, setting out how it intended to meet the recommendations. The report and action plan are available from the Ministry of Defence website (**www.mod.uk**).

- *The Data Handling in Government Report.* On 23 November 2007, the Prime Minister also commissioned the Cabinet Secretary, Sir Gus O'Donnell, to conduct a separate review of data handling procedures in government. The review's terms of reference were to examine the procedures in departments and agencies for the protection of data, their consistency with current government-wide policies and standards and the arrangements for ensuring that procedures are fully and properly implemented. The Cabinet Secretary was also asked to make recommendations on improvements that should be made. The final report (an interim report having been published on 20 December 2007) is available on the Cabinet Office website (**www.cabinetoffice.gov.uk/reports/ data_handling.aspx**).

These reviews were in addition to one commissioned prior to the HMRC incident coming to the Government's attention, in which the Information Commissioner and Dr Mark Walport, Director of the Wellcome Trust, were asked to examine data sharing in the public and private sectors and recommend improvements in security and accountability. The final report is available on the Ministry of Justice website (**www.justice.gov.uk/reviews/ datasharing-intro.htm**).

Following publication of the Poynter, IPCC and Burton reports, the Information Commissioner released a strongly-worded statement confirming that he would take enforcement action against HMRC and the Ministry of Defence. At the time of publication, the terms of the enforcement notices had not been finalised, but the Information Commissioner stated that he will 'require HMRC and the MOD to use their best endeavours to implement all the recommendations outlined in the reports' (see ICO press release 'HMRC and MOD data security breaches' 25 June 2008, available from the ICO website).

The various reports referenced above do not have as their focus compliance with data protection law *per se* (indeed, there are very few express references to the DPA in them). However, the contents of the reports (and the reports that will follow them) operate to affect existing and future compliance standards (for example, by providing reference points for what are 'appropriate' measures), help shape the public's expectations of standards to be adopted in the public and private sectors, and will influence policy-making in the area.

7.14.7   Information Security Breaches Survey 2008

The Department for Business, Enterprise and Regulatory Reform, and its predecessor the Department for Trade and Industry, has sponsored research into information security breaches since 1991 and published the results with a view to helping UK businesses better understand the risks they face. The Executive Summary to the Information Security Breaches Survey 2008 (the ninth such survey) highlights the finding that 'many companies are not doing enough to protect themselves and their customers' information'. This is illustrated by the following statistics:

- 10% of websites that accept payment details do not encrypt them;
- 21% spend less than 1% of their IT budget on information security;
- 35% have no controls over staff use of instant messaging;
- 48% of disaster recovery plans have not been tested in the last year;
- 52% do not carry out any formal security risk assessment;
- 67% do nothing to prevent confidential data leaving on USB sticks, etc.;
- 78% of companies that had computers stolen did not encrypt hard discs;
- 79% are not aware of the contents of BS 7799/ISO 27001; and
- 84% of companies do not scan outgoing e-mail for confidential data.

A copy of the survey is available from the Information Security section of the BERR website.

Endnotes

1 Any monitoring to check for compliance with the security policy must be carried out in accordance with applicable legislation, including the DPA and the Regulation of Investigatory Powers Act 2000. Guidance on monitoring in this context is set out in Part 3 of the Information Commissioner's Employment Practices Code (on monitoring at work). See also **7.4.4**.
2 Ibid.
3 Ibid.
4 2002/16/EC Commission Decision of 27 December 2001 on standard contractual clauses for the transfer of personal data to processors established in third countries, under Directive 95/46/EC. The Decision became effective on 3 April 2002. The text of these clauses can be found at **http://ec.europa.eu/justice_home/ fsj/privacy/modelcontracts/index_en.htm** under the heading 'Standard Contractual Clauses for Data Processors established in Third Countries'.
5 Version 2.0, 30 June 2006. The document is available on the ICO website.
6 Annex 1 (Safe Harbor Privacy Principles) of Commission Decision of 26 July 2000 on the adequacy of the protection provided by the Safe Harbor Privacy Principles and related frequently asked questions issued by the US Department of Commerce.
7 Ibid.

8 By reg.5(4), a measure is 'appropriate' only if, having regard to the state of technological developments and the cost of implementing it, it is proportionate to the risks against which it would safeguard.

9 Regulation 5(2) states that if necessary, this measure 'may be taken by the service provider in conjunction with the provider of the electronic communications network by means of which the service is provided, and that network provider shall comply with any reasonable requests made by the service provider for these purposes'.

CHAPTER 8

Data exports

Eduardo Ustaran

8.1 WHY ARE DATA EXPORTS AN ISSUE?

8.1.1 Legislative background

Article 25 of the Data Protection Directive (95/46/EC) placed a controversial requirement on the governments of EU Member States: to ban the transfer of personal data to any country outside the European Economic Area (which consists of the EU Member States together with Iceland, Liechtenstein and Norway) unless that third country ensures an adequate level of privacy protection.

Implementing this provision while promoting a truly borderless economy posed a real challenge for all EU governments. In the UK, this requirement was incorporated as the Eighth Principle of the DPA, which states:

> Personal data shall not be transferred to a country or territory outside the European Economic Area unless that country or territory ensures an adequate level of protection for the rights and freedoms of data subjects in relation to the processing of personal data.

Similar provisions have been incorporated in most European data protection laws. This has prompted international concern about the future of global operations involving flows of personal data.

8.1.2 EU institutions' rationale

The Recitals of the Directive are not particularly helpful in explaining the reason behind this prohibition. They recognise that cross-border flows of personal data are necessary for the expansion of international trade, but also state that the transfer of personal data to a third country which does not ensure an adequate level of protection must be prohibited.

In order to understand the basis for such a radical regime, it is necessary to bear in mind the purpose of the Directive as set out in Art.1: Member States must protect the fundamental rights and freedoms of natural persons, and in particular their right to privacy with respect to the processing of personal data. In other words, the main aim of the legal regime established by the Directive (and implemented by the DPA) is to create a framework that protects and shields individuals' personal information from misuses and abuse.

However, such a framework would be very fragile if the protection afforded by it were to fall apart as soon as the personal information leaves the boundaries of the countries subject to EU data protection law. Therefore, the European institutions responsible for drafting and adopting the Directive tried to preserve the effect of the new regime by blocking any attempts to weaken the protection afforded to individuals. In practice, this has created a situation that effectively imposes EU data protection standards in jurisdictions outside Europe.

8.1.3 Scope of the problem

Bearing in mind the high standards of privacy protection imposed by the Directive, it is difficult to see how countries without the same strict legislative approach to this issue can avoid falling foul of this provision. As a result, the Directive has been seen as a serious barrier to international commerce. While the Directive seeks to facilitate the flow of personal data between EU Member States, global commerce has become seriously affected. For some large multinational organisations, this issue has meant the adoption of EU data protection practices across their operations irrespective of where the data processing activities actually take place.

Figure 8.1 sets out the assessment process recommended when dealing with data exports. A comprehensive list of relevant primary resources is provided at **8.9**.

8.2 WHEN ARE INTERNATIONAL DATA FLOWS NOT REGARDED AS DATA EXPORTS?

The concept of transfer is not defined by the Directive or the DPA. However, the Information Commissioner has often pointed out that transfer does not mean the same as mere transit. Therefore, the fact that personal data may be routed through a third country on the way from the UK to another EEA country does not bring such transfer within the ambit of the Eighth Principle of the DPA unless some substantive processing operation is conducted on the personal data in the third country.

In practice, there are two common situations which have been a source of concern in the past, but that are not subject to the regime dealing with data exports, namely:

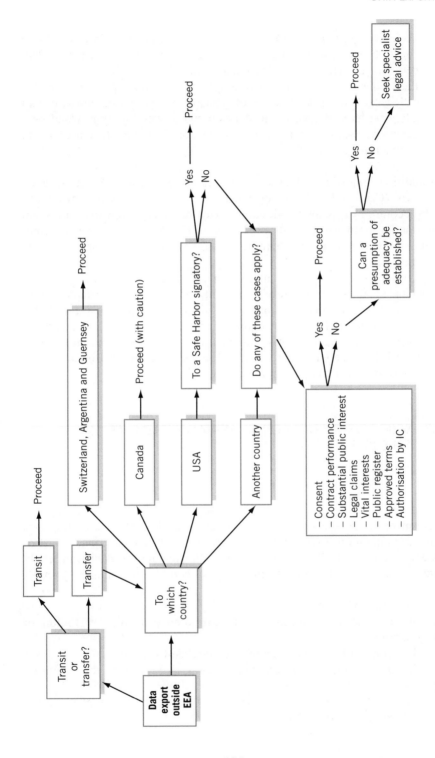

Figure 8.1 Transfer assessment flowchart

1. Technical routing of packet-switch technology (such as Internet e-mail and web pages) which may involve random transfers of personal data between computer servers located anywhere in the world.
2. Electronic access to personal data by travellers who happen to be physically located for a short period of time in a place that does not afford an adequate level of protection. An example of this situation would be a person who logs on to a computer system based in the UK to access data from a foreign airport.

In addition, following the ECJ decision in the Swedish case against *Bodil Lindqvist* (Case C-101/01) in November 2003, there is no transfer of data to a third country where an individual in a Member State merely loads personal information onto a website that is hosted in that State or another Member State, so that the information can be assessed by anyone who connects to the Internet.

However, where there is an international exchange of information about individuals with the intention of processing that personal information automatically after it has been exchanged, that should be regarded as a transfer for the purposes of the DPA, even if the original exchange does not qualify as processing of personal data. An example of this would be where information is provided by someone in the UK over the telephone to someone in a third country who then enters that information on a computer.

8.3 WHAT DOES THE LAW MEAN BY AN ADEQUATE LEVEL OF PROTECTION?

8.3.1 EU official interpretation

The general rule under Art.25 of the Directive is subject to a case-by-case assessment of the adequacy of the level of protection afforded by the third country in question. According to the Directive itself, such adequacy must be assessed in light of all the circumstances surrounding the data transfer. In addition, as part of that assessment, particular consideration must be given to:

• the nature of the data;
• the purpose and duration of the proposed processing operation or operations;
• the country of origin and country of final destination;
• the rules of law, both general and sectoral, in force in the third country; and
• the professional rules and security measures which are complied with in that country (Art.25(2)).

These circumstances have essentially been replicated in the DPA (Sched.1, Part II, para.13) without any further explanation. In order to help organisations carry out that assessment in practice, the Article 29 Working Party issued quite detailed advice even before the deadline for implementation of the Directive.[1]

Following the Article 29 Working Party's advice, the analysis of the level of protection must comprise two basic elements: (a) the content of the rules applicable; and (b) the means for ensuring their effective application. Accordingly, the Article 29 Working Party identified a set of content principles and a basic enforcement mechanism, which can be regarded as a minimum requirement for the protection to be considered adequate.

The content principles include:

- *The purpose limitation principle*: data must be processed for a specific purpose and subsequently used or further communicated only in so far as this is not incompatible with the purpose of the transfer.
- *The data quality and proportionality principle*: data must be accurate and, where necessary, kept up to date. The data must be adequate, relevant and not excessive in relation to the purposes for which they are transferred or further processed.
- *The transparency principle*: individuals must be provided with information as to the purpose of the processing and the identity of the data controller in the third country, and any other information that is necessary to ensure fairness.
- *The security principle*: technical and organisational security measures must be taken by the data controller that are appropriate to the risks presented by the processing. Any person acting under the authority of the data controller, including a processor, must not process data except on instructions from the controller.
- *The rights of access, rectification and opposition*: individuals must have a right to obtain a copy of all data relating to them, and a right to rectification of such data where they are shown to be inaccurate. In certain situations, individuals must also be able to object to the processing of their personal data.
- *Restrictions on onward transfers*: further transfers of the personal data by the recipient of the original data transfer must only be permitted where the second recipient (i.e. the recipient of the onward transfer) is also subject to rules affording an adequate level of protection.
- *Sensitive data*: where 'sensitive' categories of data are involved, additional safeguards should be in place, such as a requirement that individuals give their explicit consent for the processing.
- *Direct marketing*: where data is transferred for the purposes of direct marketing, individuals should be able to 'opt-out' from having their data used for such purposes at any stage.

- *Automated individual decision*: where the purpose of the transfer is to make an automated decision in the sense of Art.15 of the Directive, the individual should have the right to know the logic involved in this decision, and other measures should be taken to safeguard the individual's legitimate interest.

The enforcement mechanism required need not be based on a supervisory authority model, as is typically the case within EU Member States. What the Article 29 Working Party is concerned about is a system that meets the underlying objectives of a data protection procedural system, namely:

- *The delivery of a good level of compliance with the rules*: a good system is generally characterised by a high degree of awareness among data controllers of their obligations, and among individuals of their rights and the means of exercising them. The existence of effective and dissuasive sanctions can play an important role in ensuring respect for the rules, as can systems of direct verification by authorities, auditors or independent data protection officials.
- *The provision of support and help to individuals in the exercise of their rights*: individuals must be able to enforce their rights rapidly and effectively, and without prohibitive cost, which means that there must be some sort of institutional mechanism allowing independent investigation of complaints.
- *The availability of appropriate redress to the injured party where rules are not complied with*: this is a key element, which must involve a system of independent adjudication or arbitration that allows compensation to be paid and sanctions imposed where appropriate.

8.3.2   Information Commissioner's adequacy test

In June 2006, the Information Commissioner produced an updated version of his own guidance note in the area of international data transfers (the Eighth Data Protection Principle and international data transfers, 30 June 2006). The Information Commissioner's Guidance included a section called the 'adequacy test', which was aimed at assisting exporters of personal data to determine whether a transfer could be regarded as adequate in terms of data protection.

According to the Information Commissioner's Guidance, the adequacy criteria are divided into two categories: the 'general adequacy criteria' and the 'legal adequacy criteria'. The general adequacy criteria are factors which the exporting data controller will be able to identify easily; for example, the nature of the personal data being transferred and purpose for which the data will be processed. General adequacy criteria should be assessed in detail on every occasion. The legal adequacy criteria may be more difficult for the controller to assess as they are factors relating to the legal system in force in the third country.

An exhaustive analysis of the legal adequacy criteria may be unnecessary if an assessment of the general adequacy criteria has revealed that in the particular circumstances the transfer is low risk. Conversely, if the general adequacy assessment reveals a high-risk transfer (e.g. if the data are particularly sensitive), then a more comprehensive investigation of the legal adequacy criteria will be expected.

Therefore, this assessment must be made by focusing on the potential risks involved in the transfer and whether or not, in all the circumstances of the case, an adequate level of protection is likely to be ensured in the third country in question in relation to the proposed transfer.

8.4   WHICH COUNTRIES ARE REGARDED AS SAFE?

8.4.1   Procedure to designate safe countries

The Directive allows the European Commission to determine whether a third country ensures an adequate level of protection by reason of its domestic law or of the international commitments it has entered into (Art.25(6)). Therefore, the Commission has established a formal procedure to designate countries that can be assumed to ensure an adequate level of protection. The steps that are taken as part of this procedure include:

- a proposal from the EU Commission;
- an Opinion of the Article 29 Working Party;
- an Opinion of the Article 31 Management Committee delivered by a qualified majority of Member States;
- a 30-day right of scrutiny for the European Parliament to check if the Commission has used its executive powers correctly;
- the adoption of the Decision by the EU Commission.

The effect of such a decision is that personal data can flow from the EU Member States and the other EEA member countries to that third country without any further safeguard being necessary. The Commission has so far recognised Switzerland, Hungary (which is now part of the EEA), Canada, Argentina, Guernsey and the Isle of Man as providing adequate protection. At the time of publication Jersey and the Faroe Islands are in the last stages of this process.

8.4.2 Switzerland

On 7 June 1999, the Article 29 Working Party issued an Opinion stating that following a study that considered the Federal Data Protection Law and the legislation in several cantons, Switzerland ensured an adequate level of protection (Opinion 5/99). The Commission endorsed that Opinion by a formal Decision on 26 July 2000 (Commission Decision 2000/518/EC of 26 July 2000, OJ L215/1).

8.4.3 Hungary

The Article 29 Working Party also considered the relevant law in Hungary and on 7 September 1999 recommended that Hungary should be regarded as ensuring an adequate level of protection within the meaning of Article 25 of the Directive (Opinion 6/99). As in the case of Switzerland, the Commission endorsed the Article 29 Working Party's Opinion by a formal Decision on 26 July 2000 (Commission Decision 2000/519/EC of 26 July 2000, OJ L215/4). This adequacy finding is, however, no longer relevant, as Hungary is now a full EU Member State, and therefore is subject to the Directive.

8.4.4 Canada

On 20 December 2001, the European Commission recognised that the Canadian Personal Information Protection and Electronic Documents Act 2000 (PIPED Act) provided adequate protection for certain personal data transferred from the EU to Canada (Commission Decision 2002/2/EC of 20 December 2001, OJ L2/13. This Decision was preceded by an Opinion of the Article 29 Working Party of 26 January 2001 on the adequacy of the PIPED Act).

In any event, the PIPED Act does not apply to government organisations to which the Federal Privacy Act applies or that are subject to public sector privacy legislation at the provincial level. Similarly, the PIPED Act does not apply to non-profit and charitable organisations unless they engage in activities of a commercial nature.

8.4.5 Argentina

On 3 October 2002, the Article 29 Working Party issued an Opinion stating that Argentinean law complies with the basic content principles indicated in the Working Document (WP12) of 24 July 1998 and, therefore, Argentina ensures an adequate level of protection (Opinion 4/2002). This Opinion was endorsed by the European Commission on 30 June 2003 (Commission Decision 2003/490/EC of 30 June, OJ L168/19).

8.4.6 Guernsey

On 13 June 2003, the Article 29 Working Party issued another Opinion declaring that Guernsey also ensures an adequate level of protection by virtue of the Data Protection (Bailiwick of Guernsey) Law 2001, which follows closely the UK legislation (Opinion 5/2003). This Opinion was endorsed by the European Commission on 21 November 2003 (Commission Decision 2003/821/EC of 21 November 2003, OJ L308/27).

8.4.7 Isle of Man

On 21 November 2003, the Article 29 Working Party issued an Opinion concluding that the Isle of Man ensures an adequate level of protection within the meaning of Art.25 of the Directive (Opinion 6/2003). This Opinion was endorsed by the European Commission on 28 April 2004 (Commission Decision 2004/411/EC of 28 April 2004).

8.4.8 Jersey and the Faroe Islands

On 9 October 2007, the Article 29 Working Party issued two Opinions concluding that Jersey and the Faroe Islands ensure an adequate level of protection within the meaning of Art.25 of the Directive (Opinions 8/2007 and 9/2007). At the time of publication these Opinions had not yet been endorsed by the European Commission.

8.4.9 Other countries

The European Commission has recognised the need for a more extensive use of findings of adequate protection in respect of third countries (see the First Report from the Commission on the implementation of the Data Protection Directive of 15 May 2003). Therefore, the Commission has expressly included this task in the Work Programme for a better implementation of the directive and is likely to step up its activity in this area. In addition to Jersey and the Faroe Islands, other jurisdictions that may join the list of safe countries in the short- to medium-term include Australia, New Zealand and Japan.

8.5 WHAT IS THE SITUATION IN THE UNITED STATES?

8.5.1 A special case

Countries where a legislation-free approach to personal privacy is preferred, such as the United States, face a particularly difficult challenge in the context of European data imports. In light of this and considering the large volume of data transfers carried out on a daily basis between the EU and the USA, the US Department of Commerce and the European Commission devoted more than two years to develop a self-regulatory framework that would allow US organisations to satisfy the requirements of the Directive. On 26 July 2000, the European Commission finally issued a Decision stating that the so-called Safe Harbor Privacy Principles provided adequate protection for personal data transferred from the EU.[2]

8.5.2 Safe Harbor Privacy Principles

The decision by US-based organisations to abide by the Safe Harbor Privacy Principles (see **www.export.gov/safeharbor/shprinciplesfinal.htm**) is entirely voluntary. Organisations that decide to participate in the scheme must comply with the relevant requirements and publicly declare that they do so. In practice, an organisation needs to self-certify annually to the US Department of Commerce in writing that it agrees to adhere to the Safe Harbor's requirements. It must also state in its published privacy policy statement that it adheres to the principles.

The requirements established by the Safe Harbor Privacy Principles are as follows:

- *Notice*: an organisation must inform individuals of the purposes for which it collects and uses personal information, how it can be contacted, to whom it intends to disclose the information and the choices and means available to individuals for limiting the use and disclosure of that information. This notice must be made available in clear and conspicuous language before the organisation uses or discloses the information.
- *Choice*: an organisation must offer individuals the opportunity to opt out of uses or disclosures involving their personal information, where such uses or disclosures are incompatible with the purposes for which the information was originally collected or subsequently authorised by the individual. With regard to sensitive personal information (i.e. data specifying the medical or health condition, the racial or ethnic origin, the political opinions or trade union membership, the religious or philosophical beliefs or the sex life of an individual) affirmative or explicit consent – opt-in – must be obtained if the information is to be used for a purpose other than that for which it was originally collected or subsequently authorised by the individual.
- *Onward transfer*: an organisation may only disclose personal information to third parties that: (a) subscribe to the Safe Harbor Privacy Principles; (b) are subject to the Directive; or (c) enter into a written agreement

202

whereby they undertake to provide at least the same level of privacy protection provided by the Safe Harbor Privacy Principles.

- *Security*: organisations processing personal information must take reasonable security measures and precautions to avoid its loss, misuse and unauthorised access, disclosure, alteration or destruction.
- *Data integrity*: an organisation may only process information relevant to the purposes for which it has been gathered. In addition, steps must be taken to ensure that the data are: (a) relevant for the intended use; and (b) accurate, complete and current.
- *Access*: individuals must have access to personal information about them held by an organisation and be able to correct it, except where the burden or expense of providing access is disproportionate to the risks to the individual's privacy in the case in question, or where the rights of persons other than the individual would be violated.
- *Enforcement*: organisations must abide by certain mechanisms of compliance with the Safe Harbor Principles, which provide recourse for individuals and consequences for non-compliance. At the very least, such mechanisms must include: (a) a readily available and affordable independent recourse to deal with individuals' complaints and disputes by reference to the Safe Harbor Privacy Principles and award damages where applicable; (b) a follow-up procedure to verify the implementation of privacy practices; and (c) an obligation to remedy problems arising out of failures to comply with the Safe Harbor Privacy Principles.

8.5.3　Practical operation

To qualify for the scheme, an organisation must do one of the following:

- join a self-regulatory privacy programme that adheres to the Safe Harbor's requirements, or
- develop its own self-regulatory privacy policy that conforms to the Safe Harbor. (For detailed information about the self-certification process see **www.export.gov/safeharbor/helpful_hints.html**.)

Enforcement of the Safe Harbor Privacy Principles will take place in the United States in accordance with US law and will be carried out primarily by the private sector. Private sector self-regulation and enforcement will be backed up as needed by government enforcement of the federal and state unfair and deceptive statutes.

An EU organisation can ensure that it is sending information to a US organisation that participates in the Safe Harbor by viewing the public list of Safe Harbor organisations posted on the US Department of Commerce's website. (The full list is available at **http://web.ita.doc.gov/safeharbor/shlist.nsf/**

webPages/safe+harbor+list.) This list became operational at the beginning of November 2000 and contains the names of all US companies that have self-certified to the Safe Harbor Privacy Principles and any additional documentation. This list is regularly updated, so that it is clear who is in the Safe Harbor.

US organisations can also meet the adequacy requirements of the Directive if they include the Safe Harbor requirements as the substantive privacy provisions in written agreements with parties transferring data from the EU.

See Appendix 1 for the final version of the Safe Harbor Privacy Principles.

8.6 WHAT ARE THE EXEMPTIONS FROM THE BAN ON DATA EXPORTS?

8.6.1 Derogations

The principle set out in Art.25 of the Directive is not absolute, as Art.26 includes a number of so-called derogations which are, in any event, subject to the domestic laws of Member States. In the UK, Schedule 4 to the DPA refers to the cases where the Eighth Principle does not apply.

8.6.2 Consent

Data exports can lawfully be made with the consent of the individual. However, consent must be freely given and while it is possible to make consent a condition for the provision of a non-essential service, consent is unlikely to be valid if the individual has no real choice. This is particularly the case in the context of employment where, if an existing employee is required to agree to the international transfer of personal data, any consent given is unlikely to be valid if the penalty for not agreeing is dismissal.

Consent must also be specific and informed. This means that the individual must know and understand what such consent will amount to. Individuals should be informed of the reasons for the transfer and, if possible, the countries involved. In addition, any identified risks involved in the transfer should be brought to the individual's attention.

8.6.3 Contract performance

Schedule 4 to the DPA allows data transfers in cases where specific types of contracts are in place or being contemplated. In the case of a contract between the exporter and the individual to whom the data relate, a transfer may be carried out if such transfer is necessary for performance of the contract or the transfer is a necessary part of pre-contractual steps taken by the exporter at the request of the individual.

In the case of a contract between the exporter and someone other than the individual, the transfer will be lawful if the contract is entered into at the individual's request or in that person's interests and the transfer is necessary for the performance or conclusion of the contract.

The contracts covered by these provisions are not restricted to the supply of goods or services, and may apply in the case of employment contracts. However, whether a transfer is necessary for the performance of a contract will depend on the nature of the goods or services provided under the contract rather than the way in which the exporter's operations are organised. In other words, a transfer will not be necessary if the only reason for it is the fact that the exporter has chosen to structure its operations in a way that involves transferring data overseas.

Therefore, if a customer books a holiday abroad through a UK travel agent, it will be necessary for the travel agent to transfer the booking details to the foreign hotel in order to fulfil the contract with the customer. However, if for pure efficiency or cost-cutting reasons, that travel agent decides to place its customer database in a computer based outside the EEA, it cannot be said that the transfer of personal data to the computer located overseas is necessary for the performance of the contract with the customer.

8.6.4 Substantial public interest

Transfers can be carried out where they are necessary for reasons of substantial public interest. This case is most likely to apply in situations where the transfer is necessary for reasons of crime prevention and detection, national security and tax collection.

The Information Commissioner advises data exporters intending to rely on this exception to adopt a similar case-by-case test to that required by s.29 of the DPA (i.e. the crime and taxation exemption). In other words, a transfer of personal data carried out under this exception must only take place to the extent that there is likely to be substantial prejudice to the public interest if the transfer does not take place.

8.6.5 Legal claims

Transfers can be made where they are necessary:

- in connection with any legal proceedings (including prospective proceedings);

- for obtaining legal advice; or otherwise for establishing, exercising or defending legal rights.

It should be noted that the legal proceedings do not necessarily have to involve the exporter or the individual in question, and that the legal rights do not have to be those of the exporter or the individual either.

8.6.6 Vital interests

Exports of personal data can lawfully be carried out where they are necessary to protect the vital interests of the particular individual. The Information Commissioner has frequently stated that this ought to relate to matters of life and death, such as the transfer of medical records of an individual who has been taken seriously ill or been involved in a serious accident abroad.

8.6.7 Public registers

Exports of personal data can also be made in respect of parts of the information available on a public register provided any restrictions on access to, or use of, the information in the register are complied with by the person to whom the information is transferred. This allows transfers of extracts from a public register of directors, shareholders or professional practitioners, for example, but would not allow transfers of the complete register. In addition, if there are conditions of use imposed by the body or organisation responsible for compiling the register, they must be honoured by the importer and any further recipients.

8.6.8 Terms approved by the Commission

An additional derogation from Art.25 is set out in Art.26(2) of the Directive, which provides that Member States may authorise a transfer, or a set of transfers, of personal data to third countries which do not ensure an adequate level of protection where the organisation wishing to transfer the data adduces adequate safeguards with respect to the protection of the privacy rights of individuals.

Article 26(4) goes on to say that such safeguards may result from certain standard contractual clauses approved by the European Commission. After more than five years of negotiations with national regulatory bodies, influential trade associations and international organisations, on 15 June 2001, the European Commission adopted a Decision setting out standard contractual clauses ensuring adequate safeguards for personal data in this context (Commission Decision 2001/497/EC of 15 June 2001 on standard contractual clauses for the transfer of personal data to third countries, OJ L181/19 of 4 July 2001).

This Decision obliges Member States to recognise that companies or organisations using these standard clauses in contracts concerning personal data transfers to countries outside the EEA are offering adequate protection to the data. Although, in principle, Member States are bound by the Commission's Decision to allow transfers on the basis of the standard contractual clauses, the data protection authorities of each country may require that a copy of the contract is deposited with them. However, this is not a requirement in the UK.

In addition, if there is a substantial likelihood that the standard contractual clauses are not being, or will not be, complied with and the continuing transfer would create an imminent risk of grave harm to individuals, the national data protection authorities may exercise their powers to prohibit or suspend any relevant transfer.

Obligations of the exporter

According to the standard contractual clauses, an EU-based exporter of personal data must warrant and undertake:

- that the processing of personal data up to the moment of the transfer is, and will continue to be, carried out in accordance with the local data protection law;
- that, if the transfer involves sensitive personal data, the relevant individuals will be informed (e.g. via a privacy policy) that their data may be transmitted to a third country without an adequate level of data protection;
- that it will make available, upon request, to any individual to whom the data relate, a copy of the standard clauses used in the transfer contract;
- that it will respond to any enquiries of any such individual in relation to the overseas transfer and processing; and
- that it will respond to any enquiries of its national data protection authority in connection with the processing carried out by the importer of the data transferred.

Obligations of the importer

The standard clauses approved by the European Commission require the overseas recipient of the data to warrant and undertake:

- that it has no reason to believe that its national legislation will affect its performance of the contract;
- that it will process the data in accordance with the so-called nine Mandatory Data Protection Principles, which represent a minimum requirement for data protection and mirror the key requirements of the

Directive in terms of purpose limitation, data quality and proportionality, transparency, security, individuals' rights, restrictions on onward
transfers, sensitive data, direct marketing and automated individual
decisions;

- that it will deal promptly and properly with all reasonable enquiries made
  by its European partner or the individuals to whom the data relate;
- that it will co-operate with any relevant national data protection
  authority investigating the transfer or the processing carried out by the
  importer;
- that it will submit, upon request of the data exporter, its data processing
  facilities for audit;
- that it will make available, upon request, to any individual to whom the
  data relate, a copy of the standard clauses used in the transfer contract.

On 27 December 2001, the European Commission adopted a second
Decision setting out standard contractual clauses for the transfer of personal
data to 'data processors' (i.e. agents or suppliers that process personal data
on behalf of the real owner or user of the data) established in non-EEA
countries that are not recognised as offering an adequate level of data protection (Commission Decision 2002/16/EC of 27 December 2001 on standard
contractual clauses for the transfer of personal data to processors established
in third countries, OJ 6/52 of 10 January 2002).

See Appendices 2 and 3 for a copy of each respective set of the original
standard contractual clauses.

However, the European Commission stated in its First Report on the
implementation of the Directive of 15 May 2003, that it intended to adopt
further Decisions on the basis of Art.26(4) so that economic operators have
a wider choice of standard contractual clauses. Accordingly, the Commission
issued a new Decision on 27 December 2004 amending its Decision of June
2001 and adding a second version to the sets of standard contractual clauses
that can be used to legitimise international transfers between data controllers.
This second version is based on an alternative draft pioneered by the
International Chamber of Commerce.

Under the original 2001 clauses, the exporter of the data has to warrant
very difficult things, such as the fact that the processing will always be carried
out in accordance with the law of the country where the exporter is based,
and that individuals will be informed if the transfer involves sensitive
personal data. In the 2004 clauses, these obligations are replaced by more
practical and achievable tasks, such as:

- ensuring that the collection, processing and transfer is in accordance
  with the laws applicable to the exporter;
- using reasonable efforts to determine that the data importer is able to
  satisfy its legal obligations under the clauses; and

- providing the importer, upon request, with copies of relevant data protection laws and references to them (not including legal advice).

In addition, some of the obligations under the 2001 clauses have been softened by the 2004 clauses, as the exporter will only be required to respond to enquiries from individuals and data protection authorities if the importer has not agreed to do so, and confidential information may be excluded from the copy of the clauses that must be made available to individuals who request them.

The 2004 clauses dealing with the importer's obligations are very detailed and precise; however, they are also more realistic than the 2001 clauses. For example, unlike under the 2001 clauses, a data importer that enters into an agreement containing the 2004 model clauses will have to warrant and undertake that:

- it has appropriate technical and organisational security measures in place;
- it has procedures in place to ensure that any third party with access to the data (including data processors) will respect and maintain the confidentiality and security of the data;
- it will identify to the data exporter a contact point within its organisation authorised to respond to enquiries concerning the processing of the personal data, and will co-operate in good faith with the data exporter and the relevant individuals and data protection authorities within a reasonable time;
- it will provide the data exporter with evidence of financial resources sufficient to fulfil its responsibilities upon request;
- it will submit its data processing facilities, data files and relevant documentation for reviewing, auditing and/or certifying by the data exporter (or any independent or impartial inspection agents or auditors selected by the data exporter and not reasonably objected to by the data importer) to ascertain compliance with the warranties and undertakings under the agreement, with reasonable notice and during regular business hours, if reasonably requested by the data exporter;
- it will not disclose or transfer the personal data to a third party data controller located outside the EEA, except in some specific cases.

A clause that has been softened is the one dealing with the impact of local laws on the ability of the data importer to comply with its data protection obligations. Under the 2004 clauses, the data importer must warrant and undertake that, at the time of entering into the agreement with the data exporter, it has no reason to believe in the existence of any local laws that would have a substantial adverse effect on the guarantees provided, and that it will inform the data exporter (which will pass such notification on to the relevant data protection authority where required) if it becomes aware of any such laws. However, even in this case, there is no provision that allows the exporter to suspend the transfer of data or terminate the contract, as in the 2001 clauses.

Similarly, the 2004 clauses place a practical limitation on the right of access by allowing data importers to deny such access in cases where requests are manifestly abusive based on unreasonable intervals or their number or repetitive or systematic nature, or for which access need not be granted under the law of the country of the data exporter. In addition, provided that a competent data protection authority has given its prior approval, access need not be granted when doing so would be likely to seriously harm the interests of the data importer or other organisations dealing with the data importer and such interests are not overridden by the interests for fundamental rights and freedoms of the individuals.

In summary, the 2004 clauses have been a very positive development in the area of international transfers of personal data. Their pragmatism and their careful drafting has been welcomed by all parties involved in a transaction concerning data transfers and, as a result, the International Chamber of Commerce is currently working on a set of alternative model clauses for transfers to data processors.

8.6.9 Authorisation by Information Commissioner

Although Schedule 4 to the DPA enables the Information Commissioner to give its individual authorisation to specific transfers, the Information Commissioner has traditionally been reluctant to encourage potential exporters to follow this route. In fact, his original Guidance Note on international dataflows of July 1999 called *The Good Practice Approach* said that applications for authorisation made by or on behalf of exporting controllers would only be considered in extremely limited circumstances, and that the Information Commissioner would expect other derogations to be relied upon before this derogation.

It is therefore not surprising that the only authorisation ever granted by the Information Commissioner for these purposes has been a class authorisation in respect of data exports that rely on the standard contractual clauses approved by the European Commission.

However, the authorisation route gained momentum following the publication of the Article 29 Working Party's Working Document (WP74) on binding corporate rules for international data transfers of 3 June 2003.[3] The Working Party believes that as long as such corporate rules are binding (both in law and in practice) and incorporate the essential content principles identified in the Working Document (WP12) of 24 July 1998, there is no reason why national regulators should not authorise multinational transfers within a group of companies.

8.7 CAN DATA EXPORTS TAKE PLACE WITHIN A MULTINATIONAL CORPORATE GROUP?

8.7.1 Intra-group Binding Corporate Rules

Data exports within a multinational corporate group are subject to the same rules as exports outside the group. However, the EU data protection regulators acknowledge the role of the so-called Binding Corporate Rules (or BCR) as a mechanism to legitimise data exports.

The concept of using the BCR to create adequate safeguards for the purposes of Art.26(2) of the Directive was devised by the Article 29 Working Party in its Working Document WP74 adopted on 3 June 2003. To assist companies in their assessment as to whether their applications encompass all the requirements of WP74, on 14 April 2005 the Article 29 Working Party developed the Model Checklist (WP108). On the same date, the Working Party issued a Working Document Setting Forth a Co-Operation Procedure for Issuing Common Opinions on Adequate Safeguards Resulting from Binding Corporate Rules (WP107). In addition to setting out the criteria for choosing a lead data protection authority, this document sets out the required process to be followed by the lead authority and the participating data protection authorities before issuing an authorisation.

In January 2007, in response to a growing requirement from businesses and their advisers for a clarification of the application process, the Working Party issued a template application form (WP133) designed to focus applicants on the content of a BCR application and also to assist those data protection authorities reviewing applications to assess whether the required elements of WP74 are contained within the application. WP133 follows the structure of WP108 and builds on its requirements. In particular, WP133 effectively does away with the requirement in WP108 for a 'background paper' in which an applicant is required to summarise how the required elements of WP74 have been satisfied in the application.

In June 2008, the Working Party issued three additional documents which must be carefully considered when seeking to rely on the BCR to legitimise data exports. These comprise a table setting out the consolidated approval criteria for the BCR (WP153), a sample framework for the structure of the BCR (WP154) and a set of frequently asked questions (WP155). The most important of the three documents is undoubtedly WP153. Although this draws on existing Working Party papers (notably WP74 and WP108) it clarifies the specific elements which must be contained in the BCR documentation and highlights the importance placed by regulators on particular aspects of the previous Working Party papers.

8.7.2 BCR practical requirements

The BCR must apply generally throughout the corporate group irrespective of the place of establishment of the members or the nationality of the individuals whose personal data are being processed or any other criteria or consideration. The Article 29 Working Party also stresses that there are two elements that must be present in all cases if the BCR are to be used to adduce safeguards for data exports: binding nature and legal enforceability.

In practice, the binding nature of the BCR implies that the members of the corporate group, as well as each employee within it, must be compelled to comply with the BCR. Legal enforceability means that the individuals covered by the scope of the BCR must become third-party beneficiaries either by virtue of the relevant national law or by contractual arrangements between the members of the corporate group. Those individuals should be entitled to enforce compliance with the BCR by lodging a complaint before the competent data protection authority and before the courts.

In addition, the Working Party's Documents include the following requirements:

1. The BCR must set up a system which guarantees awareness and implementation of the BCR both inside and outside the EU.
2. The BCR must provide for self-audits and/or external supervision by accredited auditors on a regular basis with direct reporting to the parent's board.
3. The BCR must set up a system by which individuals' complaints are dealt with by a clearly identified complaint handling department.
4. The BCR must contain clear duties of co-operation with data protection authorities so individuals can benefit from the institutional support.
5. The BCR must also contain provisions on liability and jurisdiction aimed at facilitating their practical exercise.
6. The corporate group must also accept that individuals will be entitled to take action against the group, as well as to choose the jurisdiction.
7. Individuals must be made aware that personal data are being communicated to other members of the corporate group outside the EU and the existence and the content of the BCR must be readily accessible to those individuals.

In 2008, the BCR came of age and established themselves as a proper and legitimate method for legitimising exports for multinationals that are serious about privacy and data protection compliance. In addition to the growing number of applications, there are several additional factors that evidence this.

One strong indicator is that the BCR were one of the top priorities for the Article 29 Working Party according to its Work Programme for 2008. In addition, in the past few years there has been a real change of approach amongst EU data protection authorities, who are now very receptive to the use of the BCR to legitimise personal data exports.

8.8 WHERE CAN FURTHER HELP BE FOUND?

8.8.1 European Commission – DG Internal Market

The Internal Market Directorate-General co-ordinates the European Commission's policy on the European Single Market, which aims to ensure the free movement of people, goods, services and capital within the EU. It is responsible for proposing new laws, and once laws are adopted by the European Parliament and Council, implementing an EU-wide legal framework for data protection. For further information, see **http:// ec.europa.eu/justice_home/fsj/privacy**.

8.8.2 International Chamber of Commerce – Commission on E-Business, IT and Telecoms (EBITT)

The Task Force on Protection of Personal Data of the EBITT of the International Chamber of Commerce analyses the impact of the regulatory frameworks in the area of privacy and data protection and formulates opinions on these issues. The Task Force has developed practical tools in the context of data protection compliance, such as alternative contractual clauses for transborder data flows and advisory tools with practical information about how to carry out data flows between regions with differing privacy regimes. For further information, see **www.iccwbo.org/policy/ebitt**.

8.8.3 CBI – e-Business Group

The e-Business Group of the CBI aims to influence the policy and regulatory background set by the UK Government and international bodies. In the field of data exports, the e-Business Group has produced a number of policy briefs dealing with issues such as contractual clauses and intra-group policies. For more information, see **www.cbi.org.uk/policymatrix.htm**.

8.9 PRIMARY RESOURCES ON DATA EXPORTS

All the following resources can be found from the **http://ec.europa.eu/ justice_home/fsj/privacy** homepage.

8.9.1   What does the law mean by an adequate level of protection?

Discussion Document adopted by the Article 29 Working Party on 26 June 1997 on first orientations on transfers of personal data to third countries – possible ways forward in assessing adequacy.

Working Document adopted by the Article 29 Working Party on 24 July 1998 on transfers of personal data to third countries – applying Articles 25 and 26 of the EU Data Protection Directive.

8.9.2   Which countries are regarded as safe?

Switzerland

Opinion 5/99 adopted by the Working Party on 7 June 1999 on the level of protection of personal data in Switzerland.

Commission Decision of 26 July 2000 on the adequate protection of personal data provided in Switzerland.

Hungary

Opinion 6/99 adopted by the Working Party on 7 September 1999 on the level of protection of personal data in Hungary.

Commission Decision of 26 July 2000 on the adequate protection of personal data provided in Hungary.

Canada

Opinion 2/2001 adopted by the Working Party on 26 January 2001 on the adequacy of the Canadian Personal Information and Electronic Documents Act.

Commission Decision of 20 December 2001 on the adequate protection of personal data provided by the Canadian Personal Information Protection and Electronic Documents Act.

Frequently asked questions on the Commission's adequacy finding on the Canadian Personal Information Protection and Electronic Documents Act.

Argentina

Opinion 4/2002 adopted by the Working Party on 3 October 2002 on the level of protection of personal data in Argentina.

Commission Decision of 30 June 2003 on the adequate protection of personal data in Argentina.

Guernsey

Opinion 5/2003 adopted by the Working Party on 13 June 2003 on the level of protection of personal data in Guernsey.

Commission Decision of 21 November 2003 on the adequate protection of personal data in Guernsey.

Isle of Man

Opinion 6/2003 adopted by the Working Party on 21 November 2003 on the level of protection of personal data in the Isle of Man.

Commission Decision of 28 April 2004 on the adequate protection of personal data in the Isle of Man.

What is the situation in the USA?

Opinion 1/99 adopted by the Working Party on 26 January 1999 concerning the level of data protection in the United States and the ongoing discussions between the European Commission and the United States Government.

Opinion 2/99 adopted by the Working Party on 3 May 1999 on the adequacy of the International Safe Harbor Principles issued by the US Department of Commerce on 19 April 1999.

Opinion 4/99 adopted by the Working Party on 7 June 1999 on the frequently asked questions to be issued by the US Department of Commerce in relation to the proposed Safe Harbor Principles.

Working Document adopted by the Working Party on 7 July 1999 on the current state of play of the ongoing discussions between the European Commission and the United States Government concerning the International Safe Harbor Principles.

Opinion 7/99 adopted by the Working Party on 3 December 1999 on the level of data protection provided by the Safe Harbor Principles as published together with the frequently asked questions (FAQs) and other related documents on 15 and 16 November 1999 by the US Department of Commerce.

Opinion 3/2000 adopted by the Working Party on 16 March 2000 on the EU–US dialogue concerning the Safe Harbor arrangement.

Opinion 4/2000 adopted by the Working Party on 16 May 2000 on the level of protection provided by the Safe Harbor Principles.

Commission Decision of 26 July 2000 on the adequacy of the protection provided by the Safe Harbor Privacy Principles and related frequently asked questions issued by the US Department of Commerce.

Working Document adopted by the Working Party on 2 July 2002 on the Functioning of the Safe Harbor Agreement.

8.9.3 What are the exemptions from the ban on data exports?

Terms approved by the Commission

Working Document adopted by the Working Party on 22 April 1998 on preliminary views on the use of contractual provisions in the context of transfers of personal data to third countries.

Opinion 1/2001 adopted by the Working Party on 26 January 2001 on the draft Commission Decision on standard contractual clauses for the transfer of personal data to third countries under Article 26(4) of Directive 95/46.

Commission Decision of 15 June 2001 on standard contractual clauses for the transfer of personal data to third countries.

FAQs summarising the main issues of the Decision adopted by the European Commission on standard contractual clauses and providing information to individuals and companies on how to best make use of the standard contractual clauses.

Opinion 7/2001 adopted by the Working Party on 13 September 2001 on the draft Commission Decision (version 31 August 2001) on standard contractual clauses for the transfer of personal data to data processors established in third countries under Art.26(4) of Directive 95/46.

Commission Decision of 27 December 2001 on standard contractual clauses for the transfer of personal data to processors established in third countries.

Commission Decision of 27 December 2004 amending Decision 2001/497/EC as regards the introduction of an alternative set of standard contractual clauses for the transfer of personal data to third countries.

8.9.4 Authorisation

Working Document adopted by the Article 29 Working Party on 3 June 2003 on Transfers of personal data to third countries: applying Art.26(2) of the EU Data Protection Directive to binding corporate rules for international data transfers.

Endnotes

1 See the Discussion Document (WP4) adopted by the Article 29 Working Party on 26 June 1997 on 'First Orientations on Transfers of Personal Data to Third Countries – Possible Ways Forward in Assessing Adequacy', which was later expanded by the Working Document (WP12) adopted on 24 July 1998 on 'Transfers of Personal Data to Third Countries – Applying Articles 25 and 26 of the EU Data Protection Directive'.

2   Commission Decision 2000/520/EC of 26 July 2000, OJ L215/7 of 25 August 2000. This Decision was preceded by seven Opinions by the Article 29 Working Party on the level of protection provided by the Safe Harbor Principles.

3   Working Document (WP74) adopted by the Article 29 Working Party on 3 June 2003 on 'Transfers of Personal Data to Third Countries: Applying Article 26 (2) of the EU Data Protection Directive to Binding Corporate Rules for International Data Transfers'.

CHAPTER 9

Rights

Gary Brooks

9.1 BACKGROUND

The Sixth Data Protection Principle (the Sixth Principle) states that 'personal data shall be processed in accordance with the rights of data subjects'. The aims of this chapter are twofold:

(a) to establish what are the rights of data subjects to which this Principle is relevant; and
(b) to explore each of these rights in turn, in order to ascertain what an organisation needs to do to at a practical level to comply with the Sixth Principle.

The DPA states that an organisation will contravene the Sixth Principle if, but only if:

(a) it fails to supply information pursuant to an individual's subject access request under s.7 (the 'right of access'); or
(b) it fails to comply with notices given under the following provisions of the DPA:
   (i) s.10 (the right to prevent processing likely to cause damage or distress);
   (ii) s.11 (the right to prevent processing for the purposes of direct marketing);
   (iii) s.12 (rights in relation to automated decision-taking).

The four rights mentioned in paragraphs (a) and (b) above must be exercised by the individual in writing and any of the individual notices or requests can be served by electronic means (e.g. e-mail), as long as the notice is served in legible form and is capable of being used for subsequent reference (DPA, s.64).

If an individual believes that an organisation has failed to honour his rights, he can write to the Information Commissioner for an assessment or a notice requiring compliance with the Sixth Principle. Alternatively, individuals may enforce their rights and/or claim compensation by commencing court proceedings.

The DPA is silent on the question of whether it is possible for an organisation to exclude the data protection rights enshrined within it. The better view is that a court would not hold that provisions of the DPA could be varied by contract. Further, it is likely that the Unfair Terms in Consumer Contracts Regulations 1999, SI 1999/2083 would operate to strike out any contract term which purported to exclude a consumer's rights under the DPA (for further detail, see J. Sanders, 'Personal Data as Currency', *Privacy & Data Protection*, Volume 2, Issue 4, pp.7–9).

In practice, two of the data protection rights are exercised far more frequently than the others, namely the right of subject access and the right to prevent direct marketing. These two rights affect almost every organisation that holds personal data and addressing compliance with these rights is an essential part of any data protection compliance programme. The primary focus of this chapter is, therefore, on the right of subject access and the right to prevent direct marketing.

9.2 RIGHT OF SUBJECT ACCESS

9.2.1 What is subject access?

The most important of all the data protection rights is the so-called right of access. Under this right, which is specifically set out in s.7 of the DPA, individuals are entitled, by making a written request to the organisation concerned, to be supplied with a copy of any personal data held about them (i.e. both electronic records and manual records held in structured filing systems). An individual can only make an access request in relation to personal data in respect of which he is the data subject. Subject access is the central pillar of the DPA and individuals are becoming increasingly aware of their right of access and more sophisticated and prolific in exercising it.

Strictly speaking, in order for the processing of their data to be fair (for the purposes of the First Principle of the DPA), individuals should be informed by the organisation of their right of access and how to exercise it. This provision was included in Art.10 of the Data Protection Directive (95/46/EC), although it did not actually find its way into the DPA. The simplest method of providing information relating to the right of access is in the text of the controller's privacy policy or data protection statement as follows:

> You have a right to access the personal data held about you. To obtain a copy of the personal information we hold about you, please write to us at [Address].

It should be noted that the data subject access right applies only to personal data processed by the data controller.

9.2.2 Additional rights to the right to obtain a copy of the data

The nature of the information to be provided to the individual in response to an access request will depend on the information requested in each case and whether any exemptions may apply to justify withholding disclosure of the information. Section 7 effectively contains a number of sub-rights in addition to the right to be given a copy of personal data. In particular individuals have the right to be informed whether they are the subject of personal data being processed by the controller and to be given a description of:

- the purposes for which the data are used;
- the recipients of such data;
- the source of such data (if known to the controller); and
- where automated decision-taking has taken place, information on the logic of such decision-taking (DPA, s.7(1)(d)).

A fee of up to £10 (certain other amounts are chargeable in the case of requests for access to credit files and education records) may be charged for dealing with the right of access. An organisation must comply with an access request promptly, and in any event within 40 days of receipt of:

- the information required to satisfy itself as to the identity of the person making the request; and
- (if relevant) the fee (DPA, s.7(2)).

9.2.3 Access requests made via an agent

An individual can make a subject access request through an agent, such as his solicitor. The Information Commissioner's Legal Guidance on the DPA states that 'if a data controller who receives such a request is satisfied that the individual has authorised the agent to make the request, the data controller should reply to it' (para.4.1.5).

However, if there is any doubt as to whether or not the individual has authorised the agent to make the request, then the controller must request a written authority from the individual concerned.

From a practical perspective, controllers should be extremely wary of requests made by an individual purporting to act on behalf of a friend, spouse or partner. Access requests made by an individual on behalf of a third party such as a friend/partner/spouse/work colleague should not be complied with until the data controller has received a satisfactory written authority or separate written request from the individual who is the subject of the request.

9.2.4   Access requests made on behalf of children

Data protection rights can be exercised by children. If the controller receives a request from a child and forms the view that the child understands the nature of the request, he is entitled to exercise the right and the controller must reply to the child.

If children are incapable of understanding or exercising their own rights under the DPA (for instance, because they are too young), parents can make subject access requests on their behalf.

In addition to their rights under the DPA, parents have their own independent right of access to the official educational records of their children under separate education regulations (Education (Pupil Information) (England) Regulations 2000, SI 2000/297). A detailed discussion of the subordinate legislation dealing with access to educational records is outside the scope of this chapter. More information on access to educational records is contained in the Information Commissioner's technical guidance note entitled 'Access to pupils' information held by schools in England', dated 24 January 2007 and available on the ICO website.

9.3   RESPONDING TO SUBJECT ACCESS REQUESTS

Once a controller has received an access request in a permanent form (which includes e-mail) and received payment of the fee, it is under an obligation to respond to the request promptly by supplying the relevant information in an intelligible form (e.g. by way of a copy) within the 40-day time limit (DPA, s.7(8)). A freshly typed record of the information may suffice, and this may be the most desirable way for the controller to provide access to information where the original documents have had to be edited to remove non-disclosable information.

However, the organisation is not obliged to comply with the request until it is satisfied as to the identity of the person making the request, which is discussed further at **9.3.1**. In addition, compliance with this right is limited by a number of factors. Before responding to a subject access request, the controller must consider whether:

- the information requested constitutes personal data;
- the privacy rights of third parties would be infringed by complying with the request;
- the supply of a copy of the personal data would involve disproportionate effort;
- the request is of a very general nature (i.e. the right of the controller to request more specific information regarding the information to be supplied);
- the request is similar to a request made previously by that individual; and

- the prevention of crime exemption or other general exemptions from the data subject access right apply.

The question of whether the request constitutes personal data is of greater significance as a result of the Court of Appeal decision in *Durant* v. *FSA* [2003] EWCA Civ 1746, since it is possible that some of the data requested will not constitute personal data and so will fall outside the scope of the right of access.

The checklist set out at Annex 9A is designed to set out the steps which the controller should take in order to respond properly to a subject access request, and in particular, to determine whether the individual is actually entitled to see the information requested, bearing in mind the above limitations. The key issues are discussed in greater depth below.

9.3.1 The identity of the individual making the request

The controller must be satisfied that the person making the request is in fact the data subject. The DPA does not require the controller to ask the individual for identification before responding to the request, unlike in other European jurisdictions where a copy of the passport or the national ID card must accompany the request for access. Having received a written request, the controller can generally rely on the signature of the individual and the fact that the address on the individual's letter matches the address known to the controller. Controllers should ensure that access requests sent by e-mail are accompanied by appropriate identification-verifying information (see bullet list below for suggested methods of checking identity).

However, where the controller is not completely satisfied that the person making the request is in fact the data subject, it can take advantage of an amendment to s.7(3) of the DPA (inserted by the Freedom of Information Act 2000, Sched.6, para.1) to request better proof from the individual. This provides that:

Where a data controller:
(a) reasonably requires further information in order to satisfy himself as to the identity of the person making a subject access request and to locate the information which that person seeks, and
(b) has informed him of that requirement,
the data controller is not obliged to comply with the request unless he is supplied with that further information.

If the controller is not completely satisfied that the person making the request is the data subject, it must revert to the individual promptly (and within the time limit) and request further information to verify the identity of the person making the request. Possible methods of checking identity in these circumstances include asking the individual:

- to give information which has been recorded as personal data by the controller and which the individual might be expected to know (e.g. a customer account number or password);
- to have their signature witnessed by another person who is over 18 and is not a relative; and
- to produce a document that might reasonably be expected to be in only that individual's possession (e.g. a photocopy of his passport).

9.3.2 Open-ended requests

Individuals frequently make open-ended requests for access, typically along the lines of 'Please supply a copy of all the personal data you have about me'. However, controllers may be able to take advantage of a mechanism in the DPA when faced with such a general request. Where a controller reasonably requires further information in order to locate the information which that person seeks and the controller has informed the individual of that requirement, the controller is not obliged to comply with the request unless it is supplied with that further information (DPA, s.7(3)).

It may therefore be open to the controller to write back to the individual and request more specific information to help it to narrow down the search. This may be particularly relevant in cases where complying with a request for a copy of all the personal data relating to the individual would involve disclosing hundreds of e-mails relating to the individual. Information which may assist the data controller might include general pointers such as the dates or range of dates upon which the e-mails have been sent and the names of the authors and recipients of the e-mails.

However, the limitation of this provision is that it presupposes that the individual has a certain knowledge of the circumstances in which his personal data are being processed by the controller, which may not always be the case.

In making an assessment as to whether or not an organisation has breached the DPA by requesting further information from the individual (thereby failing to respond to the request), the Information Commissioner must take a view as to whether the individual has failed to provide information that the data controller reasonably needs to narrow down the search. If so, then it is likely to be concluded that there has been no breach of the DPA. By contrast, where a controller appears to be making demands for information which the individual cannot reasonably be expected to give and where it appears that a copy of at least some of the personal data requested could be provided, then it is likely to be judged that there has been a breach.

However, where the individual has requested specific personal information as part of his request, e.g. 'Please supply all e-mails and internal memoranda from A to B relating to me between x date and y date', there is no scope for reverting to the individual and the controller should provide the specific information requested provided that none of the other exemptions or limitations apply.

More information on how to deal with open-ended requests can be found in **9.3.10**.

9.3.3   Subject access and e-mails

In practice, it can be difficult for organisations to locate and provide access to personal data held in e-mails. However, a data controller is able to request more specific information from the individual to help it locate the e-mail data (as discussed above). Controllers should also be aware of the Information Commissioner's views on this issue and specific guidance on the issue of subject access and e-mails, which is available from the ICO website.

Data controllers are not required to search through all e-mail records merely on the off-chance that somewhere there might be a message that relates to the individual who has made the access request. Some e-mails mention the individual but fall outside the scope of the DPA since these data are not processed by reference to the data subject. For example, e-mails which merely mention the individual (e.g. his name appears in the address list or 'cc' box) need not be provided as the individual is not the subject of the information. Therefore, as a general rule, a controller will only be obliged to search for those e-mails which are obviously about the individual and therefore qualify as personal data.

However, there are still likely to be some borderline cases where the e-mail concerned is not obviously about the individual, but the information may still qualify as that person's personal data, because the information concerned has an impact on the individual. As a result of the Information Commissioner's latest guidance on the personal data concept, more borderline information is now likely to qualify as personal data in the eyes of the regulator, when previously it would have fallen outside the scope of the legislation on the basis of the *Durant* principles (this issue is discussed at **9.3.7** and **9.3.8**).

9.3.4   Subject access and manual records

Where a subject access request pertains to information held in manual files, a controller may be able to deny access to the information on the basis that the information does not constitute 'data' since the filing system is not sufficiently sophisticated to qualify as a 'relevant filing system' under the DPA.

The *Durant* judgment has considerably limited the extent to which manual files are covered by the DPA. To qualify as a relevant filing system, the manual filing system must now effectively pass the following two-stage test:

1.   it must be clearly referenced or indexed so as to readily indicate at the outset whether it contains personal data about a particular individual; and

2. it must have sufficiently sophisticated search mechanisms to indicate exactly where specific personal data can be found (i.e. without the need for a manual search through the file).

It is clear from the judgment that the structure of the manual filing system must be sufficiently sophisticated so as to be 'broadly comparable with computerised records' in terms of ease of access to and retrievability of the data in the files. This is a key factor to bear in mind when assessing whether or not a filing system constitutes a 'relevant filing system'.

Only highly sophisticated manual filing systems now come within the scope of s.7; all other manual records do not. This has notable implications for businesses that operate large numbers of paper files, since the information held in such files will fall outside the scope of the DPA in many cases.

This aspect of the *Durant* judgment remains good law and has been followed in subsequent cases. The Information Commissioner's technical guidance note entitled 'Frequently asked Questions and Answers about relevant filing systems' (21 August 2007) endorses the court's approach and sets out a number of practical examples to assist data controllers in determining whether a particular manual file qualifies as a relevant filing system. It is believed that the regulator will update its guidance on relevant filing systems in due course, but at the time of publication, his approach mirrors that of the court in *Durant*.

The restrictive interpretation of relevant filing system in *Durant* was confirmed in *Smith* v. *Lloyds TSB* [2005] EWHC 246 (Ch). This case confirmed that when assessing whether a particular set of information qualifies as 'data' for the purposes of responding to a subject access request, the organisation must only consider how the information is held at the time the access request is received.

9.3.5 Does the information that is the subject of the request constitute personal data?

The primary consideration in responding to access requests is whether the information requested actually constitutes personal data. Due to the changing regulatory landscape at an EU level and a divergence in approach between the UK courts and the regulator on this issue, it remains very difficult in some circumstances to decide when a piece of information is caught by the legislation and when it is not. The interpretation of 'personal data' by the Information Commissioner has traditionally been very wide. Where an individual is capable of being identified from data which relate to that individual, then such data have generally been regarded by the Information Commissioner as 'personal data'. However, the Court of Appeal in *Durant* narrowed the definition of personal data, which has had an impact on how organisations should respond to subject access requests (since it is possible that some, if not all, of the information requested will not constitute personal data and so fall outside the scope of the individual's right of access). Certain information will obviously be personal data, e.g. an individual's name, address or salary information. However, the data controller may hold documents which merely mention the individual and the court in *Durant* considered the issue of whether such documents amount to personal data by establishing the following two-stage test for personal data:

1. the information must be biographical in a significant sense; and
2. the individual must be the focus of the information.

Lord Justice Auld explained the test at para.28, as follows:

> not all information retrieved from a computer search against an individual's name or unique identifier is personal data within the Act. Mere mention of the data subject in a document held by a data controller does not necessarily amount to his personal data. Whether it does so in any particular instance depends on where it falls in a continuum of relevance or proximity to the data subject as distinct, say, from transactions or matters in which he may have been involved to a greater or lesser degree. It seems to me that there are two notions that may be of assistance. The first is whether the information is biographical in a significant sense, that is, going beyond the recording of the putative data subject's involvement in a matter or an event that has no personal connotations, a life event in respect of which his privacy could not be said to be compromised. The second is one of focus. The information should have the putative data subject as its focus rather than some other person with whom he may have been involved or some transaction or event in which he may have figured or have had an interest, for example, as in this case, an investigation into some other person's or body's conduct that he may have instigated. In short, it is information that affects his privacy, whether in his personal or family life, business or professional capacity.

9.3.6 Practical implications of the *Durant* test for responding to access requests

In practice each record or piece of information that is the subject of the access request must be considered in turn and the controller must form a judgement as to whether or not it constitutes personal data

The second limb of the test established in *Durant*, whereby the individual must be the subject or 'focus' of the information concerned, is of huge significance in the context of subject access, given that individuals frequently use their access right as a means of investigating a grievance or complaint and in such circumstances, the focus of the information requested is likely to be the complaint, rather than the focus being the individual (even though that person is mentioned in the information). Such information would therefore fall outside the scope of personal data and outside the scope of the right of access.

The *Durant* principles remain good law and have been followed in subsequent court cases. Having previously endorsed the *Durant* approach in its official guidance on the case, in 2007 the Information Commissioner issued new guidance on the personal data concept which has shifted the emphasis away from the *Durant* tests towards a broader interpretation of the concept, which has significant implications for how organisations respond to subject access requests. This is discussed in **9.3.7** and **9.3.8**.

9.3.7   Interpretation of 'personal data' by the Information Commissioner

The Information Commissioner's Guidance on personal data follows the Opinion adopted by the influential EU Article 29 Working Party (see WP136, Opinion 4/2007) which was produced in an effort to come to a common understanding of the concept of personal data across the EU Member States.

The Personal Data Guidance is an attempt to reconcile the broad EU position and the narrow *Durant* tests applied by the UK courts, although it generally follows the broader approach taken by the Article 29 Working Party paper and is closer to the more logical interpretation of personal data set out in the Data Protection Directive.

The statutory definition of personal data has four elements as set out in the Guidance:

- 'any information';
- 'relating to';
- 'an identified or identifiable';
- 'natural person'.

The second element is normally the key issue in the context of subject access, i.e. determining the extent to which the 'information relates' to an individual so as to qualify as personal data. In *Durant*, the court determined that information relates to an individual if he is the focus of that information and if it is of biographical significance to that person.

The Personal Data Guidance provides a number of practical examples and a form of questionnaire/flowchart (the questions are set out below) to help the reader decide if a particular piece of information 'relates to' an individual. With each question below, if the answer is 'Yes', then the information is personal data, and if the answer is 'No', you go to the next question. If the answer to the last question is 'No', the information according to the Guidance is 'unlikely to be personal data'.

1.   Is the information 'obviously about' the individual or clearly linked to him?

By way of example, the information contained on computer disks lost by HMRC in the high-profile security breach in November 2007 (i.e name, address, National Insurance number, bank account details) is personal data, as it obviously is about or linked to the individuals concerned.

2. *What is the purpose of the data processing? Is the data used or is it to be used to inform or influence actions or decisions affecting an identifiable individual?*

The key question here is whether the data is used (or likely to be used) to learn something about the individual or to determine something about him. This is a new and potentially a very broad condition and it involves a degree of subjectivity.

An example is given in the guidance of two photographers taking almost identical photographs of revellers at a New Year celebration in Trafalgar Square. One photographer is a journalist taking the photo for his own archive library, the other is a police officer taking photos of the general crowd scene to identify potential troublemakers. In the hands of the journalist, the photo is not personal data as it is not being used to learn anything about an identifiable individual. However, the photo taken by the police officer may contain personal data as it was taken for the purpose of recording the actions of individuals who the police would seek to identify in the event of trouble, so they can take action against them.

3. *Does the information have any biographical significance in relation to the individual?*

This is the first of the *Durant* principles, as described above. The Information Commissioner takes a broad approach to this in the guidance by interpreting biographical significance as simply whether the data has any personal connotations. An example given in the Guidance is of meeting minutes showing that an individual attended. The fact that the individual attended at a particular time and place is biographical and qualifies as personal data and so would generally have to be provided to an individual in response to a subject access request, according to the regulator. The rest of the minutes are unlikely to be personal data about the attendees though, unless they focus on such individuals (see next question).

4. *Does the data focus or concentrate on the individual as its central theme, rather than on some other person, or some object, transaction or event?*

This is the second of the *Durant* principles. However, there is a very significant change as a result of the Article 29 Opinion which is that information can 'relate to' an individual (and therefore qualify as personal data) even if it does not focus on a specific person. If information has qualified as personal data under any of the previous headings, then it is not necessary to consider focus. The previous ICO guidance (based on *Durant*) had stated that 'information that has as its focus something other than the individual will not be personal data'. The new Guidance correctly recognises that this is not the case, with 'focus' simply being one factor which is sufficient for the information to be personal data, but one which is not actually necessary in each case. The significance of this change in the context of subject access requests is discussed further in **9.3.8**.

5. *Does the information have an 'impact' on the individual, whether in a personal, family, business or professional capacity?*

There is a degree of overlap here with the 'Purpose' test above. The Information Commissioner says that if there is a 'reasonable chance' that the information will be processed to learn, record or determine something about that individual, then it will qualify as personal data, even if it was not the data controller's intention to process the data for this purpose.

This test seems to be very broadly interpreted by the Information Commissioner, who is following the approach of the Article 29 paper, which states that 'the impact does not have to be significant, merely that the individual may be treated differently from other people on the basis of that information'.

Having reached the end of the questionnaire, it is hard to see many circumstances where borderline information will fall outside the scope of the definition, a point which will be illustrated in the case study in **9.3.8**.

9.3.8 Implications of the Information Commissioner's new interpretation of personal data for dealing with subject access requests

It is important to note that the Court of Appeal's interpretation in *Durant* (as applied in subsequent cases) remains good law in the UK and that the Information Commissioner's guidance is not legally binding. However, in practical terms, it is the Information Commissioner as the data protection regulator with whom businesses have to deal in the event of a data protection complaint or investigation. The regulator's interpretation of personal data (and how *Durant* fits into the concept) cannot realistically be ignored.

The new approach of the regulator on the 'relates to' aspect of the personal data definition is having a significant (and potentially adverse) impact on those companies that are faced with difficult and wide-ranging subject access requests, typically made in the context of a dispute or grievance. Until now, businesses have often been able to take a robust approach based on *Durant* and fend off (at least in part) such wide-ranging requests by stating that the information does not relate to the individual because its focus is not on the individual, but on his complaint or the broader matter in which he is involved and therefore it falls outside his right of access.

The new Guidance, however, makes it clear that information can 'relate to' an individual (and therefore qualify as personal data) even if it does not focus on a specific person, which can make it hard to decide if certain information is covered. For example, there are practical difficulties for businesses in deciding to what extent video images of general crowd scenes (of the type recorded by CCTV) should be provided in response to subject access requests.

Let's take a hypothetical case study: Mr Smith makes a written complaint to a retailer, having purchased eggs as a customer which were salmonella-infested. The retailer carries out an investigation into the complaint. Whilst the investigation is ongoing, Mr Smith makes a subject access request to the retailer for 'everything you hold about me, including all e-mails and internal correspondence'.

There are internal e-mails between staff members about how to deal with Mr Smith's complaint, which mention his name. Do these e-mails relate to Mr Smith so as to constitute his personal data? Under the *Durant* two-stage test, it is not likely that the content of the e-mails is biographical, or focuses on Mr Smith, rather the e-mails are likely to focus instead on the subject of his complaint and so these e-mails would not qualify as his personal data.

However, working through the questionnaire in the Personal Data Guidance and looking at the final question in particular, the data contained in the e-mails are likely to have an 'impact' on Mr Smith's rights and interests, since the outcome of the retailer's investigation would have such an impact even if its purpose was only to evaluate the complaint. It may be then, that such information would qualify as personal data under the regulator's test (when under *Durant* principles it would clearly fall outside), but the position is not clear and depends on how widely this 'impact' condition is interpreted.

This divergence between the narrow approach of the courts and the broad approach of the regulator to the interpretation of personal data is unsatisfactory and creates uncertainty for data controllers in deciding whether information has to be provided in response to a subject access request.

In conclusion, with regard to how to interpret 'personal data' when dealing with subject access requests, the cautious data controller will follow strictly the Information Commissioner's broader approach to personal data, given that it is the regulator with whom the business has to deal in the event of an individual complaint.

However, it is perfectly legitimate when dealing with a particularly onerous subject access request which is clearly made in the context of a dispute or litigation, to adopt a robust, risk-based approach in relation to that information which relates to the broader matter/dispute by arguing that it is not personal data based on *Durant* principles (*Durant* is, after all, still binding law).

9.3.9 Third-party information

In many circumstances, responding to an access request may involve providing information relating to another individual who can be identified from that information (third-party information). For example, if the individual has requested copies of e-mails relating to him, e-mails by their very nature are likely to contain personal data relating to third parties. This can give rise to a conflict between the right of access of the person making the request and the right to respect for the private life of the third party. When dealing with such requests, the controller must be extremely sensitive, and give proper consideration, to this potential conflict before deciding whether to disclose third-party information. It should be noted that the issue of third-party information arises only where the data controller cannot comply with the subject access request without disclosing third-party information. As Lord Justice Auld commented in *Durant*, 'the data controller, whose primary obligation is to provide information, not documents, can, if he chooses to provide that information in the form of a copy document, simply redact such third-party information because it is not a necessary part of the data subject's personal data'.

The factors to which the controller must give consideration in deciding whether, or to what extent, it is legally required to disclose third-party information in response to an access request are set out in s.7(4) of the DPA as follows:

> Where a data controller cannot comply with the request without disclosing information relating to another individual who can be identified from that information, he is not obliged to comply with the request unless:
> (a) the other individual has consented to the disclosure of the information to the person making the request, or
> (b) it is reasonable in all the circumstances to comply with the request without the consent of the other individual.

Step 1 – Provide as much information as possible without revealing the identity of a third party

The controller should consider to what extent it is possible to communicate the information sought without disclosing any third-party information. In considering whether a third party can be identified from the information being disclosed, the controller should take into account not only the information being disclosed but also any other information which it reasonably believes is likely to be in or to come into the possession of the person making the request (DPA, s.8(7)). The controller should give as much information as possible without revealing the identity of the third party.

The Information Commissioner's Legal Guidance states that if a controller can protect the identity of the third party just by deleting the actual name or referring to, for example, Mr X, the controller must provide the information amended in this way (para.4.1.4). CCTV footage of an individual (in a shop, for example) will typically reveal the images of other individuals so that where possible, steps must be taken to blur the identities of these third parties before disclosing the footage in response to an access request. Controllers should refer to the Information Commissioner's Code of Practice on CCTV for information on how to respond to CCTV subject access requests, which is available on the ICO website.

However, it may be the case that the individual making the request will still be able to identify the third party even if the third party's name is deleted, or it may not be possible to disguise the third party's identity. In such circumstances, the controller must not disclose the third-party information without considering steps 2 to 5 below.

Step 2 – Has the third party consented to the disclosure of his information?

Although not directly required by the DPA to do so, the data controller should take reasonable steps to seek the consent of the third party to the disclosure of his information to the person making the request. If the third party does consent, the controller will be obliged to comply with the request. Where the controller is unable to obtain consent or consent has not been given, the controller must consider steps 3 and 4 below.

Step 3 – Is it reasonable in all the circumstances to disclose without the third party's consent?

Where consent to the disclosure of third-party information has not been given or the data controller is unable to seek consent, the controller should assess whether it is reasonable in all circumstances to disclose without consent (DPA, s.7(4)(b)).

Section 7(6) highlights four factors to be taken into account by the data controller in determining whether it is 'reasonable' to comply with the access request without the consent of the third party (these factors are not exclusive):

    (a) any duty of confidentiality owed to the other individual,
    (b) any steps taken by the controller with a view to seeking the consent of the other individual,
    (c) whether the other individual is capable of giving consent, and
    (d) any express refusal of consent by the other individual.

The Information Commissioner has provided further guidance on the issue of deciding whether it is reasonable to disclose the information without the third party's consent (available on the ICO website). In addition to the statutory factors mentioned above, when assessing whether it is reasonable to disclose without the third-party's consent, the controller should consider factors such as the nature of the third party information, whether it is sensitive and whether its release will damage the third party.

The court in *Durant* said that it is appropriate to ask what, if any, legitimate interests the individual has in disclosure of the identity of another individual named in or identifiable from personal data.

Section 7(4) contemplates a two-stage thought process. Is the information about the third party necessarily part of the personal data that the individual has requested? If so, how critical is the third-party information to the legitimate protection of the privacy of the individual making the request, when balanced against the existence or otherwise of any obligation of confidence to the third party or any other sensitivity of the third-party disclosure sought?

Where the third party is a recipient of the data and he might act on the data to the disadvantage of the person making the request, the latter's right to protect his privacy may weigh heavily and obligations of confidence may be non-existent or of less weight. Equally, where the third party is the source of information, the person making the request may have a strong case for his identification if he needs to take action to correct some damaging inaccuracy, though consideration for the obligation of confidence to the source or some other sensitivity may have to be weighed in the balance.

Step 4 – Is there a duty of confidence owed to the third party?

Of the factors to be taken into account in deciding whether it is reasonable to disclose without the third party's consent (as set out in step 3), perhaps the most significant is whether a duty of confidence arises between the data controller and the third party. Controllers should note that the fact that there may be a duty of confidence does not amount to an absolute basis on which to refuse access – it is merely one factor to be taken into account in determining whether it is reasonable to disclose. There may be circumstances where it may still be reasonable to disclose third-party information even where a duty of confidentiality clearly exists.

Whether there is a duty of confidence is a question of fact to be determined in each case and will be determined by the existing law of confidence. Even if the third party's identity is known to the individual making the request, this does not prevent a duty of confidentiality arising in respect of the third party information.

EXAMPLE

Miss X applies for a job at OIC Ltd. Her job application is unsuccessful. Miss X makes a subject access request to OIC Ltd to request a copy of a reference which was obtained by OIC Ltd from her previous employer. (Miss X believes that the reference was unfavourable and may have prejudiced her job application.) OIC Ltd asks the author of the reference if he consents to the disclosure of the reference to Miss X. The author refuses to consent on the basis that there was an expectation and understanding between the author and OIC Ltd that the reference would remain confidential. OIC Ltd has managed to ascertain that Miss X knows the identity of the author so that it cannot comply with the request simply by masking the author's identity. Should OIC Ltd comply with Miss X's access request?

The issue here is posed by s.7(4), namely whether it is reasonable 'in all the circumstances' to disclose the third-party information (relating to the author of the reference) without the consent of the third party. There appears to be an expectation of confidentiality on the part of the author of the reference and a duty of confidence exists between OIC Ltd and the author. OIC Ltd can point to the fact that disclosing the reference would breach the duty of confidence with the third-party author. OIC Ltd can also rely on the fact that the author has refused to give his consent to the disclosure of the reference (see DPA, s.7(6)(d)). OIC Ltd concludes that the combination of these factors makes it unreasonable for it to disclose the reference without the third-party author's consent and it therefore correctly withholds the reference.

The Information Commissioner's Technical Guidance Note entitled 'Dealing with subject access requests involving other people's information' (10 August 2007) states that where a clear duty of confidence arises between the controller and the third party, it will usually be reasonable to withhold the third-party information. If the third-party individual has consented to the disclosure, then it must be disclosed and in such circumstances there will be no breach of the duty of confidence owed to that individual.

In summary, the Information Commissioner's view is that where consent has not been given and the controller is not satisfied that it would be reasonable to disclose third-party information without it, the safer course for the controller is to withhold the information. (For further guidance see the Guidance Note, available from the ICO website.)

9.3.10 Disproportionate effort

A data controller is not obliged to supply a copy of the information requested where the supply of a copy in permanent form is not possible or would involve 'disproportionate effort' on the part of the controller, or where the data subject agrees otherwise (DPA, s.8(2)).

It will be a question of fact in each case whether supplying a copy of the information would involve disproportionate effort. In practice, the factors that a controller must consider are as follows:

- the cost of provision of the information;
- the length of time it may take to provide the information;

- how difficult or otherwise it may be for the controller to provide the information; and
- the size of the organisation to which the request has been made.

The fact that the controller has to expend a substantial amount of effort and/or cost in providing the information does not necessarily mean that the Information Commissioner will reach the decision that the controller can legitimately rely upon the disproportionate effort ground. In certain circumstances, the Information Commissioner would consider that a quite considerable effort could reasonably be expected.

All of the factors must therefore always be balanced against the prejudicial effect to the individual of not providing a copy of the information. For example, in the context of a subject access request made by an employee, an employer should only rely on the disproportionate effort exemption from providing a copy in exceptional circumstances, given the significance of employment records and the fact that denying an individual access to his employment record is likely to have a prejudicial effect on him.

If the controller seeks to rely on the disproportionate effort argument, it should document the reasons for its decision and explain these to the individual via a written response.

A crucial point is that the disproportionate effort exemption only applies to the obligation to provide a permanent copy of the information, according to s.8(2). Therefore, even if the controller can rely on the disproportionate effort exemption, it must consider whether there is an alternative method of making the information available to the individual, for example by inviting him to attend the controller's premises in order to view the physical files there.

Proportionality as it applies to the search for personal data – the Ezsias *case*

Ezsias v. *Welsh Ministers* [2007] All ER (D) 65 (Dec) has established that proportionality should apply not just to the supply of a copy of the data, but also to the extent to which organisations have to commit time and expense in searching for the data when responding to a subject access request. This case is a welcome development for organisations faced with particularly onerous subject access requests, although the decision is somewhat controversial and it remains to be seen whether this principle will be followed in subsequent cases. (To remain updated with developments on this case, see *Privacy & Data Protection* (**www.pdpjournals.com/privacy_data_protection**). See also 'Implications of the Ezsias case for subject access: proportionality may apply to searches of data' in Volume 8, Issue 5 of that journal.)

Mr Ezsias worked as a consultant surgeon in a Welsh hospital and was dismissed from his employment in 2005. In response he commenced proceedings in the Employment Tribunal on the basis that he was a 'whistleblower' and therefore his dismissal was automatically unfair. He wrote to the Welsh Assembly asking them to investigate these matters.

In order to obtain information to assist in his Employment Tribunal claim, Mr Ezsias then made five wide-ranging subject access requests to the Assembly, the last of which was for 'all materials and documents whether in paper or electronic format ... memos, letters notes (including e-mails), records (whatever medium they were recorded) which are connected to me, any decision, consideration etc related to me . . .'.

The Assembly applied the *Durant* tests and withheld much of the information on the basis that it was not his personal data under the DPA (i.e. that the focus of such data was not on Mr Ezsias but on the broader matter in which he happened to be involved). Crucially, the Assembly restricted the scope of its search for personal data to certain departments.

Mr Ezsias was not happy with the Assembly's response and considered that its search was insufficient and that he had therefore not been provided with all the information to which he was entitled. He therefore sought a court order requiring the Assembly to provide him with the further personal data for the stated purpose of assisting his Tribunal claim.

On the question of whether the Assembly was justified in withholding information by restricting the scope of its search, the judge held that the DPA only requires the data controller to carry out a 'reasonable and proportionate search' for the information requested and the Assembly had satisfied this requirement on the facts. The Assembly's decision to exclude certain departments from the scope of the search for information was considered to be 'reasonable and proportionate', at least in part because the Assembly was able to satisfy the court that it was unlikely that any other department would hold any personal data relating to Mr Ezsias.

The judge referred to both the £10 administration fee and the £600 fee limit (the latter is relevant only to public authorities when complying with subject access requests for unstructured personal data) as giving 'some context for reasonableness in the context of [the] search'.

The judge's reasoning seems to be that it could not have been the intention of the EU legislators or the UK Parliament for the subject access right to place an obligation on data controllers to act in a way which was 'unreasonable or disproportionate'.

On the issue of whether the requested information was personal data, it

236

is of interest that the court followed the prior decision in *Durant* (as it was bound to do) and it did not cite the Information Commissioner's Guidance Note. Instead, the court held that in almost all cases the disputed information withheld by the Assembly related to Mr Ezsias's complaint and not to him as an individual and so it did not qualify as personal data under *Durant* principles.

The judge also explained that the DPA gives a right of access to data, not to disclosure of documents, and that Mr Ezsias had not understood this distinction in seeking to use the right of subject access as a litigation tool. He stated that the court may exercise its discretion against a claimant using subject access as a litigation tool, since the disclosure process under the Civil Procedure Rules is the more appropriate method of obtaining documents.

How to deal with a wide-ranging subject access request

When faced with a broad subject access request for 'all information about me', determining what is a reasonable and proportionate search will be a question of fact in each case. It is up to the data controller to set the parameters of what is a reasonable search and, if a particular business area or set of data is to be excluded from the search, the organisation must be able to quantify the potential time, cost and effort involved in deciding not to search the excluded location and provide the data. It is a high threshold and there will still certainly be cases where a reasonable and proportionate search is costly, onerous and time-consuming. The following practical points should be considered when faced with a broad subject access request.

Find out from the requester what information he really wants and define the parameters of the search accordingly (as explained in **9.3.2**). This has always been a useful and legitimate tactic and can result in limiting the range of dates for the search or only searching certain departments or e-mail inboxes, for example.

If it is not possible to narrow the confines of the search by reaching agreement with the requester as suggested above, an assessment should be made as to whether the level of effort and expense involved in searching for and producing copies of the requested information is disproportionate. It may be that some of the information requested can be located and provided to the individual relatively easily, but the sheer amount of information requested is such that searching for and providing the remainder of the information would involve the organisation expending a level of effort and expense which is wholly disproportionate and unreasonable.

There is certainly now greater scope for relying on the disproportionate effort argument in a wider context, i.e. for the search activities, as well as the supply of the data, particularly if the organisation is dealing with a persistent requester who is using the right of access as a litigation weapon. If seeking to rely on disproportionate effort to deny access to information, the data controller must quantify in detail the likely cost, time and effort involved in searching for the required information and record this in writing. Similarly, the organisation must be able to justify why any databases/manual filing systems are excluded from the search (on the basis that they are unlikely to contain personal data or that the costs/effort involved in searching them is disproportionate).

If seeking to rely on the disproportionate effort argument, it should be recognised that the Information Commissioner takes a narrow view of what constitutes disproportionate effort (in terms of the level of difficulty, costs and time involved).

9.3.11 Similar requests

A data controller does not have to comply with a subsequent similar or identical request from an individual unless 'a reasonable interval' has elapsed since the controller dealt with the previous request. The DPA says that in considering what is a 'reasonable interval' regard shall be had to 'the nature of the data, the purpose for which the data are processed and the frequency with which the data are altered' (DPA, s.8(4)). There is no set period within which repeat requests are prohibited.

9.3.12 General exemptions

In some cases, personal data can be legitimately excluded from the scope of an access request if the information falls within one of the general exemptions in the DPA. Subject access is one of the 'subject information provisions' (DPA, s.27(2)(b)), and so many of the general exemptions will apply to subject access requests. For example, legally privileged information, confidential references given by the controller, certain price-sensitive data and some self-incriminating data may be withheld. A full list of the general exemptions which apply to subject access is provided in Annex 9B.

In practice, the most common exemption allows personal data to be withheld where disclosure to the person making the request would prejudice the prevention or detection of crime.

9.3.13 Practical problems and solutions

Individuals are increasingly using subject access to further a complaint or grievance. The typical scenario is when a customer with a complaint or a disgruntled ex-employee with a grudge against the organisation concerned makes a detailed subject access request in the knowledge that the organisation will have to resort to spending a considerable amount of management time in locating the information requested in order to comply with the request. It was clearly not the intention of the Data Protection Directive for subject access to be used for vexatious purposes. However, there is nothing in the DPA or the Directive that requires an individual to provide a motive for making an access request, since it is an absolute right and the data controller must respond to the request. This is discussed further in **9.3.14**.

Controllers faced with numerous access requests should ensure that they have a proper data retention and destruction policy. For example, if a controller were to adopt a policy to delete CCTV images at the end of each week, then the likelihood of the controller having to comply with repeated subject access requests from individuals for their CCTV images is reduced because the controller would no longer hold the data requested at the time the request is made. Proper data retention and destruction policies assist the business in complying with its obligations under the Fifth Principle of the DPA.

Controllers need to have appropriate procedures in place to ensure that they are able to respond to requests within the 40-day time limit. Staff should be educated so that they are able to recognise, and know how to deal with, access requests and controllers may find it useful to have standard acknowl-edgement letters and also a standard form on which to ask individuals to provide further details to help find the information requested. Checklists for dealing with subject access requests (see Annex 9A) are also useful as a starting point in producing a subject access response procedure.

9.3.14 Subject access in litigation

Subject access is increasingly being used as a tactical measure in litigation as a means of obtaining evidence circumventing the pre-action disclosure rules, particularly in cases where the individual making the request is the potential claimant, e.g. in unfair dismissal (as in the case of Mr Ezsias above) or personal injury cases. It is important to note that the right of subject access is freestanding and there is nothing to stop an individual exercising it in the context of litigation, as Mr Ezsias did in relation to his unfair dismissal case, as discussed above.

If a data controller receives a request from an individual who seems to be bearing a grudge or requesting a range of specific documents, the controller should promptly make the necessary checks to determine whether the indi-vidual is in actual or threatened litigation with the controller. Where the controller suspects that the request is being used as a weapon in litigation against it, it may legitimately limit the scope of its compliance with the request by relying wherever possible on the limitations to the right of access regarding both third-party information and disproportionate effort. In addition, the controller may be able to rely on the privilege exemption, which includes both solicitor/client and litigation privilege.

However, perhaps the most significant method of limiting the scope of compliance with a subject access request made by an individual in con-templation of litigation is for the controller to argue that the information concerned does not constitute personal data and therefore falls outside the scope of the request. In cases where a controller considers that a subject access request is being used by an individual as a tool to obtain information in connection with a complaint or potential claim against the organisation or a third party, it is likely that at least some of the information will fall outside the scope of the DPA despite the fact that the individual is mentioned in the record, since the focus of the data would be the actual dispute or complaint, rather than the individual.

As a consequence of the Information Commissioner's new broader approach to the interpretation of personal data, however, more of the information requested by an individual in the context of a dispute is likely to qualify as personal data (if the regulator's flowchart is followed). However, as mentioned in **9.3.8**, it is perfectly legitimate when dealing with a particularly onerous subject access request which is clearly made by an individual in the context of a dispute or litigation, to adopt a robust, risk-based approach in relation to that information which relates to the broader matter/dispute by arguing that it is not personal data based on *Durant* principles. The Information Commissioner is obliged to follow the interpretation of the DPA established by the courts. Obviously, the data controller must be aware that the Information Commissioner may ultimately disagree with the controller's interpretation of personal data and order disclosure of the information after an exchange of arguments/correspondence.

Whilst *Durant* may assist data controllers in arguing that some or all of the information requested does not constitute personal data, it does not provide authority for organisations to simply refuse to comply with subject access requests made by individuals who have commenced or who are contemplating litigation. This point is made by the Information Commissioner in his technical guidance note entitled 'Subject access requests and legal proceedings' (29 May 2005):

> The right of subject access is one of the cornerstones of Data Protection legisla-tion. If a data controller were able to avoid complying with a subject access request in circumstances where the data subject was contemplating or had begun legal proceedings it would seriously undermine this fundamental right.
>
> However, the courts do have discretion as to whether to grant an order under section 7(9) and may be reluctant to exercise that discretion where it is clear that the purpose of the request is to fuel separate legal proceedings and, importantly, where the discovery rules under the Civil Procedure Rules would provide a more appropriate route to obtaining the information sought. The Commissioner is also likely to take such matters into account when considering whether to exercise his enforcement powers under section 40.

It is clear from cases such as *Ezsias* and *Durant* that the courts are more sympathetic than the Information Commissioner to the position of data controllers in cases where the right of subject access is being used to further a dispute or claim by the individual. Whilst the right of access will always be a fundamental privacy right, these decisions are recognition that something does need to be done in exceptional cases to redress the balance in favour of data controllers who are sometimes faced with a wholly disproportionate burden where the right of access is being used as a litigation weapon. Perhaps reform of the subject access provisions of the EU Data Protection Directive is the preferred way of redressing this balance, as this is not just a UK problem.

Compliance with the right of access may, in rare cases, potentially expose the controller to civil litigation from the individual who is the subject of the request. Difficulties can arise where disclosure of information to the individual would reveal information which is offensive or defamatory in nature relating to the individual who is the subject of the request. The typical case is where the organisation receives an access request from a troublesome customer who has previously made a complaint and in dealing with the complaint, the organisation's customer services representatives have previously typed derogatory comments about the customer in internal e-mails or memoranda. Having exercised his right of access, the customer is generally entitled to be provided with all the e-mails and other documents containing opinions and other information relating to him (provided he is the focus of the information concerned). Once the individual has received these documents, it may result in him bringing a claim for defamation, for example.

The immediacy and informality of e-mail in particular can lead to potential claims for defamation and breach of confidentiality. Controllers should therefore ensure that all employees are made aware that they should be objective when making reference to other individuals in written communications (particularly e-mails) and refrain from making comments about individuals which are subjective or derogatory in nature since these comments are potentially disclosable to the individual in the event that he makes an access request.

9.3.15   Consequences of non-compliance

Not complying with an individual's access request could expose the business to the scrutiny of the Information Commissioner should the individual request an assessment of his case under s.42. Under the DPA, where the Information Commissioner considers that an organisation was not justified in withholding the information and has contravened the right of access, it may issue a formal Enforcement Notice requiring full disclosure. An individual can also apply to a court for a specific order to make the controller give the information which it has failed to provide (DPA, s.7(9)).

241

9.4 RIGHT TO PREVENT DIRECT MARKETING

In practice, the data protection right which is most likely to be encountered by businesses is the right of individuals to require the cessation of direct marketing. Section 11(1) of the DPA states the following:

> An individual is entitled at any time by notice in writing to a data controller to require the data controller at the end of such period as is reasonable in the circumstances to cease, or not to begin, processing for the purposes of direct marketing personal data in respect of which he is the data subject.

The DPA does not prevent a business from sending anyone a marketing communication, provided that the individual has been informed that his data will be used for direct marketing purposes (to comply with the information provision obligation in the First Principle of the DPA) and provided that the business is also able to meet one of the 'fair processing' conditions in Schedule 2 to the DPA in respect of this use of personal data. However, s.11 provides that individuals have the right to object to the use of their data for direct marketing purposes and businesses must therefore honour all 'opt-out' requests.

This right, as with all other rights in the DPA, must be exercised in writing. However, it need not be in any particular form and, unlike the right of subject access, there is no requirement for a business to respond to the individual as a result of receiving it.

Giving individuals the opportunity to opt out of marketing communications (e.g. via a tick box) is standard data protection practice that pre-dates the DPA and it is a legal requirement to provide an opt-out address when sending electronic marketing communications (this is discussed in **9.5.7**). In addition, offering a way to facilitate the exercise of this right also contributes to complying with the obligation to process data 'fairly' as set out in the First Principle of the DPA.

'Direct marketing' is defined in the DPA for the purposes of s.11 as meaning the communication (by whatever means) of any advertising or marketing material which is directed to particular individuals. The Commissioner adopts a broad interpretation of what constitutes 'direct marketing' as covering a wide range of activities which will apply not just to the offer for sale of goods or services, but also the promotion of an organisation's aims and ideals. This would include a charity or a political party making an appeal for funds or support and, for example, an organisation whose campaign is designed to encourage individuals to attend a public meeting or rally.

Since the adoption of the original Data Protection Directive (95/46/EC), the advent of SMS and e-mail have provided new marketing opportunities for businesses engaged in direct marketing activities. However, just as the technology has developed, so too has the legislation governing how these means of communication can be used to send promotional information. While the right to opt out is enshrined in the DPA, it is necessary to consider each different means of communication in turn as stricter rules apply to the sending of unsolicited marketing communications sent by e-mail and SMS in particular.

A table summarising the law relating to the various modes of direct marketing is set out in the table at Annex 9C.

9.5 HOW TO COMPLY WITH THE RIGHT TO PREVENT DIRECT MARKETING

In addition to honouring the individual's opt-out right (as enshrined in the DPA), organisations engaging in direct marketing must also comply with three other complementary regulatory regimes (the second of which is a self-regulation regime, rather than a legal requirement as such):

1. the Privacy and Electronic Communications (EC Directive) Regulations 2003, SI 2003/2426 (PEC Regulations) which cover the use of the telephone, fax, e-mail and SMS for marketing purposes;
2. the British Code of Advertising, Sales Promotion and Direct Marketing produced and enforced by the Committee of Advertising Practice (the CAP Code);
3. The Consumer Protection from Unfair Trading Regulations 2008 (CPUT Regulations); and
4. the Electronic Commerce (EC Directive) Regulations 2002, SI 2002/2013 (E-Commerce Regulations).

9.5.1 The Privacy and Electronic Communications (EC Directive) Regulations 2003

The PEC Regulations provide a further layer of regulation for marketing telephone calls, faxes, e-mails and SMS. The PEC Regulations replaced the Telecommunications (Data Protection and Privacy) Regulations 1999, SI 1999/2093 and implemented in the UK Directive 2002/58/EC on the processing of personal data and the protection of privacy in the electronic communications sector (E-Privacy Directive).

9.5.2 The British Code of Advertising, Sales Promotion and Direct Marketing

In addition to the legal regime established by the DPA and the PEC Regulations, all UK organisations carrying out direct marketing or any other non-broadcast marketing communications must comply with the self-regulation regime in the form of the British Code of Advertising, Sales Promotion and Direct Marketing (the CAP Code). The 11th edition of the CAP Code was launched by the Committee of Advertising Practice in March 2003 and it is administered and enforced by the Advertising Standards Authority (a copy of the CAP Code is available at **www.cap.org.uk**).

The CAP Code stresses the importance of transparency and individuals' consent in the context of direct marketing and has been updated to cover the use of new media (in particular, e-mail and SMS) for promotional purposes. In practice, the CAP Code effectively mirrors the DPA and the PEC Regulations, so that organisations carrying out direct marketing will generally be complying with the CAP Code if their marketing operations are carried out in accordance with the established legal regime.

The application of the DPA, the PEC Regulations, the CAP Code, the CPUT Regulations and the E-Commerce Regulations will now be considered by examining how they apply to the following methods of direct marketing: post, telephone, fax, automated calling systems, e-mail and SMS.

9.5.3   Marketing by post

Direct marketing by post should be carried out in compliance with the DPA. Section 11 requires a controller to honour any request from an individual not to receive marketing communications by post. Before sending a marketing mail shot, an organisation must ensure that it does not send it to individuals who have previously indicated that they do not wish to receive marketing communications. A failure to honour an individual's opt-out request may lead the Information Commissioner to take enforcement action against the company.

In addition, businesses should ensure that their mailing lists are screened against the register maintained by the Mailing Preference Service (MPS); this is a best practice issue and is not a requirement of the DPA. The MPS is run by the Direct Marketing Association and forms a central register of individuals who have indicated that they do not wish to receive written marketing communications. If a company mails an individual who is registered on the MPS, it will be breaching the CAP Code, which mirrors s.11 in requiring businesses to honour opt-out requests. The Advertising Standards Authority has been willing to take enforcement action against companies for failing to honour an individual's opt-out right in breach of the CAP Code (see **www.asa.org.uk/asa/adjudications/public** for details of adjudications concerning postal marketing).

9.5.4   Telephone marketing

With regard to telephone marketing, the PEC Regulations state that a business cannot make unsolicited marketing calls to an individual's phone number where that individual has either told the business that he objects to such calls or where the phone number has been registered on the Telephone Preference Service (TPS) (reg.21). The TPS is a central register of individuals who have indicated that they do not wish to receive marketing calls (**www.tpsonline.org.uk/tps**). Unlike with the MPS, businesses are required by law to consult the TPS register before engaging in telephone marketing to individuals. Corporate subscribers were not given a right to register with the TPS in the PEC Regulations. However, as a result of a subsequent amendment to the PEC Regulations, UK businesses are now eligible to register their phone numbers on the TPS (see the Privacy and Electronic Communications (EC Directive) (Amendment) Regulations 2004, SI 2004/1039). Registration is free for corporate subscribers, as it is for individuals. However, corporate subscribers are required to register in writing (individuals may also register by phone) and the corporate TPS subscription has to be renewed annually.

Since the PEC Regulations came into force, the Information Commissioner has taken enforcement action against numerous organisations who have made unsolicited marketing calls to numbers that are registered on the TPS or to individuals who have previously indicated to the organisation that they object to receiving marketing communications. Typically, the Commissioner requires the organisation to sign a formal undertaking to cease making unsolicited marketing calls in breach of the legislation and this undertaking is then published on the ICO website (see, for example, the undertaking signed by the Carphone Warehouse Group Plc on 18 November 2006).

9.5.5 Fax marketing

The PEC Regulations have not changed the existing law in relation to fax marketing. It is unlawful under the PEC Regulations to send an unsolicited sales and marketing fax to an individual (which includes consumers, sole traders and, except in Scotland, partnerships) without their prior consent (opt-in) (regs.20(1) and 20(2)). The Information Commissioner has been willing to take enforcement action against companies who have sent unsolicited marketing faxes without obtaining the recipient's consent.

A lesser level of protection extends to corporate subscribers, who have the right to opt out of receiving marketing faxes by notifying the sender that such communications should not be sent to that number (reg.20(1)(b)) or by registering on the Fax Preference Service. The Fax Preference Service must be consulted and respected prior to sending marketing faxes to businesses and individuals.

Since 2003, the Information Commissioner has issued formal enforcement notices against a large number of companies and individuals for unsolicited marketing faxes in breach of the PEC Regulations (see, for example, the case of Recovery Services Limited of 6 February 2008, published in the Enforcement section of the ICO website).

9.5.6 Automated calling systems

Automated systems which operate direct marketing functions without human intervention are unlawful unless the individual has notified the caller that he consents to such communications being made (PEC Regulations, reg.19).

In 2006, the Information Tribunal upheld a decision of the Information Commissioner against the Scottish National Party (SNP) in the leading case to date on reg.19.

Prior to the General Election in 2005, the SNP made a considerable number of automated calls to households in Scotland. These households were played a message from Sir Sean Connery urging them to vote for the SNP but they had not given their consent to such automated calls. Furthermore the SNP, despite trying to avoid doing so, had made some automated calls to voters registered with the TPS. The Information Commissioner's Office had consistently made it clear to political parties that it regarded canvassing calls as 'direct marketing' and therefore within the remit of the PEC Regulations.

The Commissioner commenced enforcement action against the SNP for breaching the PEC Regulations and the SNP appealed to the Information Tribunal. The Tribunal found that the 'Regulations do apply to political parties and their campaigning activities' and that a phone call seeking support or funds amounts to 'direct marketing'. The SNP had therefore contravened reg.19 by not obtaining the consent of the voters before making the automated calls. It noted that the SNP had made an effort to avoid calling those voters registered with the TPS; however, this is not applicable in the case of automated calls, and this was cited as evidence of the SNP believing that the Regulations did apply to it.

As well as indicating that breaches of the strict rules surrounding auto-mated calls will not be tolerated, this case serves as a reminder to businesses that the regulator is prepared to take a broad view on what is 'direct marketing'. Any communication intended to promote the aims or ideals of an organisation will qualify as marketing and it is clear from the Tribunal's decision that the PEC Regulations apply to all not-for-profit organisations and political parties.

9.5.7 E-mail and SMS

Prior consent general rule

For the purposes of this section, the term 'e-mail' meaning 'electronic mail' will also include SMS and MMS messages (as the same rules apply to all

these forms of electronic marketing). Unlike marketing by post and telephone, as a general rule under the PEC Regulations, the use of e-mail for
direct marketing purposes is now only allowed on an opt-in basis (i.e. with
the recipient's prior consent) (reg.22(2)). This provision is a notable departure
from the opt-out regime established by the DPA and is aimed at regulating
the use of unsolicited e-mail or 'spam' for marketing purposes.

The PEC Regulations make a distinction between 'individual subscribers'
(e.g. john.smith@hotmail.com) and 'corporate subscribers' (e.g. john.smith@
company-name.com). An individual using his work e-mail address is a corporate subscriber (provided his employer is a company, limited liability partnership or partnership in Scotland). The prior consent rule set out in reg.22
only applies to e-mails sent to individual subscribers, although e-mails sent to
corporate subscribers will still have to provide an opt-out opportunity and
comply with the basic requirements of reg.23 (see the section on p.249 'Making
the sender's identity clear and providing a valid and visible address'). This
chapter will concentrate on unsolicited marketing e-mails sent to individual
subscribers, as it is here that the PEC Regulations have the most significant
impact. In practice, most businesses ignore the distinction between individual
and corporate subscribers and adopt the highest common denominator
approach to this issue, treating e-mail marketing campaigns as being carried
out entirely to individual subscribers even if some of the e-mail addresses in
their database are actually work addresses, not least because it is impractical
to segment the database. In addition, it can often be difficult to determine
whether a particular address is a work or personal one.

The PEC Regulations only apply to messages sent over a 'public electronic
communications network' and until recently, it was thought that marketing
messages sent via Bluetooth technology are sent over such a network and
are therefore also subject to the legislation. However, the Information
Commissioner somewhat surprisingly announced in a statement dated 11
October 2007 that his view is that Bluetooth messages are not in fact sent
over a public electronic communications network and that it is for government to decide whether the law should be changed to cover such marketing.

Opt-out exception

There is an important exception to the general prior consent rule, which is
sometimes called 'soft opt-in'. The term 'soft opt-in' is confusing as this
exception is essentially an 'opt-out' approach. The PEC Regulations allow
marketing e-mails concerning a business's own 'similar' products and services
to be sent to customers without an opt-in consent, provided that customers
are given the opportunity to opt out of such e-mails when their data are
collected and on the occasion of each subsequent e-mail (reg.22(3)). The
opt-out mechanism must be available free of charge (excluding the normal
cost of sending the opt-out reply message) (reg.22(3)(c)).

This exception only applies to e-mails sent by a business to its customers advertising its own 'similar' products or services. Despite the fact that this issue of unsolicited e-mail marketing was discussed at length across the EU institutions for several years before the adoption of Directive 2002/58/EC, the wording of the exception to the opt-in principle is somewhat imprecise and controversial. There can be considerable practical difficulties for businesses in assessing whether their products or services are 'similar' in nature, since there is no guidance on how to interpret this intrinsically ambiguous word in either the Directive or the PEC Regulations. However, the Information Commissioner has published clear guidance on its interpretation of the PEC Regulations (see the latest version 3.1 of 08/10/2007) that assists organisations in determining to what extent they are marketing their own 'similar' products and services by e-mail (and therefore whether or not they can rely on the opt-out exception). The regulator has adopted a purposive approach to this issue and the 'reasonable expectations' of the customer are the decisive factor in determining whether a business can legitimately rely on the opt-out exception.

This means that an individual should not receive marketing information which that person would not reasonably expect to receive. The Information Commissioner illustrates this with the following example:

> it is reasonable to assume that someone who buys on an online supermarket and does not object to receiving marketing e-mails, will expect to receive e-mails promoting the diverse range of goods available at that supermarket.

To expand further, it follows that the more steps a business can take at the outset of the customer relationship to inform customers of the nature and range of the products and services which they can reasonably expect to be offered, the easier it will be for the business to conclude that all of those products are 'similar' in nature. Marketing products in a consistent way (e.g. under its own brand) and adopting an integrated marketing approach (i.e. advertising a variety of goods and services within the same mailing) are likely to assist an organisation in being able to rely on the opt-out exception.

What constitutes a customer relationship for the purposes of the opt-out exception?

Regulation 22(3)(a) states that an organisation can rely on the opt-out exception where it 'has obtained the contact details of the recipient of the electronic mail in the course of the sale or negotiations for the sale of a product or service to that recipient'.

The Directive does not make it clear whether the exception should apply to prospective customers (i.e. those who have registered an interest in a product or service without buying it). However, the PEC Regulations demonstrate a broad approach and it is clear from the Information Commissioner's guidance on this issue that there is no requirement for an actual purchase to have taken place for there to be a direct relationship with the individual for the purpose of applying the exception. So, where an individual takes a number of steps to register with a retail website, for example, the business will be regarded as having obtained the individual's contact details in the course of the 'negotiations for the sale' of a product or service.

The Information Commissioner's interpretation of what constitutes 'negotiations for the sale' is linked to the concept of 'inducement'. For example, where a competition is part of the inducement to raise interest in a product or service, this will be regarded as part of the negotiations for a sale. However, if someone makes an e-mail enquiry about opening hours or the location of a store, this is unlikely to be part of a negotiation for the sale of a product or service.

The Information Commissioner's guidance explains that charities, political parties and not-for profit organisations will not be able to benefit from the opt-out exception in reg.22(3). According to the regulator, the expression 'in the course of the sale or negotiations for the sale' only applies to commercial relationships. These types of organisations are therefore required to design their websites and data collection mechanisms so that individuals actively request to be sent information about such causes electronically.

Making the sender's identity clear and providing a valid and visible address

In the case of all marketing e-mails (whether sent on an opt-out or an opt-in basis), the identity of the sender of the e-mail must not be disguised or concealed (reg.23(a)) and the sender must make its identity clear in the message, e.g. 'AB Limited'. This measure is designed to stop the favourite ploy of unscrupulous marketers who employ false e-mail addresses to disguise their true identities.

Similarly, there is a requirement that the sender of a marketing e-mail or SMS message must provide a 'valid address' so that the individual can contact that address in order to exercise his opt-out right (reg.23(b)). The Information Commissioner's guidance explains that in an online environment, this requirement could be satisfied by providing an e-mail address, and in the context of SMS marketing, a short code number can be used as a 'valid address' as long as the individual does not incur costs other than the cost of sending the message (that is, using the short code does not incur premium rate charges).

Unlike the opt-in rule in reg.22, these two requirements in reg.23 apply to all unsolicited marketing e-mails, irrespective of whether they are sent to individual or corporate subscribers.

Practical significance of the opt-in requirement

As a consequence of reg.22, controllers must ensure that consent is positively obtained if third-party products or services are to be advertised by e-mail or SMS.

In addition, common practices such as sending marketing e-mails on behalf of business partners or other third parties will breach the PEC Regulations unless the e-mail addresses of the recipients belong to individuals who have previously consented to all types of e-mail marketing. The practice of list selling (where a business makes a profit from selling e-mail addresses to other businesses that use those addresses for direct marketing) is now only possible if the individual 'solicits', i.e. actively invites e-mail marketing from third parties. This issue will be examined below.

9.5.8   Solicited communications versus consent

The PEC Regulations are concerned with unsolicited marketing communications. Solicited communications are outside the scope of the PEC Regulations. The Information Commissioner's guidance on the PEC Regulations explains that a 'solicited communication' is one that is actively invited. An 'unsolicited marketing communication that someone consents to receiving' is one that has not been specifically invited but that the recipient is happy to receive and has positively said so (i.e. an 'opt-in' consent). This distinction is crucial in the context of businesses that pass e-mail addresses to third parties for direct marketing purposes.

Regulation 22(2) prohibits unsolicited electronic marketing communications unless the recipient has notified the 'sender' that he consents to receiving those communications. Given that such consent must be given to the 'sender', sending marketing e-mails to addresses provided by a third party would be prohibited by the PEC Regulations. In order to overcome this problem (which does not exist in the wording of the Directive), the Information Commissioner has pointed out that third-party lists can be compiled and used legitimately where the individual expressly 'solicits marketing by e-mail'. Therefore, it is very important that both sellers and buyers of e-mail lists appreciate this distinction and their respective responsibilities in this regard.

The following wording is an example of how to give an individual the opportunity to solicit marketing information by e-mail:

> Please contact me by e-mail with information about your products and services and those of carefully selected third parties [ ]

The use of the words 'please contact me' conveys the fact that the individual is taking the initiative to request or 'solicit' e-mail marketing, rather than merely giving his consent to receiving unsolicited marketing communications.

9.5.9   Case law on unsolicited e-mail marketing

Regulation 30(1) of the PEC Regulations allows a person who has suffered damage as a result of a failure to comply with its provisions to sue for compensation for that damage (the marketing communication must originate in the UK for an individual to be able to sue under this legislation). Three notable cases on e-mail marketing have been decided before the courts and these are discussed below:

Nigel Roberts v. Media Logistics (The Times, 28 December 2005)

In October 2005, an individual named Nigel Roberts became the first person to successfully obtain compensation for a breach of the PEC Regulations. Roberts received an e-mail sent to his private e-mail address from a company called Media Logistics. The e-mail promoted the services of another company selling contract car hire services. Despite having had no prior relationship with Media Logistics, Roberts had received several e-mails from the company, the last of which resulted in him making a complaint. He wrote to Media Logistics stating that he had never had any dealings with them and had never given his consent to receive marketing e-mails and that the e-mail was therefore in breach of the PEC Regulations.

He requested four things to prevent him suing the company: (i) an apology; (ii) details of who provided his personal information to Media Logistics; (iii) details of all personal information held by the company (i.e. items (ii) and (iii) together constituted a subject access request); and (iv) damages to compensate him for his losses. He said that the actions of Media Logistics had caused annoyance, inconvenience and expense in the form of interference with the proper functioning of his e-mail, the need for additional disk storage and a subscription to an e-mail filtering service, delay in his receipt of legitimate e-mail, and time wasted sorting legitimate e-mail from junk e-mail.

After an exchange of correspondence, where he did not receive satisfactory responses to his four requests, Roberts proceeded to bring a damages claim under the PEC Regulations in Colchester County Court. He did not approach the Information Commissioner, as the regulator does not have the power to award compensation to individuals, rather he can only order the data controller to stop sending the spam and then await a breach of that order, at which point the company can then be fined in a court for failing to comply with the Information Commissioner's enforcement notice.

The court ruled in favour of Roberts and a date was set for a damages hearing. Settlement negotiations then took place between the parties by mail and Roberts eventually settled the claim out of court for £300 (the maximum amount available in the small claims court where he chose to bring the claim).

Roberts still wanted to know how Media Logistics got his e-mail address and so pursued this aspect of his subject access request directly with them.

After more correspondence, the source of the data was eventually revealed as a now insolvent data broking company. Interestingly, at that point, Media Logistics tried to argue to Mr Roberts that it had acted in good faith and that Mr Robert's e-mail address was in fact a business e-mail address and therefore that it was lawful to send the marketing e-mail to him without having obtained his prior consent. It is true that if Mr Roberts' e-mail address had in fact been a company e-mail address, Media Logistics' e-mail activity would not have been subject to the prior consent requirement in the PEC Regulations, being an e-mail sent to a 'corporate subscriber'. However, the reality was that there was no way to tell from Roberts' address in isolation whether it was a business or personal address and the address was in fact a personal one and therefore attracted the full protection of the PEC Regulations.

The case is significant, being the first successful compensation claim under the PEC Regulations, although it does illustrate the considerable degree of effort required for an individual to bring a spam case to a successful conclusion. The amount of compensation obtained would not appear to act as a deterrent to spammers, but it was the maximum amount available under the small claims procedure chosen by Roberts. However, it is important to note that because it was an out-of-court settlement, the amount of compensation is not binding in future cases as the court never actually had an opportunity to decide whether Mr Roberts was entitled to receive compensation and if so, how much. He could have chosen to pay a higher court filing fee and then he would have been able to sue for an amount not exceeding £5000. Had Mr Roberts chosen to do this, it is again unclear how much compensation (if any) the court would have awarded, given the obvious difficulty in proving that the e-mails from Media Logistics had actually caused the losses claimed by him, since he is likely to have received larger quantities of spam from other sources, typically from outside of the UK.

Gordon Dick v. Transcom Internet Services Limited (Court Reference: SA1170/06)

The second spam case brought by an individual before the UK courts involved the sending of a single unsolicited e-mail by Transcom to Mr Dick advertising its ISP services. The e-mail was sent without Mr Dick's prior consent and he had no prior relationship with the company.

Dick took action against Transcom in Edinburgh Sheriff Court alleging breach of the DPA and the PEC Regulations. The DPA allows an individual to sue for compensation for damage and distress due to the unlawful obtaining of personal data. An e-mail address can constitute personal data where it reveals the individual's name (for example, john.smith@company-name.com).

Whilst Transcom did not defend the case in court, Dick successfully sued for damages of £750, the maximum sum that can be claimed under Scotland's small claims court procedure, together with expenses of £617.

Microsoft v. Paul McDonald, trading as Bizads UK

The High Court case of *Microsoft Corporation* v. *Paul McDonald t/a Bizads UK* [2006] All ER (D) 153 is perhaps the most significant 'spam' case to date because it established that ISPs have the right under the PEC Regulations to bring an action against the sender of an unsolicited marketing e-mail.

As a part of its ongoing efforts to protect the integrity of its Hotmail e-mail service from the activities of spammers, Microsoft identified a number of apparently unrelated spam campaigns advertising small businesses in the UK. Having carried out an initial investigation, Microsoft identified a website run by a UK entity trading as 'Bizads' as the source of these campaigns. The Bizads website sold lists of up to 10,000 e-mail addresses at a time to businesses for e-mail marketing purposes, claiming that the lists were comprised of individuals who had consented to the receipt of e-mails advertising business investment opportunities, i.e. the company was holding itself out as complying with the opt-in requirement in reg.22(2) of the PEC Regulations, which states that a person shall neither transmit, nor 'instigate the transmission of', unsolicited communications for the purposes of direct marketing by e-mail unless the recipient of the e-mail has notified the sender that he consents to such communications being sent.

Microsoft devised a sting operation and created a number of 'target accounts' (with no genuine customers behind them) specifically in order to capture spam e-mails. Microsoft's target e-mail addresses appeared in the Bizads lists and Microsoft could prove that at least some of these e-mail accounts had not consented to receiving the unsolicited marketing e-mails.

Mr McDonald was the operator of Bizads and so was not himself sending unsolicited marketing e-mails, but rather his company was harvesting e-mail addresses and selling them on to other businesses. Microsoft argued that this sale of e-mail addresses amounted to the 'instigation of the transmission of unsolicited e-mail' in breach of reg.22(2). The first issue before the court was therefore whether the practice of list selling (where consent had not been properly obtained) amounted to 'instigation' of the transmission of unsolicited marketing e-mails. Mr Justice Lewison adopted a broad approach to this matter and determined that the absence of consent from the e-mail account owners on the lists together with a statement on the Bizads website that the people on the list had in fact subscribed to receive business opportunities via e-mail and are 'waiting for your offer' was enough to constitute 'instigation' of the transmission of unsolicited e-mails.

The next issue was whether Microsoft had standing to bring a claim under the PEC Regulations given that it is the individual subscriber (i.e. the recipient of the unsolicited marketing communication) who has the statutory right to bring an action. Microsoft was bringing the action on its own behalf as a provider of the Hotmail service, and not on behalf of its customers.

The judge dealt with this issue by looking at the recitals to the E-Privacy Directive (2002/58/EC). He adopted a purposive approach to the interpretation of the Directive by finding that its underlying policy objective was not only to protect individual subscribers, but also the providers of electronic communications' systems. In giving Microsoft a right of action, the court recognised that Microsoft had suffered damage both in terms of a loss of goodwill and also as a result of the huge expense incurred in dealing with the volume of spam infiltrating its networks.

Another groundbreaking aspect of this judgment was the fact that the judge used the court's discretionary powers to grant Microsoft an injunction to prevent Mr McDonald from engaging in further illegal spamming activities. The injunction was granted despite the fact that the PEC Regulations only provide a compensation remedy for the recipient of the marketing communication.

The case is highly significant – for the first time, the courts have allowed ISPs a right of action not only against spammers but also against those who sell lists of e-mail addresses that have been compiled in breach of the prior consent requirement in the PEC Regulations. ISPs have both the financial resources and the technological capabilities to investigate and identify unscrupulous spammers and to take action against them and so the judgment is to be welcomed.

Implications of the approach of the courts and the regulator for breaches of the law on direct marketing

Despite the success of Mr Roberts and Mr Dick in the cases discussed above, experience since 2003 indicates that individuals generally have neither the inclination nor the financial means to bring a court action against a spammer (it seems easier to press 'delete').

Given that the Information Commissioner does not have the powers or the resources to fine spammers, it will be interesting in light of *McDonald* to see whether Microsoft or any other large ISPs take action against persistent spammers and those who harvest e-mail addresses, acting as a form of an additional 'quasi-regulator' in policing compliance with the PEC Regulations. It is of interest that on 13 November 2007, the EU legislators issued a Proposal for a Directive to amend the existing E-Privacy Directive in order to give legal persons (i.e. companies) a right of action against spammers, which would codify the right of action that the UK High Court gave to Microsoft in *McDonald*.

The greater risk to a business which does not comply with the direct marketing rules is the negative publicity that can arise from individual complaints or from an investigation by the regulator. Both of these cases were widely reported in the national press.

In terms of the regulator's approach to investigating breaches of the direct marketing rules, whilst this area is viewed as important, it is not the highest priority. The Information Commissioner's 2008 strategy paper entitled 'Data Protection – Protecting People' reveals that the priority is investigating data protection breaches that result in 'harm' being caused to the individual – spam generally does not cause significant harm or loss to the individual, instead it is typically more of an annoyance. The regulator is only likely to act in the event of a complaint from an individual or a request for assessment, and is not likely at present to proactively investigate and assess the level of compliance exhibited by UK businesses.

However, that it is not to diminish the importance of organisations complying with the law affecting direct marketing. The Information Commissioner has taken enforcement action against a relatively large number of companies since the introduction of the PEC Regulations, particularly in relation to breaches of the rules governing fax and telephone marketing. Whilst the regulator does not have the ability to award compensation, he does have the power to stop a company from sending direct marketing communications in breach of the DPA and/or the PEC Regulations, which is clearly a very significant sanction.

In addition the Infomation Commissioner can require the offending business to introduce procedural changes both to the way it collects personal information and the way in which it carries out its direct marketing activities in order to achieve compliance with the legislation. The decisions of organisations that have been found to have breached the direct marketing rules are also published on the Information Commissioner's website, leading to negative publicity for the organisation concerned and no sensible organisation would want to risk being portrayed in the media as not taking individuals' privacy seriously.

9.5.10   Opt-in or opt-out for e-mail marketing?

Businesses must decide whether to adopt an opt-in or opt-out approach (or a combination of both) to their e-mail marketing operations depending on the nature of their business and whether they intend to send marketing e-mails on behalf of third parties. With ever-increasing control and regulation of direct marketing, adopting an opt-in approach is the easiest way to ensure compliance with legal obligations. In addition, various other EU Member States favour a stricter opt-in approach to direct marketing by e-mail, so that it makes sense for a pan-European business to adopt an opt-in approach in respect of all new customers. Indeed, a consent-based approach to electronic marketing is fast becoming the norm for most online businesses, many of whom take the view that it is preferable to have a high value marketing database of people who actually want to hear from the company and who are likely to be stronger sales prospects than people who have simply failed to read the small print and tick the opt-out box.

However, there is still scope in the UK for businesses to rely on an opt-out approach when marketing their own similar products to their customers by e-mail, provided that an opt-out mechanism is provided in every e-mail sent by the business. Nevertheless, an opt-in consent must always be obtained if the organisation wishes to use e-mail to advertise the products or services of business partners or other third parties.

Examples of opt-in/opt-out mechanisms

An opt-in approach requires the individual to take a positive action (e.g. ticking a box, or entering an e-mail address for the specific purpose of receiving e-mail marketing or responding to an e-mail to say yes) – see Box 9.1.

BOX 9.1   Opt-in and opt-out precedents

Opt-in

We would like to send you information by e-mail about the products and services of our business partners and other organisations that we think may be of interest to you. Please tick this box if you would like to receive this information [ ]

Opt-in

By providing us with your e-mail address, you consent to receiving e-mails about our products and services, unless you would prefer not to receive them by ticking this box [ ]

Opt-out

We will occasionally send you e-mails containing information about our products and services that we think may be of interest to you. Please tick the box if you do not wish to be contacted in this way [ ]

9.5.11   Consumer Protection from Unfair Trading Regulations 2008

The Consumer Protection from Unfair Trading Regulations 2008 (CPUT Regulations) came into force on 26 May 2008 as a new piece of consumer protection legislation that regulates unfair commercial practices and provides a further layer of regulation by making the sending of spam and other unsolicited direct marketing a criminal offence. The CPUT Regulations aim to prevent traders misleading, behaving aggressively or otherwise acting unfairly towards consumers.

The CPUT Regulations contain a blacklist of 31 practices that are deemed 'unfair' in all circumstances and one of these practices is

> making persistent and unwanted solicitations by telephone, fax, e-mail and other remote media, except in circumstances and to the extent justified to enforce a contractual obligation.

This new offence complements the existing law affecting direct marketing as set out in the DPA and the PEC Regulations, but adds criminal sanctions. An 'unwanted solicitation' is presumed to be one which is sent to an individual who has previously indicated that he/she does not wish to receive marketing information from the contact or who has registered his/her telephone number with the Telephone Preference Service. This is illustrated by the following example, given in the OFT's guidance on the CPUT Regulations:

> A direct seller telephones consumers to sell them products, but does not record when consumers have explicitly asked to be removed from their contact lists. The trader calls back consumers several times, who have asked him not to. This would breach the [CPUT Regulations].

Clearly, a one-off failure to honour individuals' opt-out requests will not attract criminal liability under the CPUT Regulations, but the authorities will instead be targeting companies who persistently flout the rules on sending unsolicited direct marketing communications. The OFT guidance gives solicitation for the purposes of debt collection as an example of a situation which would be allowed (as such contact is justified in enforcing a contractual obligation).

Local authority Trading Standards Services and the OFT have a duty to enforce the CPUT Regulations, using the 'most appropriate means'. A company found guilty of sending spam in breach of the CPUT Regulations could face a fine not exceeding the statutory maximum (£5,000) on summary conviction, or a potentially unlimited fine, or up to two years' imprisonment (or both) on an indictment. An officer or manager of the company who consents to (or acts negligently in relation to) the offence can be found personally liable and fined or sentenced for up to two years in prison. Consumers affected by a breach of the CPUT Regulations do not have the right to bring a claim for compensation, although it is expected to be reviewed by the Government in due course.

9.5.12 Electronic Commerce (EC Directive) Regulations 2002

The final piece in the jigsaw of legislation affecting the use of e-mail and SMS for marketing purposes is in the form of the Electronic Commerce (EC Directive) Regulations 2002, SI 2002/2013, which implement the Electronic Commerce Directive (2000/31/EC). The E-Commerce Regulations require an unsolicited commercial e-mail and SMS message to be 'clearly and unambiguously identifiable as such as soon as it is received' (reg.8), although they do not prescribe how this requirement should be met. However, the intention of the Directive is that the recipient of the e-mail must be able to tell that it is a commercial communication from the header of the e-mail (i.e. without having to actually open it). For example, the name of the company should appear in the 'sender' field, instead of what would appear to be an individual's e-mail address (as is typically the case).

In addition, if the e-mail/SMS message is advertising a promotional offer or competition, it must clearly identify the offer/competition as such (e.g. by stating 'Great offers at nameofthebusiness.com' in the 'subject' field of the e-mail) (E-Commerce Regulations, reg.7). Both the PEC Regulations and the E-Commerce Regulations effectively prohibit UK-based senders of unsolicited commercial e-mail from disguising the source of their messages and from giving false e-mail headers.

9.6   RIGHT TO COMPENSATION

An individual who suffers damage, or damage and distress, as the result of any contravention of the requirements of the DPA by a controller, has the right to claim compensation. 'Damage' means financial loss or physical injury. The data controller has a defence if it is able to prove that it had taken such care as was reasonable in all the circumstances to comply with the relevant requirement of the DPA (s.13). All claims for compensation must be made to the court as the Information Commissioner has no power to award compensation.

The right to compensation is discussed in detail in Chapter 3. Damages for distress alone can only be claimed where the contravention relates to the processing of personal data for the 'special purposes' (referred to in Chapter 3 and which comprise journalistic, artistic or literary purposes). Again, it is a defence for the data controller to prove that it had taken such care as in all the circumstances was reasonably required to comply with the requirement concerned. There are, however, reduced circumstances in which a contra-vention may occur since processing only for 'special purposes' is, in certain circumstances, exempt from all but one of the Principles and some sections of the DPA.

If the individual can prove that damage has been suffered, the court may also award compensation for any distress which has also been suffered by reason of the breach of the DPA.

In *Michael Douglas & Catherine Zeta-Jones* v. *Hello! Ltd* [2003] EWHC 786 (Ch), the Douglases were successful in claiming compensation (albeit limited in amount) as a result of *Hello!*'s breach of the DPA (*Hello!* had published photographs of the Douglases at their wedding without their consent). The judge in this case only awarded nominal damages for *Hello!*'s breach because in his view the key question was 'if the obligations under the DPA had been performed would it truly have made any difference?'. The judge speculated that if *Hello!* had complied with the DPA by asking the Douglases to consent to the publication of the photographs (and the Douglases had refused), *Hello!* would have elected to publish the photos in any event, i.e. the damage and distress suffered by the Douglases was not by reason of a contravention of the DPA.

Some commentators have argued that this decision has restricted the scope of the s.13 right to compensation. The better view is that the above analysis concerning the right to compensation is incorrect. It seems that the true reason that the judge did not make a substantial damages award for *Hello!*'s data protection breach was stated at para.239 of his judgment, that he 'did not see [the DPA] as adding a separate route to damage or distress beyond a nominal award'. That is, he was trying to prevent the DPA being used by the Douglases as a means of making a double recovery, as they had already been awarded compensation under the law of confidence.

Damage means pecuniary loss or physical injury. *Johnson* v. *MDU (No.2)* established that s.13 does not permit the recovery of compensation for 'general damage' such as the loss of the individual's reputation. Such compensation can only be claimed under a separate cause of action, such as defamation.

What is clear from the spam cases decided under the PEC Regulations (discussed above) and decisions such as *Ezsias* and *Johnson* is that there must be a direct causal link between the breach of the data protection legislation and the damage suffered by the individual. It can be very difficult for a claimant to prove that he has suffered financial loss and, where such loss has occurred, that it was caused by the data protection breach. With more than 10 years having passed since the introduction of the DPA, we are still therefore awaiting a data protection case where significant damages are awarded.

9.7   RIGHT TO RECTIFY INACCURATE PERSONAL DATA

The processing of inaccurate data by an organisation is a breach of the Fourth Principle. The DPA gives individuals a special right to rectify any inaccurate personal data relating to them, which, unlike the other rights, is exercised by way of an application to the court, rather than via a written request to the data controller. Data are inaccurate if they are 'incorrect or misleading as to any matter of fact' (DPA, s.70(2)).

An individual may apply to the court for an order requiring the controller to rectify, block, erase or destroy such data relating to that individual which are inaccurate together with any other personal data relating to the individual which contain an expression of opinion which the court finds is based on the inaccurate data (DPA, s.14). If an opinion is inaccurate, but not related to inaccurate data held by the controller, the individual will have no remedy.

A court may also make a rectification order if it is satisfied, on the application of an individual, that the individual has suffered damage by reason of any contravention by a data controller of any of the requirements of the DPA in respect of personal data, entitling the individual to compensation under s.13, and that there is a substantial risk of further contravention in respect of those data in such circumstances.

There are very few recorded examples of this right being exercised against controllers before the courts. In *P* v. *Wozencroft* [2002] 2 FLR 1118, the claimant had applied for a residence order for his child. His claim was partly refused by the court, so the claimant then applied to the court for a s.14 rectification order claiming that two reports (relating to him) by the data controller (a psychiatrist) were inaccurate. In considering the application, Wilson J. noted that s.14 'is engaged only if the court is satisfied that personal data are inaccurate; and even then, a discretion arises as to whether to order their rectification'. In this case, the judge refused to exercise his discretion and make the rectification order essentially because the claimant had had the opportunity at the original hearing to challenge the reports in open court, but failed to do so. It seems therefore that if there is a more appropriate forum for challenging the accuracy of the personal data, this will be a factor in determining whether or not the court should make a rectification order.

If the court does use its discretion to make a rectification order, the court may, where it considers it reasonably practicable, order the data controller to notify third parties to whom the data have been disclosed of the rectification, blocking, erasure or destruction. In deciding whether it is reasonably practicable to require such notification the court shall have regard, in particular, to the number of persons who would have to be notified.

If the court finds that the data are incorrect, but that they accurately record the information given to the controller by the data subject or a third party, the court may consider the requirements set out in the interpretation of the Fourth Principle, namely:

- whether the data controller took reasonable steps to ensure that the data were correct, having regard to the purpose or purposes the data were obtained and further processed; and
- if the data subject has already notified the data controller of his view that the data are inaccurate, and whether the data indicate that fact (DPA, Sched.1, Part 2, para.7).

If the court considers that these requirements have been complied with, the court may, as an alternative, order that the data be supplemented with a statement of the true facts approved by the court. If the court considers that any or all of the above requirements have not been complied with, the court may make such order as it sees fit. If the individual has suffered damage or damage and distress as a result of the data controller's processing of inaccurate data, compensation may be awarded.

In practice, all an organisation can do to ensure that an individual does not exercise his s.14 right is to ensure that it has appropriate internal procedures in place to keep personal data accurate and up to date.

9.8 RIGHTS RELATING TO AUTOMATED DECISIONS

An individual is entitled, by written notice, to require a data controller to ensure that no decision which significantly affects that individual is based solely on the processing by automatic means of personal data of which that individual is the data subject (DPA, s.12).

The DPA includes specific examples of the purposes for which such auto-mated decision-taking might be employed, i.e. evaluating matters relating to the data subject such as his performance at work, his creditworthiness, his reliability or his conduct. This is not an exhaustive list.

Where no notice has effect and where a decision which significantly affects an individual is based solely on such automatic processing, the data controller must notify the individual that the decision was taken on that basis as soon as reasonably practicable. In addition, within 21 days of receiving such notification, an individual is entitled by written notice (the 'data subject notice') to require the data controller to reconsider the decision or to take a new decision on a different basis. Within 21 days of receiving the data subject notice, the controller must give the data subject a written notice specifying the steps the controller intends to take to comply with the data subject notice.

The DPA provides for an exemption from the above provisions of certain decisions reached in this way. These are called 'exempt decisions'. To qualify as an exempt decision certain conditions must be met as follows. First:

(a) the decision must be taken in the course of steps taken for the purpose of considering whether to enter into a contract with the data subject:

 –   with a view to entering into such a contract; or
 –   in the course of performing such a contract; or

(b) the decision must be authorised or required by or under any enactment.

Second:

(c) the effect of the decision must be to grant a request of the data subject; or

(d) steps must have been taken to safeguard the legitimate interests of the data subject (for example, by allowing the data subject to make representations).

The court may make an order requiring a person taking a decision in respect of the individual (referred to in the DPA as 'the responsible person') to reconsider the decision or to take a new decision which is not based solely on processing by automatic means. The court will only make such orders if it is satisfied that the responsible person has failed to comply with the data subject notice.

Data controllers will need to determine whether they use any systems (either their own systems or those provided by others) that will be affected by this provision. They should take steps to ensure that:

(a) individuals who have objected are not subject to decisions made by automated systems;
(b) appropriate information notices can be given to individuals to notify them where decisions are made by such systems; and
(c) they have procedures to take account of any objections raised and to allow decisions to be reconsidered with human intervention.

9.9 RIGHT TO PREVENT PROCESSING CAUSING DAMAGE OR DISTRESS

Data controllers should not process personal data where the processing is likely to cause substantial damage or distress to a data subject.

If an individual believes that a controller is processing personal data in a way that causes, or is likely to cause, substantial unwarranted damage or substantial, unwarranted distress to him or to someone else, s.10 of the DPA gives the individual a right to send a notice to the data controller requiring it, within a reasonable time, to stop the processing (the 'data subject notice').

This right to serve a data subject notice applies whether the individual objects to the processing taking place at all, or whether the objection relates specifically to processing for a particular purpose or in a particular way.

When a controller receives a data subject notice it must, within 21 days, give the individual a written notice stating either:

• that it has complied with the data subject notice, or intends to comply with it; or
• the extent to which it intends to comply with the data subject notice (if at all) and explaining the parts of the data subject notice it considers to be unjustified in any way.

There is no guidance in the DPA regarding the degree of damage or distress which must be caused for it to be deemed 'substantial'. It is for a court to decide in each case whether the damage or distress is substantial and unwarranted. The Information Commissioner takes the view that a data subject notice is only likely to be appropriate where the particular processing has caused, or is likely to cause, someone to suffer loss or harm, or upset and anguish of a real nature, over and above annoyance level, and without justification.

However, a controller can legitimately process such data, despite receiving a data subject notice, where any of the following apply (DPA, Sched.2, paras.1–4):

- the individual has previously given a valid consent to the processing (although consent may be withdrawn);
- the processing is necessary for the performance of a contract with the individual, or necessary for the taking of steps at the request of the data subject with a view to entering a contract;
- the processing is required to fulfil a non-contractual obligation; or
- the processing is necessary in order to protect the vital interests of the individual.

Of all the data protection rights, the right to prevent processing causing damage or distress is the one which is least likely to be encountered by organisations in practice, given its narrow application and the fact that individuals are generally unaware of their right to serve a data subject notice.

Subject access response checklist

Follow this checklist each time that individuals ask to be provided with the information that you have about them.

When using the checklist, you should bear in mind the following points:

- It is easier to deal with access requests if (a) you have appointed a person or team to co-ordinate the provision of information and (b) there are appropriate procedures in place to channel the requests to the appointed co-ordinator.
- Ensure easy access to data held in the organisation and know where they are held.
- A maximum fee of £10 may be charged to provide access.
- It may be a good idea to have a standard form of disclosure covering the items mentioned in step 11.

Checklist to deal with access requests

1. Ensure that date-stamped data subject access requests are promptly sent to the appointed Subject Access Response Co-ordinator.
2. Identify criteria constituting reasonable information for the identification of individuals (e.g. name, postal address, e-mail address and password used).
3. Has the individual making the request provided reasonable information to satisfy you as to his/her identity?

    (a) If so, go to step 4.
    (b) If not, you should ask for further information.

4. Has the request been made in writing (including e-mail)?

    (a) If so, go to step 5.
    (b) If not, there is no need to comply with the request, but the reason for not complying should be given.

5. Has the prescribed fee been paid?

   (a) If so, go to step 6.
   (b) If not, there is no need to comply with the request, but the reason for not complying should be given.

6. Is the request open ended?

   (a) If so, you are entitled to ask the individual for further information to help you locate the information. You do not have to comply with the request until you have been provided with the further information.
   (b) If not, go to step 7.

7. Taking each piece of information in turn, is the information obviously about the individual or clearly linked to him/her?

   (a) If Yes, it is personal data and go to step 8.
   (b) If No or if unsure, is the information used (or likely to be used) to learn something about the individual or to determine something about him? If so, it is personal data and go to step 8.
   (c) If No or if unsure, is the information biographical (i.e. it tells you something significant about the individual)? If so, it is personal data and go to step 8.
   (d) If No or if unsure, then does the data focus or concentrate on the person making the request as its central theme, rather than on some other person, or some object, transaction or event? If Yes, it is personal data and go to step 8.
   (e) If No or if unsure, does the information have an 'impact' on the individual, whether in a personal, family, business or professional capacity? If Yes, it is personal data and go to step 8.
   (f) If No, or if unsure, the information is not personal data and does not have to be provided to the individual.

8. Can you comply with the request without disclosing information relating to another individual (e.g. by deleting the identities of any third parties)?

   (a) If so, go to step 9. If not, see (b).
   (b) If not, has the other individual consented to the disclosure? If so, go to step 9. If not, or if you are unable to obtain the consent of the other individual, see (c).
   (c) Is it reasonable to comply without the consent of the other individual? If so, go to step 9. If not, there is no need to comply with that part of the request which identifies the third party, but the person making the request must be informed of this.

9. Does the supply of a copy of the information require a 'disproportionate effort', bearing in mind the prejudicial effect on the individual of not providing a copy of the information?

   (a) If so, there is no need to supply a copy of the information requested, but the individual must be informed of the reasons why supplying a copy of the information would involve a disproportionate effort. Consider whether there is an alternative method of making the information available.
   (b) If not, go to step 10.

10. When was the request made? If the same individual made an identical or similar request less than [one month] ago, you do not need to comply with the second request or subsequent request(s) in the same month. If more than [one month] has lapsed since the last request made by that individual, go to step 11.

11. Do any of the general exemptions (e.g. crime prevention, legal privilege) apply? If so, there is no need to comply with the request, but the reason for not complying should be given to the individual. If not, go to step 12.

12. Has the individual making the request specified that his/her request is limited to data of a prescribed description? If so, you may limit the access to the data accordingly. Otherwise, supply the information indicated in step 13.

13. Ensure the following information is supplied in a comprehensible form and in writing:

   (a) confirmation that personal data about the individual are being processed;
   (b) a description of the personal data;
   (c) a description of the purposes for which the data are processed;
   (d) a description of the sources of the data;
   (e) a description of the potential recipients of the data;
   (f) a copy of all of the data held about that individual (unless the request is limited as specified in step 12).

Keep a record of what has been supplied, to whom, how supplied and when.

ANNEX 9B

Subject access exemptions

Section 28:   Provides an exemption to protect national security.

Section 29:   Covers personal data processed for:

(a) the prevention or detection of crime;
(b) the apprehension or prosecution of offenders; or
(c) the assessment or collection of any tax or duty or of any imposition of a similar nature.

Section 30:   Provides powers for the Lord Chancellor to make orders providing exemptions in relation to health, education and social work records. Orders relating to all three categories of record have been made.

Section 31:   Covers personal data processed for the purposes of discharging a wide range of regulatory functions.

Section 32:   Covers personal data processed for journalistic, literary or artistic purposes.

Section 33:   Covers personal data processed only for research, statistical or historical purposes, subject to certain conditions.

Section 34:   Covers personal data which are statutorily made available to the public.

Section 38:   Provides a power for the Lord Chancellor to make orders providing exemptions where disclosure of information is statutorily prohibited or restricted, subject to certain conditions.

Schedule 7

Paragraph 1:   Covers confidential references given by data controllers in relation to education, employment or the provision of services.

Paragraph 2:   Provides an exemption to protect the combat effectiveness of the armed forces.

Paragraph 3:   Covers personal data processed for the purposes of making appointments of judges and QCs, and the conferring of honours or dignities.

Paragraph 4: Provides a power for the Lord Chancellor to make orders providing exemptions in relation to Crown appointments. An order designating a limited number of appointments has been made.

Paragraph 5: Covers personal data processed for the purposes of management forecasting or management planning.

Paragraph 6: Provides an exemption for personal data processed for corporate finance services.

Paragraph 7: Covers personal data consisting of records of the data controller's intentions in relation to negotiations with the data subject.

Paragraph 8: Modifies the 40-day maximum period for dealing with subject access requests in relation to examination marks.

Paragraph 9: Covers examination scripts.

Paragraph 10: Covers personal data in respect of which legal professional privilege could be claimed.

Paragraph 11: Provides an exemption for circumstances in which by granting access a person would incriminate himself in respect of a criminal offence other than one under the DPA.

Direct marketing requirements checklist

	Opt-in	Opt-out
Telephone		*Individuals* and *corporate subscribers* have the right to opt out of marketing calls. The Telephone Preference Service register must be consulted and respected prior to making calls to both individuals and corporate subscribers (**www.tpsonline.org.uk**). (Privacy and Electronic Communications (EC Directive) Regulations 2003 and the Privacy and Electronic Communications (EC Directive) (Amendment) Regulations 2004)
Fax	The prior opt-in consent of *individuals* is required. Individuals can register with the Fax Preference Service for further protection. (Privacy and Electronic Communications (EC Directive) Regulations 2003)	*Corporate subscribers* have the right to opt out and the Fax Preference Service register must be consulted and respected prior to sending marketing faxes (**www.fpsonline.org.uk**). (Privacy and Electronic Communications (EC Directive) Regulations 2003)
Postal mail		Right for *individuals* to opt out (Data Protection Act 1998).

	Opt-in	Opt-out
E-mail	*General rule*: Individual's prior opt-in consent is required. (Privacy and Electronic Communications (EC Directive) Regulations 2003) Service providers must ensure that unsolicited commercial communications are 'clearly identifiable as such'. (Electronic Commerce (EC Directive) Regulations 2002)	*Exception*: Opt-out is sufficient in relation to marketing of own 'similar' goods/services to existing customers, but an opt-out mechanism must be provided when the data are collected and on the occasion of each marketing e-mail. (Privacy and Electronic Communications (EC Directive) Regulations 2003)
Text messages (SMS)	*General rule*: Individual's prior opt-in consent is required. (Privacy and Electronic Communications (EC Directive) Regulations 2003)	*Exception*: Opt-out is sufficient in relation to marketing own 'similar' goods/services to existing customers, but an opt-out mechanism must be provided when the data are collected and on the occasion of each marketing SMS message. (Privacy and Electronic Communications (EC Directive) Regulations 2003)
Automated calling	Individual's prior opt-in consent is required. (Privacy and Electronic Communications (EC Directive Regulations 2003)	

CHAPTER 10

Law firm compliance

Gayle Trigg[1]

10.1 INTRODUCTION

Law firms do not have special immunity from the DPA. They are subject to the same regime and, arguably, are better placed than most to understand the requirements of the DPA and, therefore, comply with them. There are, however, certain peculiarities about the way law firms are set up and the way in which legal services are delivered that can make data protection compliance quite complicated. This is examined in more detail throughout this chapter.

Law firms are subject to a host of legal and regulatory obligations and requirements as well as particularly strict confidentiality obligations both at common law and under Solicitors Regulation Authority rules. Perhaps it is because law firms and solicitors are so heavily regulated in any event that there is a perceived attitude of 'we are probably complying anyway'. This chapter should disarm solicitors of this opinion.

There have been no detailed surveys or reviews of law firms' compliance with the DPA to date although there is anecdotal evidence that indicates that data protection compliance training within law firms could be improved. In recent times, the Information Commissioner has announced a crackdown on solicitors who fail to comply with the most basic of obligations under the DPA, notification, and solicitors obtaining information through private investigators for the purposes of litigation were also highlighted in the ICO's report 'What Price Privacy?'.

It is not difficult to imagine the unease with which a law firm or solicitor would try to explain non-compliance to the Information Commissioner if required to do so.

This chapter examines some of the more common data processing activities in which a law firm and solicitors may be involved, and aims to set out ways in which these may be best managed. It is not intended to provide a ready-made solution for all law firms. Data protection compliance should not run a law firm's business; a law firm's data protection compliance must be set within the context of that law firm's specific business processes.

---

[1]   Based on an original contribution by Cinzia Biondi.

References are made in this chapter to the views of the Information Commissioner. Such views have not been given formally in writing in specific response to detailed queries in relation to the matters raised in this chapter. Instead, they have been obtained from Information Commissioner's Guidance and codes of practice, conference/seminar presentations and interviews given by the Information Commissioner, Deputy Information Commissioner and Assistant Commissioners. In relation to a handful of issues raised in this chapter, the Information Commissioner's information helpline was consulted directly for general views and/or for clarification purposes.

10.2   WHO IS THE DATA CONTROLLER?

There is continued debate over the precise role of a law firm vis-à-vis its client files in terms of who is data controller of the personal data contained in such files and processed in the context of such. This issue will be examined in more detail below. Before then, it is necessary to clarify the nature of the legal status of law firms as this will help in determining which person (natural or otherwise) within such organisations is capable of being a data controller.

It is important to bear in mind at this stage the meaning of some of the key terms:

1. *Data controller* is a person who (either alone or jointly or in common with other persons) determines the purposes for which and the manner in which any personal data are, or are to be, processed.
2. *Data processor* in relation to personal data, means any person (other than an employee of the data controller) who processes the data on behalf of the data controller.
3. *Personal data* means data which relates to a living individual who can be identified from data alone or with any other information which is in the possession of, or is likely to come into the possession of, the data controller.
4. *Data* means information in electronic or manual form as long as, in the case of the latter only, it is arranged in a systematic manner which allows specific information about a particular individual to be readily accessible (that is, it is a 'relevant filing system').

The definitions of 'personal data' and 'relevant filing system' have been the subject of much debate resulting from the Court of Appeal decision of *Durant* v. *Financial Services Authority* [2003] EWCA Civ 1746. A brief commentary on this case can be found at the end of this chapter (**10.9**), and for further detailed information on the definitions, see Chapter 2.

10.2.1   The make-up of law firms

Law firms can take several guises. Leaving aside the issue of client files for the time being, in some instances, such as where there is a sole practitioner, the question of who is the data controller is more straightforward (the sole practitioner of course). The question is not, however, as easy to answer with larger law firms which operate their business under different legal structures.

A law firm established as a partnership (regardless of its size) is not a separate legal entity distinct from the partners comprising such partnership and, as such, has no legal personality. A law firm set up as a partnership cannot, therefore, be a data controller on whom legal responsibilities and liabilities can be placed. Where a law firm, or more accurately those within a law firm, processes personal data for purposes and in the manner determined by itself, the data controller in relation to such processing is each of the partners comprising such law firm. They are essentially joint data controllers over the same personal data.

Partners are free, under a partnership agreement, to set out the boundaries of their individual liability for each other's actions among themselves as they see fit although, under general partnership law, each partner within a partnership is jointly and severally liable for loss or injury caused to third parties and jointly liable for the obligations of a partnership, without limitations on the liability. On this basis, it would appear that each partner could be held liable for a breach of the DPA committed in the context of the partnership's business. There is, however, a curiosity about the DPA which could be used to cast doubt on a partner's liability.

Under the DPA, the data controller is the person liable for any breach of the DPA. There is no concept of joint and several liability for joint data controllers under the DPA. It is not, therefore, clear (and it does not appear to have been tested to date) as to how liability/responsibility as a joint data controller under the DPA will interact with the general liability position of partners.

The Information Commissioner has suggested that, in practical terms, where personal data have been processed in contravention of the DPA in the context of a law firm set up as a partnership, it would not seek to determine which of the partners was responsible for a particular non-compliant practice. It would work on the principle that the entity (albeit non-legal entity) of the partnership has to amend its practices as a whole and would expect the partners to have a collective responsibility in such matters.

This would appear to be a sensible and practical approach. While, however, this approach may be acceptable to partners in the event of informal dealings with the Information Commissioner, or even where the Information Commissioner takes formal proceedings such as issuing an Enforcement Notice, it may not be so palatable where criminal proceedings or civil actions are being brought under the DPA. In these circumstances, partners may try to test whether such proceedings or actions are legally competent against a joint data controller (partner) who is proven not to be directly responsible for the relevant breach giving rise to the criminal proceedings or civil actions.

A limited liability partnership (LLP) is not, despite its name, a partnership governed by partnership law. It is, in fact, a corporate body incorporated by registration with the Registrar of Companies and is governed by the Limited Liability Partnerships Act 2000.

An LLP has a legal personality of its own and can be held liable for legal wrongdoings in its own right. In an LLP, partners are technically known as members, although the law firms that have become LLPs continue to use the traditional title of 'partners'.

In data protection terms the LLP is the data controller in respect of personal data processed by the LLP and it, not its members, would be liable for breaches of the DPA.

It should be remembered, however, that s.61 of the DPA still applies. Section 61 states that:

(1) where an offence under this Act has been committed by a body corporate and is proved to have been committed with the consent or connivance of or to be attributable to any neglect on the part of any director, manager, secretary or similar officer of the body corporate or any person who was purporting to act in such a capacity, he as well as the body corporate shall be guilty of that offence and be liable to be proceeded against and punished accordingly.

(2) Where the affairs of a body corporate are managed by its members subsection (1) shall apply in relation to the acts and defaults of a member in connection with his functions of management as if he were a director of the body corporate.

The phrase 'body corporate' is not defined in the DPA. Its normal legal meaning is an incorporated body/person which is recognised as a legal entity in its own right and not an entity without legal personality such as a partnership. Section 61, therefore, extends the reach of liability beyond the legal entity of the LLP itself and out to each of the members of an LLP.

It is common practice among law firms for service companies to be established and such service companies, which are separate legal entities, to be the employer of the employees who work within the law firm and, therefore, also the provider of salary and employee benefits. Any personal data processed in the context of this legal entity are the responsibility of such service company which is, in most instances, the data controller. Depending on how the arrangements between a law firm and such service company are set up, it may be possible to argue that the service company is a data processor for the partners in a law firm. In this case, appropriate data processing contractual provisions (including those required under the DPA) should be in place between the partners and the service company (see Chapter 7).

In addition, the staff pension scheme offered by law firms is usually administered through trustees. Such body of trustees is considered a separate legal entity owing direct duties of trust, confidence and compliance with laws such as the DPA to those whose personal data are being processed for the purposes of pensions administration.

Already it is clear that in the context of one business which offers legal services there can be at least three different types of data controllers of the same or different personal data. An understanding of how personal data are used by each such type of data controller is essential in order for the relevant data controller to exercise properly its duties and obligations under the DPA. The most problematic area concerns employee data, where the everyday working relationship and performance issues are managed by the partners but the legal employment relationship rests with the service company.

10.3 CLIENT FILES: IS A LAW FIRM A DATA CONTROLLER OR A DATA PROCESSOR?

We have already noted that a data controller is a 'person' who (either alone or jointly or in common with other persons) determines the purposes for which and the manner in which any personal data are, or are to be, processed. Does a law firm fall into this category?

At first glance, it seems clear that a law firm would not have personal data contained in a client file – whether that be information about a soon-to-be ex-spouse in a divorce action or details about employees who are part of an organisation which is the subject of an acquisition – unless the client instructs the law firm to act on the client's behalf.

However, lawyers have a certain level of decision-making power in steering the client to use information, including personal data, for legal purposes. This is certainly an analogous situation to that where an organisation might appoint a third-party IT company to provide ICT and data processing solutions on an outsourcing basis. It is frequently argued that the decision to appoint such a service provider is itself the decision as to how and for what purpose the data are to be processed – thereby satisfying the definition of data controller – despite the fact that the service provider may decide on how its systems are configured to facilitate the relevant processing activities. Solicitors, and therefore law firms, will not be free to do what they wish with information obtained from clients – the information remains confidential to the client. Should a client cease to instruct a solicitor/law firm, there would be no further reason for a solicitor to process personal data in relation to the legal matter on which the solicitor was advising. Therefore, it is certainly persuasive that a solicitor is a data processor of client information – whether such client is a body corporate or an individual.

However, in a note regarding the notification of barristers' chambers in 2005, the ICO suggested that in a number of circumstances, individual barristers may well be data controllers in respect of documents they produce which contain personal data, for example opinions, pleadings and letters.

There are also circumstances in which the law firm will be taking the lead in determining the manner and purpose of personal data processing. These might include situations where the law firm specifies a type of investigation prior to litigation. Other personal data obtained by a law firm as a result of accepting the instructions of, and advising, a client are collected and processed by the law firm for its own purposes. As such, the law firm (i.e. the partners or the LLP) is the data controller and must comply with the DPA in relation to the processing of such data. The personal data and related purposes to which this may apply are shown in Table 10.1.

10.4   PROCESSING PURPOSES AND NOTIFICATION REQUIREMENTS

One of the first administrative matters to which a law firm must attend under the DPA is its notification requirement – notification is discussed in general terms in Chapter 4. To the extent that a law firm is the data controller of personal data processed by it, such processing activities must be notified with the ICO unless the law firm can avail itself of one the relevant exemptions: see Data Protection (Notification and Notification Fees) Regulations 2000, SI 2000/188. In practical terms, notification is a relatively quick and simple process and does not involve a significant cost (currently £35 per annum, although an increase in these fees and a proposal to introduce tiered charging is under consultation at the time of publication). As such, taking the time to evaluate whether certain exemptions are avail-

Table 10.1 Personal data and related purposes

Personal data	Purpose
Client contact details	Billing and administration of relationship
Contact details of various individuals at client organisations	Marketing: sending legal updates; inviting to seminars/events
Contact details of other professional advisers (although these are obtained for the purposes of providing advice to a client, law firms often use such information for future business purposes)	Business networking: marketing
Third parties assisting law firm, e.g. enquiry agents (see later in this chapter for potential difficulties with such relationships)	Monitoring performance where business relationship exists

able for certain criteria of personal data may not be a cost-effective exercise – particularly as organisations are encouraged by the ICO to notify even if they are exempt.

A law firm which constitutes a partnership may, by virtue of s.18(4) of the DPA and reg.5 of the Notification Regulations (SI 2000/188), notify in the name of the law firm rather than listing each individual partner as data controller of the personal data. An LLP must notify in its own name.

Traditionally, law was a business area confined to a discrete jurisdiction. But international activities have now become commonplace for many law firms. Where personal data are to be transferred overseas, then a note to that effect, specifying the specific destination where possible or worldwide if applicable, must be set out in the firm's register entry. It should be noted that where the website is used for data processing activities (for example, e-employment portals in international law firms or deal rooms) the Notification Guidelines issued by the Information Commissioner (available from the ICO website) state that worldwide transfer must be declared.

A law firm will need to consider carefully the split of its business activities which involve the processing of personal data before submitting a notification. Although a partnership may be providing legal services and processing personal data in that context, the service company, as a separate legal entity established for the specific purposes of staff payroll and benefits administration, may also need to notify, as will the pension administration company or trustees (subject to the application of the exemptions).

It is a strict liability criminal offence not to submit a notification when required to do so and not to keep such notification up to date and accurate as processing purposes change (DPA, ss.17(1) and 21(1)).

There are standard templates available on the Information Commissioner's website for law firms to use for notification purposes. It is the law firm's responsibility to ensure that the appropriate template is chosen. The opportunity is afforded to amend these templates as required by the peculiarities of any given law firm processing activities. Annex 10A at the end of this chapter sets out typical purposes for which a law firm might submit a notification.

There are certain items set out in Annex 10A which do not seem obvious, for example, crime prevention and prosecution of offences. This is required where law firms use CCTV cameras on their premises. Typically, law firms use CCTV security measures in their offices and car parking facilities in order to provide security for vehicles and ensure the safety of staff, clients and any other visitors. Images from CCTV cameras can constitute personal data and as such the operation of such CCTV is a processing activity which must be notified.

Another purpose which may be overlooked is the undertaking of credit checks in relation to clients, employees and other business associates. Although this is not a primary business pursuit of a law firm, it may nevertheless form part of its activities from time to time. As such, the processing must be declared in the law firm's notification.

10.5   DATA RETENTION ISSUES FOR LAW FIRMS

The Fifth Principle of the DPA states that personal data must not be held longer than is necessary for the purposes for which such data were first obtained. For further detail on the Fifth Principle, see **6.4**.

Retention of data is an issue which affects all organisations. It is an issue which takes time to resolve and proper management controls to be in place in order for the data retention policies, once devised, to be properly executed.

It is inherent in the observance of the Fifth Principle that data controllers are specifically aware of the purposes for which data are originally obtained. This requires a specific analysis of data collected and the purposes for which such data are used. One positive aspect of this process is that such information can help law firms decide on its records and data management policy as well as the underlying technology and systems which would best achieve the processing of data in a logical and manageable fashion.

Once data or certain sets of data have been classified in terms of the purposes for which they are used, law firms can start to consider the appropriate retention periods to apply. This will involve deciding at which point certain data can be closed, archived and subsequently destroyed. The means of destruction must also be considered – when destroying information, law firms have to consider their duty of confidentiality in respect of client data and will need to comply with the security obligations in the Seventh Principle (see Chapter 7). Should solicitors breach the duty of confidentiality in relation to their retention and destruction process they will not only be breaching that duty but probably also the First Principle, which states that data must be processed fairly and lawfully (see Chapter 5). Some organisations such as the Cabinet Office have set up accreditation schemes for commercial organisations that provide destruction services.

The Law Society's guidance (in *The Guide to the Professional Conduct of Solicitors 1999*, published by the Law Society, now superseded by the Solicitors' Code of Conduct 2007) provided information on the best way to ensure confidentiality when arranging for all files to be destroyed. Where destruction cannot take place on site by law firm staff, the firm should seek appropriate third-party assistance. These third parties will be data processors for the law firm, so it is essential that there is a contract in place which sets out the manner in which the data are to be destroyed and to ensure that there are adequate technical and organisational measures to protect the security of such data, that is, obligations equivalent to those imposed on data controllers by the Seventh Principle of the DPA (see Chapter 7).

This guidance has now been superseded by the Solicitors Regulation Authority Solicitors' Code of Conduct 2007, which unfortunately provides little guidance on this issue, simply requiring that law firms must make arrangements for the effective management of the firm, including the safekeeping of documents and assets entrusted to the firm.

Before destroying a file containing personal data, it is essential to consider who owns the relevant documents. No documents should be destroyed without the prior consent of the owner. The issue of destruction should be addressed in a law firm's terms of business with a client. It should make clear at what stage files will be destroyed and set out whether such destruction is dependent on the client claiming the file before the end of such period or whether the law firm will actively seek the client's consent to destroy at a relevant future stage. The mechanism is not prescribed as long as it is practical to manage (which suggests the former method is more appropriate) and it has been clearly communicated to the client in the contract with the law firm.

Once the retention periods and destruction policies have been established, the question is how to manage these in the most effective manner. Technology is bound to help in this respect. There are technical solutions which will allow law firms to allocate particular retention periods to particular data sets. At a certain time before a file is due to be closed, archived or destroyed in accordance with the parameters inputted into the software application, an alert will be sent to the appropriate person, who might be an IT manager or an HR manager depending on the record in question. At this stage such authorised person may either (i) authorise the closure, archiving or destruction to take place (assuming that the policy has been set up for positive approval to be given before the action takes place); or (ii) pull out certain data or records within data sets to avoid automatic closure, archival or destruction when the relevant time period has elapsed. The best mechanism for a law firm will be one which can be easily implemented and managed in the context of its particular business systems.

Retention and destruction policies and practices also raise security issues. For example, with files which have been archived off site, have all the potential environmental conditions been considered? If there was to be a fire, would the records survive? Where third parties have been contracted to destroy files, to what extent are they to be given a level of discretion including exactly when or how files should be destroyed? The answer should be none. Law firms should set down clear retention periods (not ranges) and specific destruction methods which any contractor should be contractually obliged to follow.

Table 10.2 gives an example of how a law firm may decide to record its data retention policy and procedures.

Table 10.2 Retention Policy Matrix Example

Data/record set	Personal data contained in the data set	Due date for closure (and reason)	Due date for archiving (and reason)	Due date for destruction (and reason)	Method of destruction	Action required
HR recruitment: unsuccessful candidates	CVs; cover letters; psychometric test results; interview notes – including personal sensitive data	3 months following date on which letter of decision sent out (thereby allowing reasonable time for individuals to challenge their decision)	6 months from date on which letter of decision sent out (assuming that this information should be archived at all)	12 months from date on which decision was communicated to the applicant unless applicant has been advised that his/her details will be retained for future vacancies. Vetting information (i.e. information obtained from third parties) to be destroyed as soon as possible but in any event within 6 months	Burning using 'Paper Destruction Limited'	Automatic destruction by 'Paper Destruction Limited' unless intervention made
Client file: divorce action	Client contact details; family details – including sensitive personal data	x months from date of closure of matter plus all fees/costs paid by client	x months from date of closure unless issue has arisen	6 years from date of matter completing unless on review at the end of 6 years it appears that a negligence action may be looming, in which case 15 years	Burning using 'Paper Destruction Limited'	Automatic destruction by 'Paper Destruction Limited' unless intervention made

©Wragge & Co LLP

280

10.5.1 Relevant retention periods

Some retention periods will be the same in law firms as they are in other organisations, particularly in the area of HR records.

There are several factors which will impact on the decision of which retention period to apply, such as legal and regulatory requirements, continuing business objectives, internal management and auditing retention requirements and financial auditing requirements. This chapter reviews some issues which are particularly applicable to law firms.

Business objectives

Personal data are primarily obtained for the purpose of providing legal services to a client. It follows, therefore, that the general position should be that such data should be retained for as long as the contract for the provision of such services remains in force. However, the nature of the client relationship may be such that there will be several files opened in relation to different matters for a client. Once all of the services in relation to a particular file have been provided to the client, including any post-completion matters and settlement of all fees due to the law firm, it may be appropriate to close the file and store for future reference.

Law firms must also consider their marketing activities. Although these are of a secondary business nature to providing legal services they are an important aspect of a law firm's business. These activities would be considered non-obvious purposes and must be specifically addressed within the data protection notice given to clients, whether in the terms of business or otherwise. Likewise, any other ancillary activity, for example, financial health checks carried out on clients, must be brought to the individual client's attention.

Legal/regulatory purposes

All law firms and solicitors in England and Wales are subject to regulation by the Solicitors Regulation Authority. The SRA sets out Practice Rules and guidance on various issues affecting everyday activities undertaken by law firms and by solicitors within such law firms. Breaching the Rules can lead to disciplinary action.

As mentioned above, in its 1999 Guide, the Law Society gave guidance on the ownership, storage and destruction of documents. Annex 12A to the Guide deals with retention of files. The guidance given was as follows:

> The Society cannot specify how long individual files can be retained. It may be advisable to retain all files for a minimum of six years from when the subject matter was *wholly* completed. At the end of the *six*-year period, you should review the files again according to the nature of the particular transactions, and

the likelihood of any claims arising. In cases where a party was under a disability at the time of the action or where judgement for provisional damages has been obtained, files should be retained for a minimum period of six years from the date on which the client would have a course of action, or final judgement has been obtained (author's emphasis).

In essence, the Law Society reinforced the limitation periods for various types of legal claims as set out in the Limitation Act 1980. A prudent organisation will always ensure that all records to any matter will be kept for the relevant limitation period as a bare minimum. Some of the most commonly applicable limitation periods are:

- three years for personal injury claims;
- six years for normal contractual claims; and
- 12 years for claims relating to a contract by deed (usually land transactions).

Under the Limitation Act 1980 a special time limit for negligence actions applies where facts relevant to the course of action are not known at the date of accrual. It prevents bringing of such actions after six years from the date on which the course of action accrued or three years from the date on which the claiming party knew or ought to have known the facts, whichever is the later (Limitation Act 1980, s.4A). Section 14B provides an overriding time limit of 15 years from the defendant's (in this case law firm's) breach of duty. In a matter where a law firm considers there may be a negligence action looming, it should consider to what extent it should ensure that the files are retained for the period of 15 years.

There is also tax legislation which affects the retention of data. Under the Value Added Tax Act 1994, records and papers relevant to VAT liability have to be kept for six years. According to the Law Society's guidance:

> This obligation could cover all the papers in a solicitor's file, and subject to HMRC agreeing the contrary in any particular case, the whole file should therefore be kept for this period. This obligation may be discharged by keeping the papers on microfilm or microfiche but HMRC detailed requirements should be first checked with the local VAT office.

The Money Laundering Regulations 2007, SI 2007/2157, breach of which is a criminal offence punishable by imprisonment or fine or both regardless of whether money laundering has in fact taken place, contains provisions which are relevant to data retention. Part 3 deals with record-keeping procedures. The general position is that information obtained in relation to evidence of a person's identity (with whom a law firm transacts on a one-off basis or has a longer-term business relationship) and the records containing details relating to all the transactions carried out by that person in the course of relevant financial business must be kept for the prescribed period.

The prescribed period is in all cases at least five years but the commencement point of this five-year period can differ. In brief, the general position is that in relation to evidence of a person's identity, the period runs from the date of either (i) the ending of the business relationship; or (ii) the completion of the activities taking place in the course of the one-off transaction (including any post-completion administrative requirements such as invoicing the client).

There are further specifics which impact on these retention rules and the 2007 Regulations should be consulted in order to ascertain with certainty the precise retention period in relation to a particular record.

The Money Laundering Regulations as well as other laws which make up the UK's package of anti-money laundering legislation have further impact in relation to data protection compliance by law firms, particularly in the area of balancing the obligation not to tip-off an individual about whom a Suspicious Transaction Report has been made and the data subject's access rights under s.7 of the DPA. See **10.6** for further details.

Internal management

There will be various business, management and financial reasons for which a law firm will, as with any other commercial organisation, want to hold on to certain data (which may include personal data). To the extent that any such activities are undertaken, and such are not obvious, a law firm's data protection notice must clearly set out the processing to be undertaken.

10.6   COMPETING LEGAL OBLIGATIONS

Under the DPA, law firms are required to respond to a data subject access request by providing information about the personal data held and by providing a copy of such where relevant (the subject access right is discussed generally in Chapter 9). Firms are also required to keep personal data secure and not to disclose such data to any third party not entitled to obtain the same unless appropriate legal authorisation, whether under the DPA or otherwise, exists.

Law firms, and solicitors within law firms, are, however, subject to certain other legal obligations which may interfere with their obligations under the DPA. In each instance of an apparent competing legal obligation, the law firm must carefully consider its position under the DPA to ensure that any exemptions of which it may attempt to avail itself are applicable and can be justified should the stance ever be tested.

10.6.1   Solicitors Act 1974

The Solicitors Act 1974 requires law firms and solicitors to hand over possession of certain documents to the Law Society and/or to allow the Law Society
to otherwise examine client files (s.44B (examination of files) and para.9 of
Sched.1). Any person who refuses, neglects or otherwise fails to comply with
the requirement to pass such documents to the Law Society, will be guilty of
an offence and liable, on summary conviction, to a fine.

Additionally, Rule 20.06 (Production of Documents and Information) of
the Code of Practice requires solicitors to disclose information and documents to the Solicitors Regulation Authority (SRA) for the purpose of ascer-
taining whether the solicitor is complying with rules, codes or guidance made
or issued by the Board of the Solicitors Regulation Authority.

10.6.2   Financial Services and Markets Act 2000 (FSMA)

Under FSMA, the Financial Services Authority (FSA) has become the single
regulator and takes over from the Law Society in respect of regulatory activities falling under the FSMA. Under FSMA law firms are subject to the
general requirement to hand over documents to the FSA. There are similar
provisions in tax legislation which require the handing over of documents to,
for example, HMRC.

10.6.3   Anti-Terrorism Crime and Security Act 2001

The Anti-Terrorism Crime and Security Act 2001, which amended the
Terrorism Act 2000, makes it an offence not to disclose information to a
constable as soon as reasonably practicable if a party knows or believes that
it may be of material assistance in preventing an act of terrorism or securing
the apprehension, prosecution or conviction of another person in the UK for
an offence involving terrorism. There is a defence available, where the solicitor
can prove that he had a reasonable excuse for not making the disclosure. The
inserted s.21(A)(5) of the Terrorism Act 2000 is important for law firms as it
specifically states that disclosure by a professional legal adviser of information which he obtains in privileged circumstances or believes or suspects that
the information is obtained in privileged circumstances is not required.
Section 21(A)(6) explains the circumstances in which such an adviser is
deemed to have obtained information in privileged circumstances. In the
absence of legal privilege, disclosure would have to be made, otherwise a
person may be guilty of an offence and be liable to conviction on indictment
to imprisonment for a term not exceeding five years, to a fine or to both or
on summary conviction, to imprisonment for a term not exceeding six
months, or to a fine not exceeding the statutory maximum or to both.

10.6.4 UK anti-money laundering legislation

Under the Money Laundering Regulations 2007 and other legislation such as the Terrorism Act 2000 (discussed above) and Proceeds of Crime Act 2002, law firms are placed under obligations to advise the relevant authorities of activities which relate to money laundering, terrorist and other criminal activities. Such suspicious activity reports (SATs) must be made without advising the individual about whom the report is made; this act of tipping-off is regarded as a criminal offence.

The Money Laundering Regulations also state that it would also be an offence for law firms to continue to advise a client where they believe the client to be prepared to commit a criminal offence, which includes an offence under the DPA. In such circumstances law firms must seek consent to continue to advise on the matter from the Serious Organised Crime Agency. Failure to obtain this approval to continue to advise would amount to a criminal offence and imprisonment may result.

10.6.5 How are the competing obligations reconciled with the obligations under the Data Protection Act 1998?

In s.29 of the DPA, it states that an exemption from certain of the DPA's requirements will apply to the processing of personal data for the purposes of any of:

- the prevention or detection of crime;
- the apprehension of prosecution of offenders; or
- the assessment or collection of any tax or duty or of any other imposition of a similar nature.

To the extent that the application of any of the First Principle (except to the extent to which it requires compliance with the conditions in Schedules 2 and 3) and s.7 (the data subject access request provisions) would be likely to prejudice any of the matters mentioned above (the 'purposes'), then such Principle and section need not be complied with.

This is the basis for allowing law firms to withhold from individuals who have submitted a subject access request the fact that a SAT has been made if to so advise would constitute the offence of tipping-off. This is not, however, a blanket authority for law firms to disregard data subject access requests. First, a law firm must consider whether the referral does indeed constitute a tipping-off offence. Then it must consider whether in that particular case disclosure of the SAT would be likely to prejudice any of the purposes. It must then decide whether any of the justifications under Schedule 2 and/or Schedule 3 can still apply. If these tests are not satisfied then a law firm cannot avail itself of the s.29 exemption. It is ultimately the law firm's decision, as data controller, as to whether or not they have been satisfied. It is advisable that law firms keep a record of the steps they have taken in determining whether disclosure of a SAT would involve tipping-off and/or the applicability of the s.29 exemption.

Section 29(3) states that personal data can be disclosed where the disclosure is for any of the purposes and the application of the First Principle and s.7 would be likely to prejudice the purposes. The same tests as stated above apply in relation to this disclosure exemption.

In addition, s.35 of the DPA states that personal data is exempt from the *non-disclosure provisions* where the disclosure is:

- required by or under any enactment, by any rule of law or by the order of a court;
- necessary for the purpose of, or in connection with, any legal proceedings (including prospective legal proceedings) or for the purpose of obtaining legal advice; or
- otherwise necessary for the purposes of establishing, exercising or defending legal rights (these could extend to criminal prosecutions).

The *non-disclosure provisions* are set out in Table 10.3.

Again, what appears to be blanket authority to disclose personal data without further consideration is not, in fact, the case. There are, again, some

Table 10.3 Non-disclosure provisions

Principle	Non-disclosure provision
First Principle (but not from compliance with Schedules 2 and/or 3)	Fair and lawful processing.
Second Principle	Data to be obtained for only one or more specified and lawful purposes and shall not be further processed in a manner incompatible with such.
Third Principle	Personal data to be adequate, relevant and not excessive in relation to the purposes for which they are processed.
Fourth Principle	Personal data will be accurate and, where necessary, kept up to date.
Fifth Principle	Personal data processed for any purpose or purposes shall not be kept for longer than is necessary for that purpose or those purposes.
Section 10	The right to prevent processing likely to cause damage or distress.
Section 14(1) and (3)	The right to request the rectification, blocking or erasure of personal data.

tests to be satisfied before the exemption will apply. First, that non-disclosure would prejudice the right(s) being defended and, second, that a justification under Schedules 2 and/or 3 (where sensitive personal data are involved) applies.

10.6.6 Schedules 2 and 3 justification

Potential Schedule 2 justifications to apply:

1. Consent of the data subject. A law firm's data protection notice within its terms of business (which is countersigned by the client) can specify that personal data will be disclosed where required under statute or other legal/regulatory obligation.
2. The processing is *necessary* for compliance with any legal obligation to which the data controller is subject, other than an obligation imposed by contract.
3. The processing is *necessary* for the administration of justice or for the exercise of any functions conferred on any person or under any enactment or for the exercise of any functions of the Crown or a government department.
4. The processing is *necessary* for the exercise of any other functions of a public nature exercised in the public interests by any person.

Potential Schedule 3 justifications to apply:

1. The data subject has given explicit consent.
2. The processing is *necessary* for the purpose of, or in connection with, any legal proceedings (including prospective legal proceedings) or is *necessary* for the purpose of obtaining legal advice or is otherwise necessary for the purposes of establishing, exercising or defending legal rights.
3. The processing is *necessary* for the administration of justice or the exercise of any functions conferred on any persons by or under any enactment or for the exercise of any functions of the Crown or a government department.

Some of these justifications will only apply where law firms have decided that the necessity test has been met. In reaching this decision, a law firm must, in some instances, query whether the relevant authority requesting the personal data (or records which contain personal data) would be able to achieve its aims by other means. This puts law firms in a difficult position because it almost expects the data controller to pre-try the case in which the requesting party is involved and to determine whether the information which it holds is necessary for that case.

10.7 INTERNATIONAL ACTIVITIES

UK law firms often operate internationally. Not only do they act for UK clients on international matters, perhaps by project managing legal advice from several jurisdictions, but also deal directly with clients who are based abroad. In addition, marketing activities, due to the Internet and ease of e-mail marketing, must also be considered in the international context.

Transborder data flow issues come into play where personal data are being transferred outside of the European Economic Area. The Eighth Principle of the DPA states that there should be no transfer of data outside the EEA unless an adequate level of protection exists for the rights and freedoms of the data subject in relation to the processing of personal data.

It is permissible under the DPA to transfer personal data to certain countries which have been approved. Those countries, as at the date of publication, are the Isle of Man, Guernsey, Jersey, Switzerland, Argentina, Canada (those subject to particular federal legislation only) and the US (where the recipient of information within the US has signed up to the Safe Harbor regime). There are two main scenarios to consider. One is where the client instructs the law firm to send personal data to other parties as part of the legal services being provided; the other is where a law firm itself transfers its own personal data, for example employee data, between its offices which are based all around the world.

EXAMPLE 1

Where a client instructs a solicitor within a law firm to send personal data outside the EEA, a law firm may, subject to the client being given certain information, transfer such data to the required jurisdiction. The caveat about law firms providing information to the client is quite important. Although the client has decided that certain information has to be transferred, the means by which the data will be transferred is entirely dictated by the lawyer's system. As such, where a law firm is aware that its system has suffered security breaches in the past when carrying out similar activities, it would be fair to advise the client of this fact and to give the client an option to use an alternative means to transfer the data. Where a client instructs the transfer of personal data of a third party, consent of the client is not sufficient. However, it is for the client, as data controller, to ensure that the relevant consent has been obtained if the client intends to rely on that exemption.

It would also be prudent to advise the client that the law firm is not responsible for the way in which third parties process such data. It is for the client as data controller of the data to ensure that any limitations on use of the data are expressly set out to the law firm so that it may pass on such instructions to the recipient third party outside of the EEA.

EXAMPLE 2

Where a law firm is transferring data for which it is data controller (for example, employee data or marketing data about its clients), then it is the law firm's responsibility to ensure that the Eighth Principle has not been breached.

Law firms may effect such transfer under the following exemptions as set out in Schedule 4 to the DPA:

- the law firm holds the data subject's (valid) consent;
- the transfer is *necessary* for the performance of a contract between the law firm and the data subject;
- the transfer is *necessary* for the conclusion of a contract between the law firm and a third party which the data subject has requested or it is in the data subject's interest and for the performance of such contract;
- the transfer is *necessary* for legal proceedings, obtaining legal advice or establishing, exercising or defending legal rights. This last exemption would be of particular importance where a client and a law firm wish to transfer details of a third party outside the EEA for the purposes of obtaining legal advice on whether or not the client can exercise any rights under the local jurisdiction.

10.8   USING THIRD PARTIES

Where law firms acting as data controllers wish to appoint any third parties to process data on their behalf (such as with confidential waste disposal firms) there must be a written contract in place which incorporates the obligations to process the data only in accordance with the law firm's instructions and to comply with obligations equivalent to those set out in the Seventh Principle.

Where law firms then instruct third parties to process personal data in the course of providing advice to clients (for example, enquiry agents, other lawyers in different jurisdictions, counsel, experts) they must ensure that they have the clear consent of the data controller to do so otherwise the law firm, and the individual solicitor involved, may be committing an offence under s.55 of the DPA.

Section 55 states that a person must not knowingly or recklessly without the consent of the data controller obtain or disclose personal data or the information contained in personal data or procure the disclosure to another person of the information contained in the personal data. This would not apply if:

- it was necessary for the purpose of preventing or detecting crime;
- it is required or authorised by or under any enactment, by any rule of law or by order of the court;
- a person acted in the reasonable belief that he had in law the right to obtain or disclose the data or information or, as the case may be, to procure the disclosure of information to the other person;
- a person acted in the reasonable belief that he would have had the consent of the data controller if the data controller had known about the obtaining, disclosing or procuring and the circumstances of it.

Assuming the law firm has the relevant consent, the appropriate instructions must be given to third parties to ensure that they do not commit such an offence, for example, by tracing people or checking out an individual's financial circumstances by fraudulent or dishonest means. Although it will be for the client as data controller to ensure that any such sub-data processor behaves appropriately and is properly managed, the reality is that such responsibilities fall to the law firm as, more often that not, law firms will recommend the use of particular parties with whom it has worked in the past. It is important to protect the client in such circumstances; although the client may not be committing a s.55 offence it may find itself in breach of its other obligations under the DPA as a result of subsequently using information obtained by a third party not knowing the circumstances in which it was obtained and can, as a result of that person's unlawful activity, find itself facing a civil action from data subjects or enforcement action by the Information Commissioner.

It would be a mistake to consider this to be solely the client's risk, for where the law firm is managing the process, there is an argument that it may be negligent if it fails to advise the client of the dangers of instructing such parties without the appropriate checks in place. Perhaps the best way to deal with this is for the law firm to have a general contract in place with such third parties in which the right is reserved for it and its client to issue precise instructions from time to time on how data should be processed and the manner in which they should be processed (to the extent that it can be covered in the contract from the outset) and also to obtain indemnities from such third parties in the event that they breach the obligations and cause loss or damage to the law firm and/or the client.

The importance of such third parties processing data properly is particularly significant where information has been obtained for court proceedings. If the personal data have been obtained unlawfully, whether under the DPA or otherwise, then they may be held to be inadmissible as evidence. The ramifications therefore are widespread and this justifies tight controls on third parties such as enquiry agents and tracing agents.

10.9 BRIEF COMMENTARY ON THE *DURANT* v. *FSA* CASE

10.9.1 Background

Mr Durant had been involved in litigation with Barclays Bank plc, which he lost. Mr Durant subsequently sought disclosure of documents (under DPA, s.7) held by the FSA from when it was investigating Mr Durant's complaint in its supervisory/regulatory capacity. The FSA refused to provide some of the documents on the grounds that they did not constitute personal data and/or were not part of a relevant filing system. Mr Durant brought a court action to seek disclosure of those documents. Following a decision at first instance which did not address fully the issues at hand, leave to appeal was granted. The appeal was heard on 8 December 2003.

10.9.2 The issues

The court examined four issues:

- the meaning of personal data;
- the meaning of relevant filing system;
- withholding personal data from a data subject on the grounds that third-party personal data are present; and
- the nature and extent of a court's discretion in deciding on subject access rights disputes.

Only the first two are of direct relevance for this chapter.

10.9.3 Conclusions

'Personal data' does not necessarily mean any and every document (and information contained in that document) which has the data subject's name on it. This is considered too wide an interpretation of the words 'related to' used in the definition of personal data in the DPA. It was decided that the overriding test is whether the information (note, not the document) in question affects a person's privacy, whether in his personal or family life, business or professional capacity.

Some queries and doubts immediately spring to mind: who will make this important judgement call? Does this serve only to add another layer to the subject access process? A data controller must seek out the information anyway (more likely by reference to an individual's name, this being the easiest criterion) and then sift through it for the usual items such as third-party references. Now, once all of that is done, the data controller must also consider (in the event that it does not want to provide the information to the data subject for whatever reason) whether privacy issues are at stake. Are those who deal with subject access requests on a daily, administrative basis in a position to understand the complexities involved in that decision?

The court has given a steer on this. Whether or not information can be classed as 'personal data' will depend on where the information falls in the continuum of relevance or proximity to the data subject as distinct from matters in which he may have been involved to a greater or lesser degree. There are two 'notions' (as identified by the court) to help in this task:

- is the information in itself significantly biographical?; and
- does it have the data subject as its focus, as opposed to just being a 'bystander'?

In respect of the meaning of a 'relevant filing system' the court has supported the view (widely held for some time now) that information contained in manual papers should be contained in a structure which allows specific information (e.g. health or performance history) about an individual to be readily accessible and identifiable from the outset of the search with 'reasonable certainty and speed'. A paper file on a named individual in which papers simply appear in date order, rather than by subject, is not a relevant filing system. The court stated that:

> It is plain that Parliament intended to apply the Act to manual records only if they are of sufficient sophistication to provide the same or similar ready accessibility as a computerised filing system.

Despite some concerns around the narrowed definition and its consistency with the Directive and the approach taken in other European jurisdictions, the Information Commissioner in August 2007 issued revised guidance to address the issues raised by this case, and this guidance is available on the ICO website. Guidance is still awaited in relation to the 'relevant filing system' definition.

10.10 FURTHER GUIDANCE

Those responsible for law firm compliance, for example, Office and Practice Managers, will need to keep up to date with data protection developments. The following are the main sources of further learning.

10.10.1 The Information Commissioner's Office Website

The ICO website, located at **www.ico.gov.uk**, provides the latest guidance on various aspects of data protection compliance and the latest incidences of enforcement action.

10.10.2   Training for law firms

PDP, the provider of the UK's leading data protection training courses, runs the UK's only professional training course on 'Data Protection Compliance for Law Firms'. For further information, see **www.pdptraining.com**.

10.10.3   Privacy & Data Protection

The periodical, *Privacy & Data Protection*, contains practical articles on various aspects of data protection compliance, plus up-to-date news on data protection issues, cases and enforcement activity. See **www.privacy dataprotection.co.uk**.

Potential purposes to be notified by a law firm

Purpose 1:	Legal services
Purpose 2:	Staff administration (N.B. Certain aspects of this processing may also be undertaken by a service company)
Purpose 3:	Accounts and records
Purpose 4:	Advertising, marketing and public relations
Purpose 5:	Management of customer records
Purpose 6:	Pensions administration (N.B. To be notified by the trustees of the pension scheme)
Purpose 7:	Crime prevention and prosecution of offenders/CCTV use
Purpose 8:	Education (in particular where Law Society accredited courses are provided)
Purpose 9:	Debt administration and factoring
Purpose 10:	Information and databank administration

APPENDIX 1

Safe Harbor Privacy Principles

NOTICE: An organization must inform individuals about the purposes for which it collects and uses information about them, how to contact the organization with any inquiries or complaints, the types of third parties to which it discloses the information, and the choices and means the organization offers individuals for limiting its use and disclosure. This notice must be provided in clear and conspicuous language when individuals are first asked to provide personal information to the organization or as soon thereafter as is practicable, but in any event before the organization uses such information for a purpose other than that for which it was originally collected or processed by the transferring organization or discloses it for the first time to a third party.[1]

CHOICE: An organization must offer individuals the opportunity to choose (opt out) whether their personal information is (a) to be disclosed to a third party[1] or (b) to be used for a purpose that is incompatible with the purpose(s) for which it was originally collected or subsequently authorized by the individual. Individuals must be provided with clear and conspicuous, readily available, and affordable mechanisms to exercise choice.

For sensitive information (i.e. personal information specifying medical or health conditions, racial or ethnic origin, political opinions, religious or philosophical beliefs, trade union membership or information specifying the sex life of the individual), they must be given affirmative or explicit (opt in) choice if the information is to be disclosed to a third party or used for a purpose other than those for which it was originally collected or subsequently authorized by the individual through the exercise of opt in choice. In any case, an organization should treat as sensitive any information received from a third party where the third party treats and identifies it as sensitive.

ONWARD TRANSFER: To disclose information to a third party, organizations must apply the Notice and Choice Principles. Where an organization wishes to transfer information to a third party that is acting as an agent, as described in the endnote, it may do so if it first either ascertains that the third party subscribes to the Principles or is subject to the Directive or another adequacy finding or enters into a written agreement with such third party requiring that the third party provide at least the same level of privacy protection as is required by the relevant Principles. If the organization complies with these requirements, it shall not be held responsible (unless the organization agrees otherwise) when a third party to which it transfers such information processes it in a way contrary to any restrictions or representations, unless the organization knew or should have known the third party would process it in such a contrary way and the organization has not taken reasonable steps to prevent or stop such processing.

SECURITY: Organizations creating, maintaining, using or disseminating personal information must take reasonable precautions to protect it from loss, misuse and unauthorized access, disclosure, alteration and destruction.

DATA INTEGRITY: Consistent with the Principles, personal information must be relevant for the purposes for which it is to be used. An organization may not process personal information in a way that is incompatible with the purposes for which it has been collected or subsequently authorized by the individual. To the extent necessary for those purposes, an organization should take reasonable steps to ensure that data is reliable for its intended use, accurate, complete, and current.

ACCESS: Individuals must have access to personal information about them that an organization holds and be able to correct, amend, or delete that information where it is inaccurate, except where the burden or expense of providing access would be disproportionate to the risks to the individual's privacy in the case in question, or where the rights of persons other than the individual would be violated.

ENFORCEMENT: Effective privacy protection must include mechanisms for assuring compliance with the Principles, recourse for individuals to whom the data relate affected by non-compliance with the Principles, and consequences for the organization when the Principles are not followed. At a minimum, such mechanisms must include (a) readily available and affordable independent recourse mechanisms by which each individual's complaints and disputes are investigated and resolved by reference to the Principles and damages awarded where the applicable law or private sector initiatives so provide; (b) follow up procedures for verifying that the attestations and assertions businesses make about their privacy practices are true and that privacy practices have been implemented as presented; and (c) obligations to remedy problems arising out of failure to comply with the Principles by organizations announcing their adherence to them and consequences for such organizations. Sanctions must be sufficiently rigorous to ensure compliance by organizations.

[1] It is not necessary to provide notice or choice when disclosure is made to a third party that is acting as an agent to perform task(s) on behalf of and under the instructions of the organization. The Onward Transfer Principle, on the other hand, does apply to such disclosures.

APPENDIX 2

Standard contractual clauses for the transer of personal data to third countries

Name of the data exporting organisation:

....

Address. ....

....

Tel.: .... *Fax:* .... *E-mail:* ....

Other information needed to identify the organisation:

....

....

('the Data Exporter')

and

Name of the data importing organisation:

....

Address. ....

....

Tel.: .... *Fax:* .... *E-mail:* ....

Other information needed to identify the organisation:

....

('the Data Importer')

HAVE AGREED on the following contractual clauses ('the Clauses') in order to adduce adequate safeguards with respect to the protection of privacy and fundamental rights and freedoms of individuals for the transfer by the Data Exporter to the Data Importer of the personal data specified in Appendix 1.

Clause 1

Definitions

For the purposes of the Clauses:

(a) 'personal data', 'special categories of data', 'process/processing', 'controller', 'processor', 'data subject' and 'supervisory authority' shall have the same meaning as in Directive 95/46/EC of 24 October 1995 on the protection of individuals with regard to the processing of personal data and on the free movement of such data ('the Directive');
(b) 'the data exporter' shall mean the controller who transfers the personal data;
(c) 'the data importer' shall mean the controller who agrees to receive from the data exporter personal data for further processing in accordance with the terms of these Clauses and who is not subject to a third country's system ensuring adequate protection.

Clause 2

Details of the transfer

The details of the transfer, and in particular the categories of personal data and the purposes for which they are transferred, are specified in Appendix 1 which forms an integral part of the Clauses.

Clause 3

Third-party beneficiary clause

The data subjects can enforce this Clause, Clause 4 (b), (c) and (d), Clause 5 (a), (b), (c) and (e), Clause 6 (1) and (2), and Clauses 7, 9 and 11 as third-party beneficiaries. The parties do not object to the data subjects being represented by an association or other bodies if they so wish and if permitted by national law.

Clause 4

Obligations of the data exporter

The data exporter agrees and warrants:

(a) that the processing, including the transfer itself, of the personal data by him has been and, up to the moment of the transfer, will continue to be carried out in accordance with all the relevant provisions of the Member State in which the data exporter is established (and where applicable has been notified to the relevant Authorities of that State) and does not violate the relevant provisions of that State;

(b) that if the transfer involves special categories of data the data subject has been informed or will be informed before the transfer that his data could be transmitted to a third country not providing adequate protection;

(c) to make available to the data subjects upon request a copy of the Clauses; and

(d) to respond in a reasonable time and to the extent reasonably possible to enquiries from the supervisory authority on the processing of the relevant personal data by the data importer and to any enquiries from the data subject concerning the processing of his personal data by the data importer.

Clause 5

Obligations of the data importer

The data importer agrees and warrants:

(a) that he has no reason to believe that the legislation applicable to him prevents him from fulfilling his obligations under the contract and that in the event of a change in that legislation which is likely to have a substantial adverse effect on the guarantees provided by the Clauses, he will notify the change to the data exporter and to the supervisory authority where the data exporter is established, in which case the data exporter is entitled to suspend the transfer of data and/or terminate the contract;

(b) to process the personal data in accordance with the Mandatory Data Protection Principles set out in Appendix 2;

or, if explicitly agreed by the parties by ticking below and subject to compliance with the Mandatory Data Protection Principles set out in Appendix 3, to process in all other respects the data in accordance with:

the relevant provisions of national law (attached to these Clauses) protecting the fundamental rights and freedoms of natural persons, and in particular their right to privacy with respect to the processing of personal data applicable to a data controller in the country in which the data exporter is established, or,

299

the relevant provisions of any Commission decision under Article 25(6) of Directive 95/46/EC finding that a third country provides adequate protection in certain sectors of activity only, if the data importer is based in that third country and is not covered by those provisions, in so far those provisions are of a nature which makes them applicable in the sector of the transfer;

(c) to deal promptly and properly with all reasonable inquiries from the data exporter or the data subject relating to his processing of the personal data subject to the transfer and to cooperate with the competent supervisory authority in the course of all its inquiries and abide by the advice of the supervisory authority with regard to the processing of the data transferred;

(d) at the request of the data exporter to submit its data processing facilities for audit which shall be carried out by the data exporter or an inspection body composed of independent members and in possession of the required professional qualifications, selected by the data exporter, where applicable, in agreement with the supervisory authority;

(e) to make available to the data subject upon request a copy of the Clauses and indicate the office which handles complaints.

Clause 6

Liability

1. The parties agree that a data subject who has suffered damage as a result of any violation of the provisions referred to in Clause 3 is entitled to receive compensation from the parties for the damage suffered. The parties agree that they may be exempted from this liability only if they prove that neither of them is responsible for the violation of those provisions.

2. The data exporter and the data importer agree that they will be jointly and severally liable for damage to the data subject resulting from any violation referred to in paragraph 1. In the event of such a violation, the data subject may bring an action before a court against either the data exporter or the data importer or both.

3. The parties agree that if one party is held liable for a violation referred to in paragraph 1 by the other party, the latter will, to the extent to which it is liable, indemnify the first party for any cost, charge, damages, expenses or loss it has incurred.*

[* paragraph 3 is optional]

Clause 7

Mediation and jurisdiction

1. The parties agree that if there is a dispute between a data subject and either party which is not amicably resolved and the data subject invokes the third-party beneficiary provision in Clause 3, they accept the decision of the data subject:
    (a) to refer the dispute to mediation by an independent person or, where applicable, by the supervisory authority;
    (b) to refer the dispute to the courts in the Member State in which the data exporter is established.
2. The parties agree that by agreement between a data subject and the relevant party a dispute can be referred to an arbitration body, if that party is established in a country which has ratified the New York Convention on enforcement of arbitration awards.
3. The parties agree that paragraphs 1 and 2 apply without prejudice to the data subject's substantive or procedural rights to seek remedies in accordance with other provisions of national or international law.

Clause 8

Cooperation with supervisory authorities

The parties agree to deposit a copy of this contract with the supervisory authority if it so requests or if such deposit is required under national law.

Clause 9

Termination of the Clauses

The parties agree that the termination of the Clauses at any time, in any circumstances and for whatever reason does not exempt them from the obligations and/or conditions under the Clauses as regards the processing of the data transferred.

Clause 10

Governing law

The Clauses shall be governed by the law of the Member State in which the data exporter is established, namely

....

Clause 11

Variation of the contract

The parties undertake not to vary or modify the terms of the Clauses.

On behalf of the Data Exporter:

Name (written out in full): ....

Position: ....

Address: ....

Other information necessary in order for the contract to be binding

(if any): ....

Signature...
(stamp of organisation)

On behalf of the Data Importer:

Name (written out in full): ....

Position:. ....

Address: ....

Other information necessary in order for the contract to be binding

(if any): ....

Signature...
(stamp of organisation)

APPENDIX 1 to the Standard Contractual Clauses

This Appendix forms part of the Clauses and must be completed and signed by the parties

(*The Member States may complete or specify, according to their national procedures, any additional necessary information to be contained in this Appendix)

Data exporter

The data exporter is (*please specify briefly your activities relevant to the transfer*):

....

....

....

Data importer

The data importer is (*please specify briefly your activities relevant to the transfer*):

....

....

....

Data subjects

The personal data transferred concern the following categories of data subjects

(*please specify*):

....

....

....

Purposes of the transfer

The transfer is necessary for the following purposes (*please specify*):

....

....

....

Categories of data

The personal data transferred fall within the following categories of data (*please specify*):

....

....

....

Sensitive data (if appropriate)

The personal data transferred fall within the following categories of sensitive data (*please specify*):

....

....

....

Recipients

The personal data transferred may be disclosed only to the following recipients or categories of recipients (*please specify*):

....

....

....

Storage limit

The personal data transferred may be stored for no more than (*please indicate*): ....(months/years)

DATA EXPORTER DATA IMPORTER

Name: ....

Authorised Signature ....

APPENDIX 2 to the Standard Contractual Clauses
Mandatory Data Protection Principles referred to in the first paragraph of Clause 5(b).

These data protection principles should be read and interpreted in the light of the provisions (principles and relevant exceptions) of Directive 95/46/EC.

They shall apply subject to the mandatory requirements of the national legislation applicable to the Data Importer which do not go beyond what is necessary in a democratic society on the basis of one of the interests listed in Article 13(1) of Directive 95/46/EC, that is, if they constitute a necessary measure to safeguard national security, defence, public security, the prevention, investigation, detection and prosecution of criminal offences or of breaches of ethics for the regulated professions, an important economic or financial interest of the State or the protection of the Data Subject or the rights and freedoms of others.

1. **Purpose limitation**
   Data must be processed and subsequently used or further communicated only for the specific purposes in Appendix 1 to the Clauses. Data must not be kept longer than necessary for the purposes for which they are transferred.

2. **Data quality and proportionality**
   Data must be accurate and, where necessary, kept up to date. The data must be adequate, relevant and not excessive in relation to the purposes for which they are transferred and further processed.

3. **Transparency**
   Data Subjects must be provided with information as to the purposes of the processing and the identity of the data controller in the third country, and other information insofar as this is necessary to ensure fair processing, unless such information has already been given by the Data Exporter.

4. **Security and confidentiality**
   Technical and organisational security measures must be taken by the data controller that are appropriate to the risks, such as unauthorised access, presented by the processing. Any person acting under the authority of the data controller, including a processor, must not process the data except on instructions from the controller.

5. **Rights of access, rectification, erasure and blocking of data**
   As provided for in Article 12 of Directive 95/46/EC, the Data Subject must have a right of access to all data relating to him that are processed and, as appropriate, the right to the rectification, erasure or blocking of data the processing of which does not comply with the principles set out in this Appendix, in particular because the data are incomplete or inaccurate. He should also be able to object to the processing of the data relating to him on compelling legitimate grounds relating to his particular situation.

6. **Restrictions on onward transfers**
   Further transfers of personal data from the Data Importer to another controller established in a third country not providing adequate protection or not covered

by a Decision adopted by the Commission pursuant to Article 25(6) of Directive 95/46/EC (onward transfer) may take place only if either:

(a) Data subjects have, in the case of special categories of data, given their unambiguous consent to the onward transfer or, in other cases, have been given the opportunity to object.

The minimum information to be provided to data subjects must contain in a language understandable to them:

- the purposes of the onward transfer,
- the identification of the data exporter established in the Community,
- the categories of further recipients of the data and the countries of destination, and
- an explanation that, after the onward transfer, the data may be processed by a controller established in a country where there is not an adequate level of protection of the privacy of individuals;

or

(b) the data exporter and the data importer agree to the adherence to the Clauses of another controller which thereby becomes a party to the Clauses and assumes the same obligations as the data importer.

7. **Special categories of data**

Where data revealing racial or ethnic origin, political opinions, religious or philosophical beliefs or trade union memberships and data concerning health or sex life and data relating to offences, criminal convictions or security measures are processed, additional safeguards should be in place within the meaning of Directive 95/46/EC, in particular, appropriate security measures such as strong encryption for transmission or such as keeping a record of access to sensitive data.

8. **Direct marketing**

Where data are processed for the purposes of direct marketing, effective procedures should exist allowing the data subject at any time to 'opt-out' from having his data used for such purposes.

9. **Automated individual decisions**

Data subjects are entitled not to be subject to a decision which is based solely on automated processing of data, unless other measures are taken to safeguard the individual's legitimate interests as provided for in Article 15(2) of Directive 95/46/EC. Where the purpose of the transfer is the taking of an automated decision as referred to in Article 15 of Directive 95/46/EC, which produces legal effects concerning the individual or significantly affects him and which is based solely on automated processing of data intended to evaluate certain personal aspects relating to him, such as his performance at work, creditworthiness, reliability, conduct, etc., the individual should have the right to know the reasoning for this decision.

APPENDIX 3 to the Standard Contractual Clauses
Mandatory Data Protection Principles referred to in the second paragraph of Clause 5(b).

1. **Purpose limitation**
   Data must be processed and subsequently used or further communicated only for the specific purposes in Appendix 1 to the Clauses. Data must not be kept longer than necessary for the purposes for which they are transferred.
2. **Rights of access, rectification, erasure and blocking of data**
   As provided for in Article 12 of Directive 95/46/EC, the data subject must have a right of access to all data relating to him that are processed and, as appropriate, the right to the rectification, erasure or blocking of data the processing of which does not comply with the principles set out in this Appendix, in particular because the data is incomplete or inaccurate. He should also be able to object to the processing of the data relating to him on compelling legitimate grounds relating to his particular situation.
3. **Restrictions on onward transfers**
   Further transfers of personal data from the data importer to another controller established in a third country not providing adequate protection or not covered by a Decision adopted by the Commission pursuant to Article 25(6) of Directive 95/46/EC (onward transfer) may take place only if either:
   (a) Data Subjects have, in the case of special categories of data, given their unambiguous consent to the onward transfer, or, in other cases, have been given the opportunity to object.
      The minimum information to be provided to Data Subjects must contain in a language understandable to them:
      • the purposes of the onward transfer,
      • the identification of the Data Exporter established in the Community,
      • the categories of further recipients of the data and the countries of destination, and,
      • an explanation that, after the onward transfer, the data may be processed by a controller established in a country where there is not an adequate level of protection of the privacy of individuals;
   or
   (b) the Data Exporter and the Data Importer agree to the adherence to the Clauses of another controller which thereby becomes a party to the Clauses and assumes the same obligations as the Data Importer.

APPENDIX 3

Standard contractual clauses for the transfer of personal data to processors established in third countries

Clause 1

Definitions

For the purposes of the Clauses:

(a) 'personal data', 'special categories of data', 'process/processing', 'controller', 'processor', 'data subject' and 'supervisory authority' shall have the same meaning as in Directive 95/46/EC of the European Parliament and of the Council of 24 October 1995 on the protection of individuals with regard to the processing of personal data and on the free movement of such data (the Directive);

(b) 'the data exporter' shall mean the controller who transfers the personal data;

(c) 'the data importer' shall mean the processor who agrees to receive from the data exporter personal data intended for processing on his behalf after the transfer in accordance with his instructions and the terms of these Clauses and who is not subject to a third country's system ensuring to adequate protection;

(d) 'the applicable data protection law' shall mean the legislation protecting the fundamental rights and freedoms of natural persons and, in particular, their right to privacy with respect to the processing of personal data applicable to a data controller in the Member State in which the data exporter is established;

(e) 'technical and organisational security measures' shall mean those measures aimed at protecting personal data against accidental or unlawful destruction or accidental loss, alteration, unauthorised disclosure or access, in particular where the processing involves the transmission of data over a network, and against all other unlawful forms of processing.

Clause 2

Details of the transfer

The details of the transfer and in particular the special categories of personal data where applicable are specified in Appendix I which forms an integral part of the Clauses.

Clause 3

Third-party beneficiary clause

The data subject can enforce against the data exporter this Clause, Clause 4(b) to (h), Clause 5 (a) to (e), and (g), Clause 6(1) and (2), Clause 7, Clause 8(2), and Clauses 9, 10 and 11, as third-party beneficiaries.

The data subject can enforce against the data importer this Clause, Clause 5(a) to (e) and (g), Clause 6(1) and (2), Clause 7, Clause 8(2), and Clauses 9, 10 and 11, in cases where the data exporter has factually disappeared or has ceased to exist in law.

The parties do not object to a data subject being represented by an association or other body if the data subject so expressly wishes and if permitted by national law.

Clause 4

Obligations of the data exporter

The data exporter agrees and warrants:

(a) that the processing, including the transfer itself, of the personal data has been and will continue to be carried out in accordance with the relevant provisions of the applicable data protection law (and, where applicable, has been notified to the relevant authorities of the Member State where the data exporter is established) and does not violate the relevant provisions of that State;

(b) that he has instructed and throughout the duration of the personal data processing services will instruct the data importer to process the personal data transferred only on the data exporter's behalf and in accordance with the applicable data protection law and these clauses;

(c) that the data importer shall provide sufficient guarantees in respect of the technical and organisational security measures specified in Appendix 2 to this contract;

(d) that after assessment of the requirements of the applicable data protection law, the security measures are appropriate to protect personal data against accidental or unlawful destruction or accidental loss, alteration, unauthorised disclosure or access, in particular where the processing involves the transmission of data over a network, and against all other unlawful forms of processing, and that these measures ensure a level of security appropriate to the risks presented by the processing and the nature of the data to be protected having regard to the state of the art and the cost of their implementation;

(e) that he will ensure compliance with the security measures;

(f) that, if the transfer involves special categories of data, the data subject has been informed or will be informed before, or as soon as possible after, the transfer that his data could be transmitted to a third country not providing adequate protection;

(g) that he agrees to forward the notification received from the data importer pursuant to Clause 5(b) to the data protection supervisory authority if he decides to continue the transfer or to lift his suspension;

(h) to make available to the data subjects upon request a copy of the Clauses set out in this Annex, with the exception of Appendix 2 which shall be replaced by a summary description of the security measures.

Clause 5

Obligations of the data importer

The data importer agrees and warrants:

(a) to process the personal data only on behalf of the data exporter and in compliance with his instructions and the Clauses; if he cannot provide such compliance for whatever reasons, he agrees to inform promptly the data exporter of his inability to comply, in which case the data exporter is entitled to suspend the transfer of data and/or terminate the contract;

(b) that he has no reason to believe that the legislation applicable to him prevents him from fulfilling the instructions received from the data exporter and his obligations under the contract and that in the event of a change in this legislation which is likely to have a substantial adverse effect on the warranties and obligations provided by the Clauses, he will promptly notify the change to the data exporter as soon as he is aware, in which case the data exporter is entitled to suspend the transfer of data and/or terminate the contract;

(c) that he has implemented the technical and organisational security measures specified in Appendix 2 before processing the personal data transferred;

(d) that he shall promptly notify the data exporter about:
  (i) any legally binding request for disclosure of the personal data by a law enforcement authority unless otherwise prohibited, such as a prohibition

under criminal law to preserve the confidentiality of a law enforcement investigation;

(ii) any accidental or unauthorised access; and

(iii) any request received directly from the data subjects without responding to that request, unless he has been otherwise authorised to do so;

(e) to deal promptly and properly with all inquiries from the data exporter relating to his processing of the personal data subject to the transfer and to abide by the advice of the supervisory authority with regard to the processing of the data transferred;

(f) at the request of the data exporter to submit his data processing facilities for audit of the processing activities covered by the Clauses which shall be carried out by the data exporter or an inspection body composed of independent members and in possession of the required professional qualifications bound by a duty of confidentiality, selected by the data exporter, where applicable, in agreement with the supervisory authority;

(g) to make available to the data subject upon request a copy of the Clauses set out in the Annex, with the exception of Appendix 2 which shall be replaced by a summary description of the security measures in those cases where the data subject is unable to obtain a copy from the data exporter.

Clause 6

Liability

1. The parties agree that a data subject, who has suffered damage as a result of any violation of the provisions referred to in Clause 3 is entitled to receive compensation from the data exporter for the damage suffered.

2. If a data subject is not able to bring the action referred to in paragraph 1 arising out of a breach by the data importer of any of his obligations referred to in Clause 3 against the data exporter because the data exporter has disappeared factually or has ceased to exist in law or become insolvent, the data importer agrees that the data subject may issue a claim against the data importer as if he were the data exporter.

3. The parties agree that if one party is held liable for a violation of the clauses committed by the other party, the latter will, to the extent to which it is liable, indemnify the first party for any cost, charge, damages, expenses or loss it has incurred.

Indemnification is contingent upon:

(a) the data exporter promptly notifying the data importer of a claim; and

(b) the data importer being given the possibility to cooperate with a data exporter in the defence and settlement of the claim.

Clause 7

Mediation and jurisdiction

1. The data importer agrees that if the data subject invokes against him third-party beneficiary rights and/or claims compensation for damages under the clauses, the data importer will accept the decision of the data subject:
    (a) to refer the dispute to mediation, by an independent person, or where applicable, by the supervisory authority;
    (b) to refer the dispute to the courts in the Member State in which the data exporter is established.
2. The data importer agrees that, by agreement with the data subject, the resolution of a specific dispute can be referred to an arbitration body if the data importer is established in a country which has ratified the New York Convention on enforcement of arbitration awards.
3. The parties agree that the choice made by the data subject will not prejudice his substantive or procedural rights to seek remedies in accordance with other provisions of national or international law.

Clause 8

Cooperation with supervisory authorities

1. The data exporter agrees to deposit a copy of this contract with the supervisory authority if it so requests or if such deposit is required under the applicable data protection law.
2. The parties agree that the supervisory authority has the right to conduct an audit of the data importer which has the same scope and is subject to the same conditions as would apply to an audit of the data exporter under the applicable data protection law.

Clause 9

Governing law

The Clauses shall be governed by the law of the Member State in which the data exporter is established, namely the law of England and Wales.

Clause 10

Variation of the contract

The parties undertake not to vary or modify the terms of the Clauses.

Clause 11

Obligation after the termination of personal data processing services

1. The parties agree that on the termination of the provision of data processing services, the data importer shall, at the choice of the data exporter, return all the personal data transferred and the copies thereof to the data exporter or shall destroy all the personal data and certify to the data exporter that he has done so, unless, legislation imposed upon the data importer prevents him from returning or destroying all or part of the personal data transferred. In that case, the data importer warrants that he will guarantee the confidentiality of the personal data transferred and will not actively process the personal data transferred anymore.
2. The data importer warrants that upon request of the data exporter and/or of the supervisory authority, he will submit his data processing facilities for an audit of the measures referred to in paragraph 1.

APPENDIX 1 to the Standard Contractual Clauses

This Appendix forms part of the Clauses and must be completed and signed by the parties

(*The Member States may complete or specify, according to their national procedures, any additional necessary information to be contained in this Appendix)

Data Exporter

The data exporter is (*please specify briefly your activities relevant to the transfer*):

....

....

....

Data Importer

The data importer is (*please specify briefly your activities relevant to the transfer*):

....

....

....

Data subjects

The personal data transferred concern the following categories of data subjects (*please specify*):

....

....

....

Categories of data

The personal data transferred fall within the following categories of data (*please specify*):

....

....

....

Special categories of data (if appropriate)

....

....

Processing operations

....

....

DATA EXPORTER DATA IMPORTER

Name ....

Authorised
Signature ....

APPENDIX 2 to the Standard Contractual Clauses

This Appendix forms part of the Clauses and must be completed and signed by the parties

Description of the technical and organisational security measures implemented by the data importer in accordance with Clauses 4(d) and 5(c) (or document/legislation attached):

....

....

....

Addresses and websites

BSI British Standards
389 Chiswick High Road
London
W4 4AL
Tel: +44 (0) 20 8996 9001
Fax: +44 (0) 20 8996 7001
www.bsi-global.com

Department for Business Enterprise and Regulatory Reform
Information Security Policy Team
1 Victoria Street
London
SW1H 0ET
Tel: +44 (0) 20 7215 5000
Fax: +44 (0) 20 7215 0105
www.berr.gov.uk

Facsimile Preference Service
DMA House
70 Margaret Street
London
W1W 8SS
Tel: +44 (0) 20 7291 3330
Fax: +44 (0) 20 7323 4226
www.fpsonline.org.uk
E-mail: fps@dma.org.uk

Direct Marketing Association
DMA House
70 Margaret Street
London
W1W 8SS

Tel: 020 7291 3300
Fax: 020 7323 4426
www.dma.org.uk

Information Commissioner's Office
Wycliffe House
Water Lane
Wilmslow
Cheshire
SK9 5AF
Tel: +44 (0) 1625 545 700
Fax: +44 (0) 1625 545 745
www.ico.gov.uk

Mailing Preference Service
DMA House
70 Margaret Street
London
W1W 8SS
Tel: +44 (0) 20 7291 3310
Fax: +44 (0) 20 7323 4226
www.mpsonline.org.uk
E-mail: mps@dma.org.uk

Privacy & Data Protection Journal
PDP Companies
16 Old Town
London
SW4 0JY
Tel: +44 (0) 845 226 5723
Fax: +44 (0) 870 137 7871
www.pdpjournals.com
Email: uk_office@pdpcompanies.com

Data Protection Training
PDP Training
16 Old Town
London
SW4 0JY
Tel: +44 (0) 845 226 5723
Fax: +44 (0) 870 137 7871
www.pdptraining.com
E-mail: bookings@pdptraining.com

Safe Harbor Website
www.export.gov/safeharbor

Telephone Preference Service
DMA House
70 Margaret Street
London
W1W 8SS
Tel: +44 (0) 20 7291 3320
Fax: +44 (0) 20 7323 4226
www.tpsonline.org.uk
E-mail: tps@dma.org.uk

Glossary

Approved country: A country to which you may send **personal data** without breaching the 8th **data protection principle**. At the time of writing, approved countries are: Argentina, Canada (to companies subject to the Canadian Personal Information Protection and Electronic Documentation Act), Guernsey, Isle of Man, Jersey, Switzerland, USA (to companies signed up to **safe harbor**).

Conditions for processing: The reasons for processing **personal data** which are permitted under the Data Protection Act 1998, listed in Schedules 2 and 3. One of these conditions must be fulfilled before processing **personal data** can be lawful; one condition from each schedule must be fulfilled before processing **sensitive personal data** can be lawful. One of the most common condition for processing used is that the processing is necessary for the legitimate interests of the **data controller** or third party to whom the data is disclosed, unless it is unwarranted because it prejudices the rights, freedoms or legitimate interests of the **data subject**.

Data: Any information processed or to be processed automatically (i.e. by computer) or held in a **relevant filing system**.

Data controller: The person or persons who determine the how and why of data **processing**. Only data controllers have liability under the Data Protection Act 1998; there can be more than one data controller for the same **personal data**.

Data processor: A person who processes data on behalf of a data controller. *Data processors don't need to notify the* **Information Commissioner's office**.

Data protection principles: The 8 principles set out in the Data Protection Act 1998 which underpin the obligations of **data controllers** under the Act. They are:

1. Process **personal data** fairly and lawfully, only if you meet one of the **conditions for processing**;
2. Obtain **personal data** only for specified and lawful purposes, and only process **personal data** for those purposes;
3. Ensure **personal data** is adequate, relevant and not excessive in light of those purposes;
4. Ensure **personal data** is accurate and, where necessary, up to date;
5. Do not keep **personal data** for longer than is necessary for the purposes it is processed for;

6. Process **personal data** in accordance with the **data subject**'s rights;
7. Take appropriate technical and organisational measures to protect against unauthorised or unlawful processing, or loss, destruction or damage to **personal data**;
8. Do not transfer **personal data** outside the EEA without adequate protection.

Data subject: The individual about whom personal data are processed. A data subject needn't be a UK resident.

Data subject access request: A request made by a **data subject** for access to **personal data** held by a **data controller** about him/her. **Data subjects** are entitled to obtain this information under s7 of the Data Protection Act 1998.

Enforcement notice: A notice served by the Information Commissioner on a data controller who is in breach of a **data protection principle** requiring compliance with that principle.

Exempt purpose: The purposes for which you can process **personal data** without needing to notify the **Information Commissioner's Office**. These are:

1. Staff administration
2. Advertising, marketing and public relations
3. Accounts and records.

Information Commissioner's Office: The regulator and promoter of the Data Protection Act 1998 and the Freedom of Information Act 2000.

Information notice: A notice served by the **Information Commissioner's Office** on a **data controller** to obtain information necessary to investigate a claim of a breach of the Data Protection Act 1998.

Model Terms: Model contractual terms approved by the European Commission for the transfer of **personal data** to a **third country** – outside the EEA or other **approved countries**. There are 3 versions of the **model terms** – two deal with transfers between **data controllers** and the third deals with transfers from a **data controller** in Europe and a **data processor** in a **third country**.

Non-disclosure provisions: The first **data protection principle** (except the requirement to have a **condition for processing**), the second, third, fourth and fifth **data protection principles**, the right to prevent data being processed where it will cause damage or distress and the right to require rectification, blocking, erasure or destruction of data where it contains an expression of opinion based on inaccurate data.

Notification: Registration with the **Information Commissioner's Office** that an organisation is a **data controller**. This is a requirement if the **data controller** is carrying out **processing** for any purpose which is not exempt (an **exempt purpose**).

Personal data: Any **data** which is capable of identifying a living individual and which relates to that individual. Identification can be by the information alone or in conjunction with any other information in **data controller's** possession or likely to come into such possession. Does not apply to information on deceased persons or corporations; covers photographs and images, for example, on CCTV.

Processing: Anything done with/to personal data. Includes holding, storing and even destroying **personal data**.

Relevant filing system: A systematic system of holding manual (paper) records from which specific information about a particular individual can be readily accessed; e.g. individual's employment record within a filing cabinet separated by tabs with specific headings such as 'sickness record'.

Safe Harbor: A voluntary scheme set up by the European Commission and the US Department of Commerce whereby organisations can sign up to abiding by Privacy Principles, similar to those contained in the Data Protection Act 1998. Not all US organisations can participate in **Safe Harbor**. However, a transfer of **personal data** to a **data controller** who does participate in **Safe Harbor** will not breach the 8th **data protection principle.**

Sensitive Personal data: Personal data relating to an individual's racial or ethnic origin, political opinions, religious beliefs, trade union membership, physical or mental health or condition, sexual life, alleged or actual criminal activity and criminal record.

Special purposes: Journalistic, artistic and literary purposes.

Third country: A country outside the EEA or other **approved countries** where it is not permitted to transfer **personal data** in accordance with the 8th **data protection principle**.

Courtesy of Wragge & Co.

Index